A NILOTIC WORLD

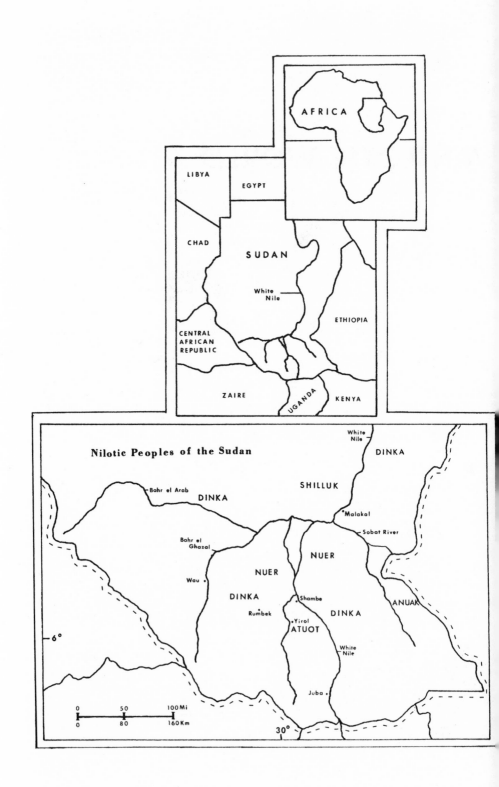

Nilotic Peoples of the Sudan

A NILOTIC WORLD
The Atuot-Speaking Peoples of the Southern Sudan

JOHN W. BURTON
Foreword by FRANCIS M. DENG

Contributions to the Study of Anthropology, Number 1

GREENWOOD PRESS
New York • Westport, Connecticut • London

Library of Congress Cataloging-in-Publication Data

Burton, John W., 1952-
  A Nilotic world.

  (Contributions to the study of anthropology,
ISSN 0890-9377 ; no. 1)
  Bibliography: p.
  Includes index.
  1. Atuot (African people) I. Title. II. Series.
DT155.2.A79B87 1987   306'.08996   86-31790
ISBN 0-313-25501-6 (lib. bdg. : alk. paper)

British Library Cataloguing in Publication Data is available.

Library of Congress Catalog Card Number: 86-31790
ISBN: 0-313-25501-6
ISSN: 0890-9377

First published in 1987

Greenwood Press, Inc.
88 Post Road West, Westport, Connecticut 06881

Printed in the United States of America

∞

The paper used in this book complies with the
Permanent Paper Standard issued by the National
Information Standards Organization (Z39.48-1984).

10 9 8 7 6 5 4 3 2 1

FOR JONA

CONTENTS

FOREWORD

The Nilotic peoples of the Sudan have been the subject of a
series of monographic studies that have attained the status of
classics in Anthropology and African Studies. John Burton's A
Nilotic World is a worthy and insightful addition to this body
of literature. Writing as a Nilote who has taken an interest
in studying his own people, I am particularly intrigued by two
features of Dr. Burton's work. One is that the manner in
which he related to the Atuot in the course of his work
signifies a narrowing of the gap between the outside field
worker and the people he or she studies. The other is that,
by identifying and studying the Atuot as a people separate
from the Dinka or Nuer with whom they have conventionally been
identified, he has positively contributed to the understanding
of their material, moral, and spiritual world. But some
people will undoubtedly argue that he has added to the
proliferation of ethnicities in a context that calls for wider
bases of national identification. In this foreword, I comment
on these two themes.

When I first met John Burton in Washington, he was
accompanied by a young Dinka diplomat, Charles Manyang, whom
he had met and befriended in New York where he [Charles
Manyang] was serving at the Permanent Mission of the Sudan to
the United Nations. We later got to know John and L'Ana
Burton quite well and grew to be friends. We have often
recalled with humor and deep appreciation the day they arrived
in Khartoum to find our compound filled with boxes of our
shipment from Washington which had just been delivered; we
were busy unpacking and settling into our new house. The
Burtons immediately joined us in the work which, as might be
expected, took days--indeed, weeks--before we could feel fully
settled. Throughout that period the Burtons physical,
technical, and (particularly in the case of L'Ana) nursery
skills were fully mobilized. We had the great pleasure of
having them with us prior and and subsequent to their field
work. In due course, the Burtons made many friends, not to
mention close acquaintances, especially with members of the
communities they were studying.

There is, of course, nothing unusual about this, for
anthropologists working in the field have generally been known
to cultivate close relations and become intimately identified

with the people they study. What I believe to be noteworthy
is that John and L'Ana Burton, a young couple with pleasant,
affable, and beneficient personalities, represent a new
generation of field workers who, by the very nature of the
increasingly unifying context in which they work, are
transcending racial and cultural barriers more than could have
been possible under the conditions of the colonial
stratification and segregation, the egalitarianism of
individual anthropologists notwithstanding.

Although Dr. Burton reports that he was invariably
addressed as "Turuk, a term commonly applied to [European or
Western] foreigners" or initially as "Dingalese, an
Englishman" by the Atuot, and thereby identified with the
rulers that were, these terms are largely descriptive, but
might also have been intended as a gesture of endearment for
the British rule, which, though initially imposed by force and
in any case inherently objectionable as foreign, gave the
Nilotics the only period of peace, security, and stability
that they have known in recent history. It is an experience
which is remembered with a degree of nostalgia and those
foreigners who are associated with it or are in any way
identified with the British tend to be greeted with special
sentiments of appreciation.

I witnessed this when my American wife accompanied me to
the southern Sudan in 1973 and participated in the tape-
recorded interviews which I conducted with Dinka chiefs. The
Atuot chief, Stephen Thongkol, from whose account Dr. Burton
quotes at length, was among those interviewed. Several chiefs
commented favorably on my wife as a representative of the
English "race." One chief began by saying, "Why don't you
translate the things you are saying so that your wife follows
what you are saying in Dinka? No thought should finish
without her knowing how her people, the people of her husband,
(think and) speak." He then proceeded to say:

> This wife of yours . . . is a pleasure to my heart.
> . . . It is their race that will one day be our good
> friends. As for this other race (the Arab), which
> says one word up there and other words go on
> underneath here, so that you laugh with a person but
> with other things hidden inside you, that is not the
> race for us. . . . The main mistake of the English
> is that they did not educate us: They were deceived
> by the Arabs who murmured (whispered) into their
> ears, saying: "If you educate these people, they
> will take the country from both of us." Now, the
> English come back only as guests, like this wife of
> mine (meaning yours and therefore ours-mine)! I
> like her very much. This is the race which in the
> past, when we saw them (the English), they had fame
> (charisma). And we, these people who are so black,
> so different from them, so different in colour, we
> are similar with them. I am very pleased that you
> have brought her. I like her with all my heart.

This racial consciousness, accompanied by moral
identification with those who were in authority and are now
being remembered with positive sentiments, is clearly
different from the type of identification that places the

outsider in a position somewhat representative of a ruling race or group. While the former can be expected to permit a greater degree of involvement with the people, the latter stratified the relationship in a manner that implied racial and cultural segregation, mutual alienation, and oftentimes resentment.

Evans-Pritchard has given us a candid account of the difficulties he encountered when he studied the Nuer, and while his case may reflect the experience of a particular individual working among a particular people, it does, to an extent, represent the atmosphere of the colonial context. Asking his reader not to judge him too harshly, Evans-Pritchard explained that the Nuer were "extremely difficult" to study. "Their country and character are alike intractable and what little I had previously seen of them convinced me that I would fail to establish friendly relations with them."

After giving details of the logistical difficulties he encountered, Evans-Pritchard went on to say,

> The local Nuer would not lend a hand to assist me in anything and they only visited me to ask for tobacco, expressing displeasure when it was denied them. When I shot game to feed myself and my Zande servants . . . they took the animals and ate them in the bush, answering my remonstrances with the rejoinder that since the beasts had been killed on their land they had a right to them."

He later moved to another area of Nuerland where his days "were happy and remunerative," and where, he writes, "I made friends with many Nuer youths who endeavoured to teach me their language and to show me that if I was a stranger they did not regard me an an obnoxious one." But just as he felt his "confidence returning" and would have remained there, a government force surrounded their camp one morning at sunrise, searched for two prophets who had been leaders in a recent revolt, took hostages, and threatened to take many more if the prophets were not handed over. "I felt that I was in an equivocal position, since such incidents might occur, and shortly afterwards returned to my home in Zandeland." It must be remembered that Evans-Pritchard had indeed been commissioned by the government to study the natives of the south in order to advise on how best they should be administered. His position was indeed "equivocal" and it was certainly brave of him to have stayed on among the Nuer even a day more after that punitive action.

On his second visit, Evans-Pritchard went to another area of the Nuer, which, in retrospect, he considered "an unfortunate" choice, for:

> The Nuer there were more hostile than those I had hitherto encountered and the conditions were harsher than any I had previously experienced. . . . Every effort was made to prevent me from entering the cattle camps. As it was seldom that I had visitors I was almost entirely cut off from communication with the people. My attempts to prosecute inquiries were persistently obstructed.

When the Nuer decided to befriend him at long last, Evans-Pritchard paradoxically found their encroachment a gross violation of his privacy:

> They visited me from early morning till late at night, and hardly a moment of the day passed without men, women, or boys in my tent. . . . These endless visits entailed constant badinage and interruption and, although they offered opportunity for improving my knowledge of the Nuer language, imposed a severe strain. . . . The chief privation was the publicity to which all my actions were exposed, and it was long before I became hardened, though never entirely insensitive, to performing the most intimate operations before an audience or in full view of the camp. . . . Because I had to live in such close contact with the Nuer I knew them more intimately than the Azande, about whom I am able to write a much more detailed account.

Evans-Pritchard's case is a good example of how the racial and cultural barriers of the colonial context were either too formidable to bridge or, when bridged, were replaced by an unnatural proximity that was irritating. Godfrey Lienhardt, who went into the field a decade later, had a far more congenial atmosphere and a less contrived relationship with the Dinka, whom he studied. This is apparent in the way he acknowledged the Dinka by name. It does not challenge the imagination to expect later generations of anthropologists in the field to have experienced far less difficulties of logistics, contacts, relationships, and substantive communication with the local peoples, as opposed to their one-sided observation as "objects" in a "social laboratory." Consider, for instance, this scene from Dr. Burton's experiences among the Atuot, which he quotes from his diary:

> We were sitting this afternoon in our hut drinking millet beer and had just been talking about how people used to attack an enemy's homestead, setting fire to the thatched roof and then shooting people with arrows as they ran from the hut seeking safety. An older man said that if a person was struck by an arrow he would urinate or defecate immedately. I said something stupid: "wouldn't that be like a witch, defecating in a homestead?" and the mood seemed to change quickly. I was told to shut off the tape recorder so it wouldn't catch people's words.

After the tape recorder was shut off the people present then offered uninhibited information about Atuot's conceptions of witchcraft. It is quite obvious from the social atmosphere and the tone of conversation that there was a genuine and uncontrived companionship between him and the Atuot. The Atuot probably feared the tape recorder as an instrument which, once it registered what was said, froze it in a manner that did not permit a flexible adjustment of words to suit the context, a very important consideration in Nilotic discourse. But it would not be stretching the point too far to say that

the tape recorder also symbolizes the ears of those regarded
as outsiders and therefore should not be privy to the
conversation. Since there was no reason to believe that
Burton would play the tape back to other members of the
immediate community, the outsiders who were intended to be
excluded conceivably went beyond the context of the Atuot and
presumably focused on the Western audience which the tape
recorder represented. The tape recorder was thus viewed as a
foreign intruder, while John Burton had become accepted as an
adopted member of the community.

Let us take yet another example from a personal
experience which Dr. Burton reports:

> One evening in August when the rains had been
> especially heavy and lightning had been particularly
> severe, the young men of our camp faced a difficult
> task when herding the cattle through the forest on
> return to the camp. As they explained, the
> thunderstorm had startled the cattle, which then
> scattered in the forest. It was past nine in the
> evening, long after the evening fires had been lit,
> when the first animals began to make their way into
> the camp. A short while later amidst what appeared
> to me as a hopelessly confused collection of men and
> cattle, a friend called to me, "Ayoicrial, thek e du
> ce ben", indicating that my ox had returned and
> could be tethered at our gol. As I understand it,
> the message was that amid about 1,500 cattle and
> sixty adult males, my own ox could now be safety
> tethered, insuring my own well-being.

Again, the environment Burton so vividly describes and the
sense of camaraderie that comes across defies conventional
dichotomy between the outside researcher and the "native
objects" of his study. Although acquiring local names among
the Nilotics is the rule and not the exception in the
experience of field workers and outside administrators, it is
interesting that the Burtons were assigned the names of Mayan
for John, the color-name of tawny ox, obviously because of his
color of skin, and Alak for L'Ana in recognition of the manner
in which her marriage had been contracted without cattle.
Their names thus recognized their distinctive features
while also symbolizing their assimilation into the local
community.

Judging also from the conversation about their marriage
which preceded the choice of the name Alak for L'Ana, the fact
that the Burtons went to Atuotland as a couple must also have
been a significant factor in their social context, for not
only did it make them appear more "normal" or less "anomalous"
among the marriage-prone Nilotics, but, in addition, because
of L'Ana's own admirable manner and winning personality, it
must have opened more avenues or channels of communication and
mutual assimilation. Although naming a child after a visiting
outsider is not a novelty among the Nilotics, the reason for
which L'Ana's name was honored among the Atuot, as reported by
her husband, is clearly significant. "As she had endeared
herself to smaller children," he writes, "especially in the
families of our own fictive identity, two women who gave birth
during our visit named their children L'Ana."

In his earlier book, <u>God's</u> <u>Ants</u>, John Burton also
acknowledged his wife's contribution to his field work in
words that underscore the point. He wrote,

> Atuot had seen a number of white males prior to our
> arrival in their country, but the sight of a white
> woman--who could actually speak the Atuot language--
> never ceased to be a source of conversation and
> reflection among our Atuot friends. In retrospect,
> I have the firm impression that a major reason why
> Atuot were so kind to us was because of the
> unrestrained hospitality L'Ana offered them.

The point I want to make is almost too obvious to require
emphasis: the greater the distance from the colonial
experience, the less the racial and cultural barriers between
European or Western ethnographers in the field and the people
they study. This in itself does not necessarily guarantee
more or better information about a people, for, as Evans-
Pritchard tells us, he was able to write more extensively
about the Azande, with whom he maintained a distance, than he
did about the Nuer, who, though initially distant, drew
closer, eventually imposing on him a high degree of intimacy.
But then, without in any way underestimating the classic
importance of his Zande studies, I believe I am right in
saying that Evans-Pritchard's works on the Nuer, from whom he
was both too distant and too close, have contributed the most
to his legendary image. The point Evans-Pritchard wanted to
make, of course, is that the hierarchical nature of Zande
society fit with the colonial regime of which he was a part,
but that while the Nuer accepted him in one way, they resisted
his claims to colonial authority. Comparing the relative
treatment he received among the Azande and the Nuer he wrote:
"Azande would not allow me to live as one of themselves; Nuer
would not allow me to live otherwise. Among Azande I was
compelled to live outside the community; among Nuer I was
compelled to be a member of it. Azande treated me as a
superior; Nuer as an equal."
What Evans-Pritchard's experience alludes to are the
dangers and potential benefits of close proximity. The danger
of losing objectivity when an observer becomes an intimate
member of the community he or she is studying is counter-
balanced by the prospects of acquiring insightful knowledge.
It is by being alert to both the dangers and the prospects
that the benefits can be maximized.
What impresses me the most about John Burton's book is
that the reader is privileged to become privy to such
intricate, complex, but lively social processes in which
people emerge not as unidentifiable guinea pigs in what I have
termed the social laboratory, but as human beings with
understandable motivations and modes of operation, and, above
all, can talk back in a mutually intelligible conversational
style with their participant-observer. Social values and
institutions, and even cultural patterns, cease to be
abstractions which are occasionally illustrated with some
human models and instead become the individualized essence of
the ongoing and also changing processes of human interaction.
And yet the reader still acquires a sense of the whole, the
system, the social order--its organizational structure, its

overriding goals and values, and its network of institutions and mechanisms, all of which combine to give individuals and groups both the motivation and the means to achieve the desired objectives in an orderly institutionalized manner. As an adopted member of the community, Burton is privileged to witness events and acquire information with the trust that it will be used not against them but more likely for the welfare of their society.

Although I have presented Dr. Burton as representative of a generation that has made considerable progress in bridging the "outside"-"inside" dichotomy, I do not want to imply that the earlier anthropologists who studied the Nilotes, some of whom I came to know very well, did not cultivate close relationships with the people they studied. Indeed, the opposite is evident in their classic works, whose conceptual framework is enriched by a wealth of detailed information about the values, institutions, and practices of the people they studied. I, for one, found Godfrey Lienhardt's works on the Dinka inspirationally insightful and most informative, even to an outsider. On the personal level, Dr. Lienhardt has also sustained close contacts, warm friendships, and unusual generosity with the Dinka, characterized by an open-door attitude which prompted me to remark on one occasion that his room at Queen Elizabeth's House in Oxford reminded me of a Dinka cattle-byre--a spacious, popular place for meeting around a fireplace.

The difference between the various generations of anthropologists in their involvement with the people they studied is also apparent in the extent to which members of the native community are or are not anticipated to be among the potential readers. Initially, products of field research were never expected to be read by members of the communities studied. Preliterate as they were, the natives could only be objects of research and not consumers of the knowledge thereby generated. Evans-Pritchard implied the point when he wrote: "I, unlike most readers, know the Nuer, and must judge my work more severely than they." Had he expected the Nuer to read the book, he would have realized that they might, indeed would, know more about themselves, at least in certain respects. Of course, Evans-Pritchard did not expect the Dinka to read his book, The Nuer, either, or he would not have commented on them from a Nuer perspective, with his own editorial addition: "All Nuer regard them (the Dinka)--and rightly so (emphasis added)--as thieves, and even the Dinka seem to admit the reproach." No wonder that throughout the years I knew Evans-Pritchard, he continued to address me in Nuer on the assumption that I was a Nuer, my persistent corrections to no avail. He could not accept me as a Dinka, knowing that I must have read his book. Unlike Evans-Pritchard, Godfrey Lienhardt anticipated that his audience would include the Dinka. This is obvious in the way he included in his acknowledgment a sentence in Dinka--koc kok kajuec (and many more people). Lienhardt indeed made this explicit when, in reproducing details of a historical myth given him by a senior chief, he wrote, "They may be of value to any Dinka who someday tries to reconstruct the history of his people." Scholars of today must prudently realize that it is no longer possible to predict where the reader will come from. The people studied must be anticipated to be among the audience to whom the results will be available.

     The other issue which calls for comment is Dr. Burton's
identification and treatment of the Atuot as a people separate
from the Dinka, who they have conventionally been assumed to
be, or the Nuer with whom they have also been sometimes
identified. Strong arguments can be presented for and against
this undertaking. From a public policy standpoint, it might
be argued that the need for solidarity within the larger
national groupings that are evolving in the process of state-
formation and nation-building militates against fostering
concepts of ethnic and cultural identification that might have
the effect of encouraging divisiveness and political
fragmentation. Viewed in this light, discovering,
reinforcing, and therefore fostering a "new" group sense of
identity may be considered antithetical, especially in
circles with which the group had previously been identified.
The significance of this can best be appreciated if it is
remembered that research and writing for the Nilotics are not
regarded as merely intellectual exercises, but as forms of
action with social consequences. Writing is seen as a form of
advocacy, which, because of its permanence, is irrefutable and
immutable. In their eyes, what is written down is
immortalized, sanctified, and becomes in due course a self-
fulfilling prophecy. It was because of this normative
connotation of scholarship and writing that the chiefs I
interviewed in 1973 felt that their words had been invested in
the service of their people. One chief urged me to "put them
in the newspapers." He went on to say:

> You Mading . . . we are very pleased. Things we
> have told you, you will give them a purpose; you
> will write them down and that is a big thing. . . .
> If this machine of yours writes and records what a
> man really says, and really records well, then if
> what we have said is bad, it will search for our
> necks; if it is good, then we will say these words
> have saved our country. . . . We trust in you fully.
> Whatever you think we have missed, (add it and) let
> it be said that we are the people who said it. Even
> if we have said something that can kill us, please
> write it down as we said it. Let us die; if we die
> and the South remains united and free, then it is
> well; let it be said that we are the people who said
> these things and that we should die for them. We
> would welcome that.

Even the order in which their ideas should be presented was
considered an establishment of priorities. "Of all things,
put down the question of water first; write it down
first. . . . Other things are machinery for cultivating the
fields and medicines for the cure of people and for the cure
of cattle."
     In the words of another chief, "I don't drink tea and I
don't drink milk. . . . When someone calls me, as you have
called me, to talk, that is the most important thing to me. I
am glad that we have now gone into the book." Viewing
research and writing as a policy statement and advocacy, to
say that the Atuot are a separate people is for the Nilotes to
will that they be and to have the advantage of making that
come true.

On the other hand, a strong case can also be made in favor of Burton's research not only on the grounds of scholarly objectivity in the quest "for the truth," but also in the interest of policy considerations. If the Atuot are indeed a separate people, then it is not only scientifically imperative to identify and study them as such, but also prudent and meritorious that their own sense of who they are and their place in the pluralistic Sudan be accorded the recognition and respect they deserve. It is indeed through such recognition and respect that the Sudan can ensure genuine unity in diversity and foster a sense of nationhood that is strengthened rather than weakened by the multiplicity of ethnic or "tribal" groups, value-institutional structures, and patterns of cultural behavior.

There was a period when the Nuer were written about and spoken of as "Dinka Nuer"; now no one questions the fact that, though a close kindred of the Dinka, they are a separate people. And so will it be with the Atuot. And perhaps the discovery may not end there. And why not? After all, we should remember that none of these people call themselves by the labels given them from the outside. As Aiden Southall has so poignantly reminded us, "Nuer and Dinka are People" and that is precisely what they each call themselves in their own languages. And what is more, except for the more enlightened among them, each major group among the Dinka consider themselves "The People," in other words, the Dinka, while applying only group names to the other Dinka tribes or labelling them "the others." Identification is therefore a fluid concept, used by different people at different times to serve different objectives.

And, of course, there are also other points of contact beyond the Nilotic world. I have often wondered why the Nuer word for themselves, "Nath," by which they mean "People," is so close to the Arabic word Nas which means the same thing-- people. The difference is easily explained by the fact that Nilotic languages have no "s" sound. Whichever group adopted the original word from the other, it spells a degree of cross-cultural fertilization which scholars have only just begun to recognize. As Professor Jay Spaulding so eloquently expressed it in a recent workshop organized by the Woodrow Wilson Center in Washington on the Problems and Prospects of Peace and Unity in the Sudan:

> If one picks up a book of, let us say, Evans-Pritchard or Monneret de Villard, and makes a deliberate effort to examine the periphery of the community in question, there are always hands reaching in awkwardly from off the screen, as it were, and individuals coming and going for incomprehensible or poorly-explained reasons.

Professor Spaulding also acknowledged some of the recent developments in the corrective direction:

> With the independence of the Sudan a new generation of scholars . . . asked that students of society shift their primary focus from the real or alleged "center" of the various communities to the very boundaries that were presumed to divide them.

The moment this mental exercise was performed, the vision of Sudanese society conjured up by the historians simply vanished into thin air.

The image that replaced it was one of a complex network of interactions among people, in which all manner of economic, political and cultural influences made themselves felt in an intricate web of reciprocal relationships.

From then on, the primary emphasis in the study of Sudanese society has shifted from a preoccupation with groups to the examination of social processes.

To emphasize the cross-boundary process of interaction as a subject of methodological investigation is not to underestimate the importance of an autonomous group with its distinctive system of cultural values and institutions, nor to minimize the sensitivities and the emotionalism associated with the primordial issues of ethnic, cultural, and linguistic identities as both uniting and divisive labels. Indeed, a significant aspect of Burton's contribution is the material he provides for understanding how the Nilotics identify and distinguish among themselves. Since he started his research on the Atuot, Dr. Burton has published some twenty-four articles and two books on the people called the Atuot. Knowing the level of his motivation, the rigor of his intellectual pursuits, and the vigor of his youth, we can confidently expect a great deal more to come in the years ahead. In the face of such overwhelming evidence, who can doubt that there are indeed a people called the Atuot?

Because of Burton's work, we may have lost the Atuot as assumed fellow Dinkas but gained them as another group of fellow Nilotes. What is important is that the cultural pattern and dynamic personality of these peoples, now reaffirmed and reinforced by fresh evidence, reflects a rich reservoir of human experience that remains largely a potential still to be tapped and more fully utilized in addressing the pressing problems of development and nation building in the pluralistic context of the Sudan.

Francis M. Deng
Washington, D.C.
May, 1987

ACKNOWLEDGMENTS

I am grateful to the Royal Anthropological Institute, the International African Institute, the Anthropos Institute, the Indiana University Press, and the editors of _Ethnology_ for permission to reprint passages from the following essays: "Ghosts, Ancestors and Individuals among the Atuot of the Southern Sudan"; "Atuot Age Categories and Marriage"; "Ghost Marriage and the Cattle Trade among the Atuot of the Southern Sudan"; "Atuot Ethnicity: An Aspect of Nilotic Ethnology"; "Women and Men in Marriage: Some Atuot Texts"; "The Names People Play: Metaphors of Self among the Atuot of the Southern Sudan"; "The Village and the Cattle Camp: Aspects of Atuot Religion"; "Ethnicity on the Hoof: On the Economics of Nuer Identity"; "Same Time, Same Space: Observations on the Morality of Kinship in Pastoral Nilotic Societies" and "Gifts Again: Complimentary Prestation among the Pastoral Nilotes of the Southern Sudan." I am also grateful to R. G. Lienhardt and F. M. Deng for permission to draw upon certain of their published works.

Professor R. Francis Johnson, Dean of the Faculty at Connecticut College, made it possible to complete this monograph in its present form, and I am forever grateful for his moral and intellectual support. Finally, I want to express my sincere thanks and appreciation to Catherine J. Marshall for her exemplary professional and editorial assistance. This project would not have been completed without her humor, stamina, and direction.

PREFACE

In anthropology, as in other scientifically inspired social studies, certain key concepts enjoy remarkably long life histories, and one way to measure change within a discipline is to examine these usages across longer and shorter intervals of time. A ready illustration is provided by the concept "culture." It is probable that many nonprofessionals believe that "culture" is what anthropologists study, as, indeed, some practitioners call themselves cultural anthropologists. A larger number of the professional audience rely upon the term as a means of accounting for and explaining the diverse ways in which humans behave. One of the leading anthropologists of the present generation, Clifford Geertz, has put forward the argument that human nature is in fact a cultural fact. From this view, one of the more primary features of the human is the manner in which belief, expectation, and experience are molded by one or another cultural tradition so that there is no such thing as a human being in the absence of a cultural tradition. Some decades before in American anthropology the concept of culture was employed to refer to habits of the mind, so that culture connoted value, social sentiments, and style. With this usage came the explicit premise that cultures were to be conceived of in holistic terms, that cultures were fully integrated systems, with one element necessarily interconnected with all others. Explaining culture meant defining and demonstrating this ordered unity. In contemporary anthropology these views no longer carry the same degree of explanatory power. Indeed, within the past decade, it has become increasingly common to encounter the argument that cultures are not integrated systems but rather abstract and sometimes conflicting guides for channeling modes of belief and behavior. Throughout the history of institutionalized anthropology, the concept of culture has provided a focal point on which practitioners have agreed to disagree. Very similar remarks and observations apply to the concepts "society" or "social structure." The perennial debate focuses on the epistemological status of these sconcepts: Are they real things that can be known, or useful analytic constructs that help to advance the process of knowing? As T. O. Biedelman recently notes (1986: vii), "Much that currently passes for brilliant innovation is merely the recrudescence of past ideas and arguments."

The concept "tribe" has an analogous history within the discipline. Only some short decades ago it was commonly accepted that tribes, like cultures, were the objects of anthropological study. The term "tribe" was used repeatedly by anthropologists conducting field research throughout the world and its standard uses encouraged the misconception that tribal societies were timeless, bounded steady state systems. Rather than accurately portraying extant social realities, this usage merely provided a convenient way to designate a focal point of study. Beginning in the 1930s and increasing at a more rapid pace in the 1950s, anthropologists wrote of the ways in which tribal societies were changing as a consequence of culture contact, independence from former colonial domination, or more direct involvement in cash- and market-oriented economies. Largely in consequence of changing social facts, anthropological theory addressing the nature of societies of this order also began to move in novel directions. For example, discussions about "tribalism" were increasingly phrased in the language of ethnicity and ethnic flexibility. Almost overnight, tribes became ethnic groups in the anthropological literature. As suggested, the changing theoretical stance was the result of changing social facts and reflected heightened sensitivities to the various ways in which systems of colonial and imperial rule created bounded tribal groups as a means of advancing their self-defined political and economic interests. It was hardly legitimate to undertake a study of "traditional" Amerindian cultures, for example, some 400 years after Spanish conquest in the new world.

From this discussion a larger series of questions emerge. Processes of domination and conquest have occurred repeatedly throughout human experience, so it is shortsighted to suggest that social change in so-called "tribal" societies was primarily a response to western contact. As Robert Lowie wrote a half-century ago, "White influence, however devastating its ultimate effect, is not a thing sui generis; aboriginal peoples have borrowed from one another for thousands of years, and the attempt to isolate one culture that shall be wholly indigenous in origin is decidedly simple-minded" (1935: xviii). Lowie was here concerned with the Crow peoples of North America. A recent detailed study of the Nuer of the southern Sudan convincingly shows that conquest, migration, and ethnic ambiguity were characteristic of this area long before the colonial era (see Kelly 1985). D. Tedlock (1982: 160) addresses a related issue from a different perspective and suggests "There is no such thing as pre-contact ethnography."

The purpose of recalling some of these points at the beginning of this study is to underscore the well-known fact that all observations about human society and human experience are historically contingent since they represent the values, interests, and knowledge of the author. Historical and anthropological knowledge are thus in one sense very relative, and anthropologists have long recognized that the data that they gather in the course of field work reflect similar biases and interests of willing informants. Those same individuals are not merely reflecting upon received wisdom, but are actively involved in its recreation and transformation.

Within the past decade anthropologists have become more
willing to concede that they, too, play a role in creating an
image of the society they seek to interpret or understand.
Thus, with renewed self-consciousness, anthropologists
increasingly struggle with questions of interpretation,
objectivity, and historical transformation. There can be no
pure ethnography.

One of the primary concerns of this study is to
understand some of the social values and sentiments of the
Nilotic Atuot-speaking peoples of the southern Sudan, who
share close linguistic and ethnological affinities with the
more numerous Nuer and Dinka. Though they possess a firm
conviction of their own cultural and linguistic identity, they
are surely more alike than different from their Dinka and Nuer
neighbors. Therefore, in the present work, as in all other
essays I have written about their social environment, implicit
comparisons are intended. The most useful and certainly the
most valid method by which to proceed is to focus on a limited
series of social facts, which are best understood as
variations on a regional theme. In this way one can recognize
the common, broader cultural attitudes that characterize the
Nilotic-speaking pastoralists of the southern Sudan and
perhaps account for the significant variations on these common
themes. So the Atuot represent a Nilotic world which is best
understood within a regional framework.

Indeed, the problematic nature of ethnic and regional
variation in the Nilotic Sudan led to my interest in living
among the Atuot with the hope of completing a course of field
research. As a graduate student, this initial interest was
encouraged and amply developed, especially by W. Arens, at
Stony Brook. During those years I became familiar with the
previously published literature on the Shilluk, Anuak, Dinka,
and Nuer, and found the occasional reference to a people
called Atuot. These references were always of a suggestive
rather than substantive nature. As I read further it became
more clear that relatively little was actually known of these
people, so that the prospect of making an initial
anthropological survey of their communities began to
materialize. In retrospect I confess a degree of romantic
fascination with this initial prospect, as a number of classic
and centrally important monographs in anthropology were based
on Nilotic ethnography. At the same time I was very conscious
of following in the footsteps of exceptionally gifted,
perceptive, and brilliant (and also British) anthropologists
who had worked in neighboring communities. On the advice of
my graduate adviser I went to the Sudanese Mission to the
United Nations, hoping to find out more regarding guidelines
or restrictions on research in the Sudan. By chance I met
Charles Manyang at the mission, a highly educated man from
Dinka country, just east of the Nile. After I described my
interests in traveling to the southern Sudan he began to show
some measure of the pride and dignity that the Nilotic peoples
hold for their "traditional" culture and world view. To
condense this narrative a great deal, I had the opportunity to
meet a greater number of Nilotic Sudanese during a year of
graduate study and research at the University of Cambridge.
Some were pursuing advanced degrees in the hope of gaining an
academic title and others sought further training to advance
their careers in various branches of the Sudanese civil and
foreign service. To my surprise, each new acquaintance had

heard my name before and knew at least something about my then
ill-defined plans to carry out research in the southern Sudan.
Without exception they supported my interests with enthusiasm
and gave my wife and me names of friends and associates who
might assist us when we arrived in their country.   When we
arrived in Juba, the capital of the southern Sudan, we found a
network of government officials equally willing to assist us.

The point of this anecdotal digression is to draw
attention to a fact I was not clearly aware of at the time.
While I was in the midst of preparing for field work in the
Nilotic Sudan, members by birth of those cultural traditions
were making a first study of my wife and me.   Anthropologists
generally report that field work is something you do.   It
might be noted as a rejoinder that field work is also
something that happens to you.   Clearly, if we had made a
different impression on the expatriot Nilotes we met, the very
possibility of living in their country could have been in
question.

With the generous support of the Social Science Research
Council and the Wenner-Gren Foundation for Anthropological
Research, my proposal to study "Ethnic and Cosmological
Boundaries of Atuot Society" was funded.   During the three
years in which I had been planning to travel to the Sudan, a
good deal of preparatory research was done, not only in
libraries, but in the company of expatriot southern Sudanese.
As Charles Manyang was a very recent arrival to the United
States, he appreciated and accepted our frequent invitations
to visit in Stony Brook.   He reciprocated with invitations for
dinner at his apartment in Manhattan where we met other
southern Sudanese now living in the United States.   Dr.
Francis Deng, the author of nearly a dozen books on the Dinka,
was then Sudanese ambassador to the United States, and he and
his wife were gracious hosts when Manyang and I visited them
in Washington.   As a "native son" and distinguished author and
statesman, Dr. Deng offered moral support and enthusiasm for
my projected study.   In Cambridge we befriended Thiang Thiep
Thiang, a Dinka colleague of Manyang, and through him we met
Paul Mabior Aliab, one of a number of Atuot then living in
England.   Thiang was a regular visitor at our college flat and
showed remarkable patience with my efforts to learn Dinka.   As
there is no dictionary or grammar of the Atuot language, Paul
Mabior Aliab agreed to help me begin to learn his natal
tongue.   We met on Friday afternoons at the Sudanese embassy
in London and usually ended the evening in the company of a
dozen or so southern Sudanese at a local pub.   Those
experiences had the double effect of allowing the opportunity
to learn something firsthand about the society that had
administered the Sudan for fifty-eight years, and to gain a
sense of the values and aspirations of the second generation
of formally educated southerners.

When we later arrived in Yirol, the administrative center
of Lakes Province and home of the Ceic and Aliab Dinka as well
as the Atuot, we were offered shelter by the acting executive
officer.   Some weeks later we began the process of rebuilding
an abandoned homestead on the fringe of this small town, and
this eventually served as a home base for our belongings and
wanderings.   From here we traveled by foot or bicycle to visit
villages and cattle camps throughout the territories where the
approximately 35,000 Atuot-speaking peoples live.   Inspired by
the image of field work as a process in which one becomes

immersed in local life, information was gathered by attempting
to participate as fully as possible in the social life of
Atuot communities. When we first arrived I spoke only a
little Dinka and even less Atuot. The majority of Atuot are
fully bilingual in the mutually distinct dialects of Dinka and
Atuot, while others profess fluency only in Atuot. With luck
and by chance we met Telar Deng, an Atuot by birth and nephew
of the then-Commissioner of Bahr-el-Ghazal Province, Isiah
Kulang. Telar was visiting Yirol on a short leave from his
post as elementary teacher in the province headquarters at
Wau. He agreed to work with us for a fixed fee, to help us
learn his language, and to act, at least for a time, as a
translator. (I should note that Telar was called upon a
number of times during our visit to serve in an official
capacity as translator in government and legal decisions
affecting Nuer, Dinka, and Atuot.) In the early stages of our
research he was constant company, though later on I sought his
advice less frequently. It has been remarked that one can
master a foreign language in two or three years of study, but
it takes a lifetime to fully command one's native tongue.
Though some Atuot friends were kind enough to offer the
opinion that I spoke their language well, I think many forgave
or ignored mistakes I made. The translation of Nilotic poetry
is an especially difficult undertaking, and I was ever
dependent upon Telar and other willing participants in that
effort. Telar was the only assistant in the field that I ever
paid. Given his knowledge of Atuot, Dinka, Nuer, Arabic, and
English, I would have done so gladly in any circumstance,
though the fee we agreed upon only compensated him for an
equivalent salary he earned as a teacher. Gabriel Gum Deng,
the late Akutei Muokjok, Barnaba Madeo Bol, Malek Majok,
Kulang Mabor, Iwer Deng, Andrew Acijok Yak, among others, were
patient and generous tutors.

I would like to add a few final, introductory comments.
This monograph draws upon a number of previously published
essays which address certain aspects of Atuot social
organization and values, and is intended to supplement a
sister volume, God's Ants: A Study of Atuot Religion. In the
effort to create a synthesis of this material, considerable
detail has been deleted from earlier essays while some
previously unpublished materials are included. I would like
eventually to write an additional monograph that will examine
Atuot oral literature and poetry: I hope the reader will
appreciate the individual and social significance of song in
this Nilotic world.
All field workers inherit long-lived moral as well as
political debts in consequence of their longer and shorter
sojourns in chosen communities. Elsewhere I have offered
testimony and gratitude to recognize my own debt to local
peoples as well as government officials who made our initial
visit to Atuot country possible and even productive. In a
very different world, all anthropologists who carry out field
work inherit the responsibility to faithfully report the
results of such study to professional colleagues. Thirty or
forty years ago, there was indeed something that approached an
"anthropological community." What is taken for theory in
anthropology in the contemporary world is a bewildering tangle
of argument and counterargument, with participants claiming
truths from inspirational fonts as diverse as evolutionary

biology to literary criticism. Somewhere in between,
ethnography must find a place, even while each passing
generation decides anew what is and what is not "good"
ethnography. Godfrey Lienhardt has remarked on the
relationship between theory and ethnography by analogy with an
elephant and rabbit stew: one elephant of ethnography to one
rabbit of theory. "It is a good recipe for a cook who can
bring out the flavor of the rabbit" (1985: 647). Clearly,
every ethnographic observation is biased by the interest and
perception of the observer, so that theory and ethnography
cannot be separated. Facts do not stand by themselves and
cannot speak for themselves. Yet there are any number of
ethnographies and surely many more journal articles so laden
with theory that the elephant is smothered by the rabbit.
Anthropology, like history, is a study in--or a process of--
interpretation. When we prove hypotheses about "culture" in
the absence of people, we demonstrate the consistency of a
scientific method. When we interpret a culture in the absence
of people, we are no longer anthropologists. Initially
inspired by a taxonomical brand of science, modern
anthropology sometimes asks us to find the other in ourselves.
If we cannot, there is no purpose to ethnography and surely no
possibility of anthropology. Conversely, if one learns from
ethnography something new about oneself, both translation and
culture are possible.

   The first chapter of this study surveys some of the
complex and perhaps still-unanswered questions surrounding an
answer to the ethnological and linguistic relationships
pertaining among the peoples called Dinka, Nuer and Atuot, and
draws upon essays previously published on the Atuot dialect of
Nilotic, British colonial rule in the southern Sudan and the
contemporary sense of ethnic identity of these peoples. The
ecological year and its relation to subsistence patterns and
modes of residence comprises the main focus of Chapter 2,
which brings together data published in essays concerning
villages and cattle camps, kinship, and morality of physical
space. The third chapter is largely concerned with processes
leading to, and consequences of, marriage, which is the key
institution in the social reproduction of social life.
Chapter 4 summarizes a body of material discussed more fully
in God's Ants, here addressed more in sociological than
theological terms. Chapter 5 offers some understanding of the
dialectic relationship between the private and public self and
the ways in which social values are established and
interpreted by individuals. The final short essay reviews
some of the current political events in Sudan as these affect,
for better or worse, the local peoples. When writing those
brief remarks I often thought of Claude Levi-Strauss's quip,
"Nothing is possible so all is possible" (1974: 260).

A NILOTIC WORLD

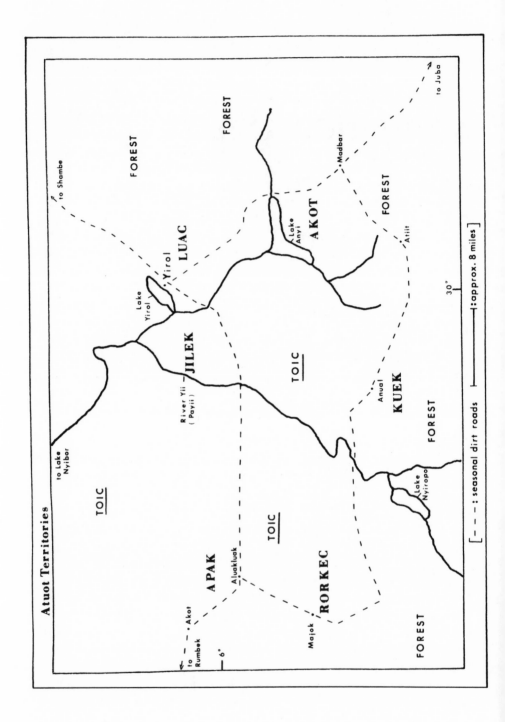

Atuot Territories

1.
A PEOPLE CALLED ATUOT

> In ordinary social situations no distinction is
> drawn between Nuer and Dinka members of a community.
> This distinction is only drawn in situations where
> purity of descent is socially relevant (Evans-
> Pritchard 1935: 18).

For a number of decades, anthropologists interested in the
field of Nilotic studies have struggled with questions
concerning ethnogenesis as well as the nature of contemporary
social relations between named ethnic groups. This chapter
offers an attempt to clarify the status of the Atuot-speaking
community within this diachronic and contemporary spectrum.
Many Atuot adults who are well-versed in such matters indicate
that they shared a common origin with the Nuer, in particular,
those who now live west of the Nile River. Atuot also share a
sense of cultural distinctiveness from the far-more-numerous
Dinka, who live on three of their geographic borders. E. E.
Evans-Pritchard (1951: 23) once remarked upon a "python-like
assimilation by the Nuer of vast numbers of Dinka through
adoption or intermarriage." Until the effects of British
administration began to take hold of local affairs, one can
reasonably suggest that the quality of relations with the
neighboring Dinka were decidedly more hostile. I will return
to this point later in the chapter after reviewing some early
accounts which make reference to the Atuot as well as data I
collected firsthand while living in their country.

THE ATUOT FROM WITHOUT

Arab traders and slavers have figured for a considerable
period in the history of western Dinka groups. A good number
of the songs F. M. Deng (1973) has translated recall the times
when their country was "spoiled" by northern invaders and,
according to K. Sacks (1979) events of this order occurred
with much greater frequency in Dinka country than among the
Nuer. In the course of field work those Nuer whom I met
invariably addressed me as <u>Turuk,</u> a term commonly applied to
foreigners since the Ottoman penetration of the Sudan. Atuot
initially called me <u>Dingalese,</u> an Englishman, an occurrence

that I interpret as supporting the observation that only the
British administrators of the first half of this century
affected traditional Atuot livelihood in any significant
manner. I found that only a handful of older Atuot men and
women were willing to speculate on this element of their
history in the nineteenth century. Indeed, I recorded only a
single incident learned from their grandfathers, which noted
how a Turkish garrison was surrounded by Atuot near their
present border with the Ceic Dinka. On that occasion, the
intruders were speared, riddled with arrows, and burned.

     Traveling through the southwestern region of Atuot
country in the 1960s, G. Schweinfurth (1873) gained the
impression that Atuot would prove to be a difficult people to
subjugate because of their skilled use of bows and arrows. R.
Gessi (1892: 213) also makes reference to a tribe "called
Atuot which is till now independent and its presence renders
travelling dangerous. The government has not yet succeeded in
subjugating it." To effect a change in this state of affairs
he "sent three hundred men armed with guns to make a simple
demonstration but my people were obliged to retreat on finding
that they were facing thousands of Atuot" (1892: 337; see also
Petherick 1869: 216; Gray 1961: 131; Beltrame 1961: 119). A
number of Atuot elders related to me that when the Turks first
landed at the Nile port of Shambe, the Ceic were enlisted as
porters. As this initial caravan approached the northern
perimeter of Atuot country, the Dinka refused to travel any
further since they recognized that Atuot were superior
warriors. J. Poncet (1863: 54) likewise noted, "les Atot [sic]
quoique peu nombreux, sont tres forts et respectes des Elliab
[Aliab] et principlement des Kitch [Ceic]." Given this
general impression of Atuot country among outsiders, the Turks
understandably made their way westward from the Nile by
skirting this general region, and proceeded into Agar Dinka
territory to establish ivory and slave trading stations in
Rumbek, a district headquarters in the contemporary Sudan (see
also Fergusson 1921: 151; Gray 1961: 37). The same general
route was followed by the first cadre of British
administrators early in the present century.

     A careful examination of extant sources on the contact
and precontact history of this general region suggests that
hostile rather than peaceable relations were characteristic
expectations. Foreigners entered this environment and made
the attempt to exploit local hostilities for their own
purposes. R. Kelly has commented at some length on the
contact period of pastoral Nilotic history. As he notes
(1985: 268), "The most important factor in opening the
southern Sudan to external influences was the first successful
navigation through the vegetation-choked channels of the Upper
Nile in 1839." For perhaps the first time in their history,
the rivers, which had always been a source of life for Nilotic
peoples, began to threaten their very existence, even though
the process initially occurred at a snail's pace. As Kelly
writes,

     The initial effects were slight. Between 1839 and
     1851 the Egyptians carried out small annual
     expeditions to trade for ivory. Contact between the
     Egyptians and the Nuer and Dinka was limited to the
     riverbanks and to the relatively few points at which
     high banks and an absence of peripheral swamp made

it possible for the boats to draw close to the land
(1985: 268).

Until the middle of the last century local peoples could avoid
contact by simply avoiding these few and scattered riverine
environments.   Soon after, however, Europeans began to arrive
in greater numbers and began to establish permanent trading
stations with increasing numbers of Egyptians and northern
Sudanese working as servants. Kelly (1985: 269) writes,

> Between 1857 and 1874 it was common practice for the
> traders' private armies to ally themselves with one
> of the groups engaged in a local conflict and to
> participate in raids in which large numbers of
> cattle and captives were taken. The situation that
> evolved soon after was one in which the cattle
> supported the operation of the stations and served
> as the currency in both obtaining ivory and
> arranging for it to be carried to the river for
> shipment. The captives supplied remuneration to the
> Arab mercenaries who sold them into slavery in the
> north.

While the alien traders sought to advance their interests
by exploiting local hostilities, local peoples perceived their
presence as a means to advance their own interests as well.
D. Johnson (1980: 210) offers a case in point. Nuar Mer, a
Dinka by birth later adopted by Nuer parents, sought to ally
himself with traders to gain armed assistance against his own
enemies. Johnson observes,

> Nuar Mer raided for both cattle and people, and he
> traded the people to the merchants for tobacco,
> sugar and other minor items. . . . Individuals who
> came into conflict with Nuar often had their
> children captured, or were sold as slaves
> themselves. Nuar got the aid of slavers to herd
> men . . . into an enclosure where they were burned
> to death in revenge for the murder of another man
> they had killed. In this way Nuar came into
> increased conflict with other Gaawar [Nuer].

Kelly (1985: 270) observes, "Nuar Mer not only perpetuated a
sustained conflict between sections of the Gaawar, but also
recruited members of other Nuer and Dinka tribes to fight
against his own people. This unprecedented pattern of
alliance was only possible as a consequence of the armed
support provided by the traders." Foreign contact thus added
further incentive to seek gain at the expense of one's
neighbors. Phenomena such as that described by Johnson for
the Nuer were probably more common throughout the Nilotic
Sudan. When the British began their temporary domination of
the southern Sudan in 1898, they understandably had it in mind
that the pastoral Nilotes were a violent, aggressive, and
warlike people, and the early years of their administration in
this region reflected this unfortunate and inaccurate
stereotype. Apart from a number of particularly severe and
bloody punitive raids carried out by British troops in their
country, the Atuot remained unadministered until 1922 when a
subdistrict headquarters was established among them aside Lake

Yirol (see Millais 1924: 161). I will return to a discussion
of the effects of this newer foreign presence later in this
chapter. At this point it will be of some value to review the
relevant literature on the Atuot that was published prior to
our visit among them.

According to J. P. Crazzolara's imaginative interpretation of Nilotic ethnology (1950), the present area of
Atuot settlement is co-terminous with what he called the
"cradleland" of the Nilotes.   I do not endorse this
interpretation even though his writings are worthy of close
examination. In his first volume on the Lwoo-speaking peoples
of eastern Africa he wrote:

> The name Dowaat is mentioned as the name of the man
> who remained in the home country at the head of a
> group of Lwoo, while the rest emigrated. The home
> country, according to general Lwoo custom, was
> probably PaDowaat, "country" or "place of Dowaat," a
> name which was then, or later became, the
> designation of the whole group which remained
> behind. Possibly or mainly under Dinka influence,
> the name underwent a gradual change: PaDowaat became
> PaDowaat and Pa-Dwot; then (P)Aduot and Atwot,
> without any violence to the phonetic laws of the Jii
> languages (1950: 31).

Crazzolara's comment is interesting, though the derivation he
reaches is decidedly based on Dinka terms and phonology. Pan
is indeed a Dinka term that can mean home or homeland, while
in the closely related Atuot and Nuer languages, cieng is the
analogous term.   Though he had no firsthand experience living
among the Atuot, Crazzolara suggested,

> The Atuot are supposed to be a group of Nuer who in
> former times thrust forcibly into Dinka country and
> settled there. The Dinka then closed in at their
> back cutting them off from the bulk of Nuer. Their
> language is said to be Nuer with a slight admixture
> of Dinka [which is of course the case, for those who
> know it, with the Nuer language]. A Bull Nuer who
> passed through Atuot country declared that he found
> no difference in their language--just ordinary Nuer
> (1950: 31).

Linguistic authorities (Tucker 1935: 878; Bryan and
Tucker 1948: 12) classify Atuot as a "dialect cluster" of the
Nuer language, and I encountered only little difficulty
speaking with western Nuer in the Atuot tongue. Emin Pasha
apparently experienced a similar fact as he wrote, "Of the
various Dinka tribes the Nuer and the Atuot speak the same
language, which differs considerably from the true Dinka"
(cited in Schweinfurth 1873: 339).
Crazzolara's remarks can be considered alongside S.
Santandrea's (1968: 112) comments on the Luo.

> The original country of the Luo was south of Yirol
> in what is now Atuotland. . . . At the time the
> Atuot started invading the land and hard fighting
> ensued . . . the Jo Luo left their land for

good . . . No details are given about the splitting
up of the various Luo tribes, except that it was
caused by the inroads of the advancing enemies, the
Atuot.

Events along this order are reflected in Atuot oral
traditions, which also suggest that the peoples resident in
the environment where they settled were primarily blacksmiths
and hunters. Families who carry on these traditions can be
found in numerous lineages of contemporary Atuot, a fact which
suggests that their migration was partly violent but also a
process of incorporation. At the time of our initial visit
among the Atuot, the so-called Luo or Jur living to the
southwest of Atuot country continued to live as hunters,
trappers, and smiths. The same traditions suggest that in the
early stages of Atuot migration into their present homeland,
Aliab and Ceic Dinka had already occupied their present
territories.

Mention is also made of the Atuot in H. C. Jackson's
(1923: 74) account of the western Nuer. He writes,

When we first hear of the Nuer they seem to have
been domiciled in what is commonly referred to as
"the island," the country west of Shambe. . . . With
them were the Atuot and to the north and west, the
Shilluk. . . . Up to this period [mid-fifteenth
century] it is perhaps not unreasonable to imagine
that the Nuer, Dinka and Atuot and Shilluk were all
more or less congregated in the area round Shambe
but were forced gradually to emigrate.

In the oral traditions of pastoral Nilotes, the initial cause
of dispute which eventually leads to separation occurs in
association with arguments over the rightful ownership of
cattle. In this sense they were forced to migrate because
continued co-residence would have led to open hostility. Were
these peoples indeed, as Jackson intimates, at one time more
benign neighbors, it is interesting to speculate that the
Dinka, Nuer, and Atuot made off with larger and smaller herds
of cattle which had once been common property. Whereas Anuak
possess an extensive cattle color terminology they tend, in
the main, smaller stock, as is generally the case for the
Shilluk.

Recent archeological research in the southern Sudan does
not directly support such an interpretation, though it gives
one grounds to imagine such a scenario. According to N. P.
David and others (1981: 50), at Dhang Rial, a site excavated
in the Ngok Dinka country, there were found traces of a
ceramic style followed by

an early iron age culture that appears at about A.D.
500. This phase, characterized by pastoralism, has
produced striking evidence of internecine warfare.
Possibly in the 14th or 15th century A.D. the
replacement of humpless by humped cattle marks the
division between the local early and later iron age.
The latter appears directly ancestral to the present
Dinka occupation. . . . The diffusion of a superior
breed of humped cattle here formed part and parcel
of a process of western Niloticization where

elsewhere it may have facilitated the expansion of speakers of Nilotic languages.

That "Nuer" and "Atuot" have emerged as distinctive ethnic categories over a period of time has been generally accepted as historical fact by authorities with firsthand experience in their country. What eludes an understanding of this co-divergent process is the cause in situ of initial migrations-- for the Atuot in a southerly direction, and for the Nuer, eastward across the Nile. It has been suggested that these processes resulted from ecological necessity resulting from "pressure" (Southall 1976) or overgrazing (Howell 1955: 207-208; cf. Wall 1976) while M. Sahlins (1961) suggested that Nuer social structure was largely the result of a lusty preference for cattle raiding. But of course Nuer also raid Nuer. Texts cited below suggest instead that movement, migrations and a certain degree of flux in social relations are a constant feature of pastoralism in this region of Africa and that in a real sense there was no homeland from which ancestral Nuer or Atuot migrated. To imagine a common homeland, one would have to know much more than is now possible about the prepastoral or protopastoral Nilotic world.

Rather than seek a cause to explain an initial series of migrations it may be more worthwhile to underscore the fact that the pastoral onus invariably entails a continual dialectic between membership in one or another social group, and exclusion from others vis-a-vis cattle (see especially Lienhardt 1975; Verdon 1982). The published ethnographies on the Sudanese Nilotes offer numerous illustrations of the process whereby members of local groups break away from larger social segments to settle in new cattle camps, in new territories. The lesson seems to be "united we fall, divided we stand." Many who have addressed this aspect of Nilotic ethnogenesis have sought an historical event which caused people to disperse due to some kind of catastrophic event. The fact that there is considerable flexibility in ethnic associations in the contemporary world, as suggested by Evans-Pritchard in the epigraph of this chapter, may well serve as a model for understanding Nilotic ethnology. The Nuer are a group of people who see to the needs of their cattle in a particular environment. The Dinka are more or less the same, as are the Atuot. In a very general sense the ethnic labels correspond on the ground to regional variations in economic and ecological adaptation. As I have hinted elsewhere, ethnicity moves "on the hoof."

In a review of the status of Nilotic studies Evans-Pritchard (1950: 6) wrote, "The Atuot seem to be a section of the Nuer who are today separated from them by Dinka tribes. Almost nothing is known of them and they would certainly repay a separate study." A decade later he noted (1960: 337) "I would suggest a study of the Atuot, for apart from the intrinsic value of such a study, it would shed a revealing light on the complex ethnological problem of the relationship of the Nuer and the Dinka." P. P. Howell (1955: 217) observed "Linguistically and to some extent culturally, the Atuot are closer to the Nuer than most Dinka tribes and they claim a common origin with the Nuer" (see also Buxton 1973: 108). In his critical appraisal of the veracity of many entries of C. G. Seligman's (1932) Pagan Tribes of the Nilotic Sudan, Evans-

Pritchard (1971: 164) stated "The Atuot are not Dinka," an observation that is confirmed by my own research. But to Evans-Pritchard's comment it must be remarked that neither are they Atuot. The ethnic designation is meaningful only in relation to who is posing the query and in regard to the social context of its application.

The criteria of language and its usage have often been employed to delimit ethnic groups in the anthropological literature and, to some extent, subject peoples utilize a similar classification. For this reason the Nuer have become known by a term which they do not (at least in the so-called traditional setting) employ for self-reference, even while they are called Nuer by both the Atuot and Dinka. Similarly, Dinka and Nuer use the term "Atuot" when making reference to a social group within which many refer to themselves as Reel, or nei cieng Reel. In some accounts of local ethnogenesis, Reel is imaged as a long-deceased ancestor who quarreled with and later parted company from the respective apical ancestors of the Nuer and Dinka. At the same time, Nuer and Atuot refer to the Dinka as Jaang, a term that connotes a degree of insult since it intimates the status "foreigner." There is an interesting demographic paradox to this usage: the Dinka are estimated to number more than one million individuals, while the Nuer are less than half as numerous and the Atuot-speaking population are the size of a smaller Nuer or Dinka tribal segment.

It has been suggested that "Dinka" is an Arab bastardization of Dengkur (see Nebel 1954: 7). Naath perhaps became known as Nuer because their existence was first brought to the attention of travelers by Shilluk, Dinka or even itinerant Arab traders. In the Atuot dialect the noun nuer also means "human being." The Nilotic interest in cattle has a wide currency in the general anthropological literature and it is in this regard that the etymological derivation of "Atuot" may be appreciated. In the Nuer language ngut atuot refers to a "bull kept for service; not to be castrated" and gatuot, "aristocrat, the most noble of the tribe" (Kiggen 1948: 334, 100). Crazzolara (1933: 49) translates the compound term gatatuot (from gat, to child) as "sons of chiefs or bulls" (see also Evans-Pritchard 1940: 179). In the Dinka language, atuot can refer to a type of cow with especially wide-spreading horns, which they imagine originate in Atuot country (Deng 1973: 106). As an adverb in the Atuot language the term reel connotes cleverness as well as a task that is difficult to perform and unpredictable in its results. A term that is almost homophonic, rial, is an ox-color denoting a predominantly dark animal with a splash of white standing out starkly against the otherwise muted hide. This usage appears cognate with R. G. Lienhardt's (1963: 87) translation of the Dinka rial as "dazzling array" or "shining beauty." Some Atuot spoke of themselves as a people who likewise stand apart or who are separated, a notion that is consistent with the ox-color metaphor. This is in turn akin to the Nuer usage of atuot (from tut, or bull) as "aristocrats" or those who have distinguished themselves from the common lot.

The preceding comments are not intended to imply that in relation to their Nuer and Dinka neighbors, Atuot speakers think of themselves as "aristocratic." However, in the contemporary world, where political sensibilities have been heightened following independence, there is a sense of

exclusiveness which one can observe in Atuot communities.
With reference to an economic approach to ethnic distinctions
it is also apparent that the evolved forms of pastoralism in
the Nilotic Sudan are essentially similar, with slight but
significant ecological variables affecting each form.
Concurrently, their economic interests, at least as far as
these involve pastoralism, demand a degree of exclusiveness in
competition for selected resources such as grazing areas in
transitional ecological zones.

One can then suggest that in view of microenvironmental
variations, differences in cultural form and practice, as well
as in linguistic usage, have developed over longer and shorter
periods of time throughout the Nilotic Sudan.   Two ready
examples come to mind. Howell (1955: 239-40) writes,

> The environmental parameters of ethnic interaction
> are relatively clear, as scarcity of dry season
> pasture or elevated land during high water
> corresponds positively with increased inter-tribal
> warfare and raiding.

In their gradual assumption of pastoralism, the Mandari, a
people whose cultural and linguistic affinities were once
closer to the Bari, have been in the process of adopting
Nilotic custom and usage over the past sixty years (see Buxton
1955, 1975).   From a broader perspective it might be
emphasized once more that the Nuer, too, "are of comparatively
recent origin as a people" (Howell 1955: 208).

THE ATUOT FROM WITHIN

The typical response to my question of local people, "Who are
the Atuot?" was a listing of the six sections or homelands of
people who speak thok Reel, the Atuot tongue: Apak, Luac,
Jilek, Akot, Rorkec, and Kuek.   As time passed during
residence in different Atuot communities, it became
increasingly clear that the Apak did not neatly conform to
this order. On the one hand, their common language might best
be termed Dinka Atuot. Even after I had learned to converse
in thok Reel it remained difficult for me to understand thong
Apau, the Apak dialect. In addition, as the historical and
mythical texts I collected from Apak elders indicate (see
Burton 1981a) while the Apak are the numerically largest Atuot
section, they are the least homogenous ethnically. Apak texts
reveal that representatives of different agnatic groups
entered this region from the Jur to the south, from Agar Dinka
territory to the north and west as well as from areas of Ceic
Dinka settlement to the east. In consequence, while the Apak
are administratively considered to be a section of the Atuot
this may well have been a consequence of British
administrative policy rather than extant social reality.   In
any case, the Apak offer a clear illustration of the fluid
nature of ethnic classification and ecological variation.
Even in the other five sections there are notable linguistic
variables. Many Atuot refer to the Rorkec and Kuek linguistic
forms as the purest type of Atuot.   Whereas virtually all
Luac, Akot, and Jilek are fully bilingual in Atuot and Dinka,
one can easily encounter individuals in Kuek and Rorkec who
speak only Atuot.   Throughout Atuot country, again excepting

Apak territory, Atuot speakers by birth highly value this
bilingual recourse. In practical matters this means that
while in the company of Agar, Ceic or Aliab Dinka, they can
turn among themselves and speak Atuot, thus immediately
excluding the others from social intercourse. It is my
impression that Atuot alone was the more common language in
these communities since the presence of administrative
officials during the colonial period ensured more peaceable
relations between and among ethnic groups. I will return to
this general point later in the chapter.

As noted, Atuot refer to their Dinka neighbors as Jaang:
In Atuot one will hear Jaang te cor wene, era nei murro, or
"those are Dinka living there and they are a different
people." With regard to the Nuer, Atuot suggested to me kok a
Nuere era kok thiako nei, "we and Nuer are closely related
people." Some older and perhaps more philosophically oriented
men told me that the Nuer are a people "who have taken our
language and made it crooked" (see Evans-Pritchard 1956:
74-75).

To preface a number of texts that provide some images of
Atuot history and ethnology, something should be said about
the indigenous perception of time past (see Evans-Pritchard
1939; Deng 1974, 1980; Lienhardt 1961). The Atuot word wal
refers to a period in the past within living memory;
"creation," or their initial migrations and separation from
other Nilotic peoples, happened ne mei, too long ago to be
certain of details or time sequences. As such, the texts can
be designated alet ne mei, "the words of ancient times."
Often the histories and narratives of clans and smaller
agnatic groups are recollections of feuds and warfare between
them, as is also the case for the Nuer, who state that "feuds
and quarrels between lineages chiefly led to their dispersal,
and they can cite many examples" (Evans-Pritchard 1940: 209;
see also Lienhardt 1958, 1975). All adults save the infirm or
senile share a similar version of a creation myth, while I
doubt that any individual possesses a comprehensive knowledge
of the more diverse origin of all Atuot clans and sections.
At the individual level, when a man composes an ox or bull
song, the names of his forebears and the events of their lives
are often central themes (see Chapter 5). It could not be
stated positively without some qualification that Atuot
express an abstract interest in the unfolding of historical
events, yet whenever a number of men and women sat with me to
recount such activities, others joined the group to listen,
occasionally interrupting to amend or dispute a narrative.

These selected texts relate on one level how ancestors
parted company with Nuer and, in another sense, how they came
to consider themselves a distinct cultural and linguistic
group. Creation (separation) is typically said to have taken
place in a cattle camp north of present-day Atuot country,
close to the Nile in western Nuerland. The camp is spoken of
with two names, Akorthaar and Akorlil. The literal
translation of the first name reads "under the tree called
akor." Akorlil can be glossed as "at the tree called akor in
the type of pasture called lil," or "the place of the fight in
lil." The Adok and Nuong peoples of western Nuerland refer to
a camp called Tharjath, "under the tree" in similar texts.
The shortened, selected narratives presented here are
representative of many others I collected in response to the
question, "Where did the Atuot first come from?" An elder

man, Barnaba Madeo Bol, who had been a government-appointed chief in Kuek country, replied,

> There is always a certain amount of envy and enmity between brothers. The words we hear from the old people when we were children say we were part of Nuer. They were brothers, Reel and Nuer, and had a quarrel over the bead called tik yang. Reel could not find the bead once and accused Nuer that his cow had swallowed it. Reel said the cow would have to be killed so the bead could be retrieved. This was done, but they found that the cow had not eaten it. Then they fought, but later settled by making an oath. They said if we stay together we will always go on killing each other. So Reel left.

By demanding such extreme action in the first place, this probably points toward a longer period of hostility. Reel is here portrayed as the one who separated. The gist of the lesson seems again to be "united we fall, divided we stand." The text continues,

> Reel left a bull tethered in the camp then rounded up the families to move by night. When Nuer later returned to the camp and heard the bull crying, he thought Reel was still about. He stayed for one day but then realized that Reel had left and was already too far away to follow. Reel went until the people came to this place and lived in the cattle camp Panther [apparently a Dinka term that can be translated "the ancient home"]. We praise ourselves by being called Reel because we despise these Dinka around us.

In passing I would like to note that a number of older adults suggested that before they lived in Akorlil or Akorthaar, all people--Dinka, Nuer, and Atuot--came from a place known as adekdit, a Dinka term that in colloquial usage refers to a body of water so vast that a bird would be unable to cross its expanse without dying.

As I indicated, this preceding text is one example of a common Nilotic form. A second variant, collected at different times among the Luac Atuot, also suggests the initial dispute between the two "brothers" involved cattle.

> At one time the father of Nuer and Reel became very old and he told his sons to come early in the morning to his bedside so he could divide his cow and calf between them. They left together but Nuer went off on his own a short while later because he had arranged to meet a woman. Reel came very early the next morning and took the calf, while Nuer appeared much later in the day because he had been with his woman. He found that only the old cow remained. Then the father died. Nuer later accused Reel of stealing the calf but Reel retorted that if Nuer did not know where it was he had better remain quiet. They killed and ate the old cow and then departed. Because they had eaten together they vowed never to fight each other (see Evans-Pritchard 1940: 127; Lienhardt 1961: 177-78).

     A possible interpretation of this short narrative is that
Reel is figured as the younger son without a wife, eager to
increase his number since he makes off with the cow calf, a
symbol of the potential growth of a family and herd.   In this
mythical world where Nuer and Atuot are personified as single
individuals, they part with a sentiment of caution bordering
on precarious restraint.   The accusation of theft points
toward strained relations and serves as an omen portending
that death would have ensued had the suspicion arisen again
(see also Lienhardt 1975: 200).   Each of these short extracts
clearly implies that it was Atuot or Reel who left Nuerland.
Common   sense   would   attest   to   this   since   the   Nuer   are
ten   to   twelve   times   as   numerous   as   native   speakers   of
Atuot.
     In the course of field work a number of additional texts
were collected with the help of Telar Deng from chiefs of the
Nuong and Adok Nuer, peoples with whom Luac and Jilek share
inland dry-season pastures.   There are once again common
themes in the texts which are summarized as follows:

     One time a cow of Jagei [Nuer] swallowed a bead
     belonging to Tuot [Atuot].   The cow had been
     tethered in the camp and left behind when the other
     cows were released for grazing because it was
     calving.   Tuot claimed that since the cow of Jagei
     had swallowed the bead, it would have to be cut open
     to bring it out.   This was done, but the bead was
     not found.   At the time no one had seen a kite swoop
     down and make off with the bead, tik yang.   Jagei
     became very angry with Tuot because the cow was to
     have given birth, but was now dead.   He demanded to
     fight with Tuot, who refused, and suggested instead
     that he would replace the dead animal with three
     healthy cows of his own.   Jagei refused and once
     more demanded to fight.   Tuot persisted for a
     settlement but to no avail.   Tuot then decided to
     leave the camp secretly to avoid a fight.   He
     tethered a bull in the camp to deceive Jagei into
     thinking he had not left.   The next day Tuot was
     already far away, leaving behind him his father Reel
     and his younger brother Thiang.   Thiang later
     refused to stay with his brother Jagei when he
     learned how he had mistreated Tuot.   Thiang crossed
     the Bahr-el-Jebel.   The father Reel stayed with
     Jagei and died in [western] Nuerland.   Tuot later
     became known as Atuot and went to live where
     Atuot now stay.   The Nuer used to be called
     Reel because their father was Reel.

     R. G. Lienhardt (1975), in a brilliant summary and
interpretation of similar narratives recorded for the
neighboring Dinka and other, more geographically distant
Nilotic peoples, suggests that "their substance is held to be
historical by those who tell them" and in this regard such
texts might correctly be termed legends (pp. 213-14).   More
important, he observes that the traditional political order of
Nuer and Dinka society (and for obvious reasons, one must
include the Atuot as well) has an important impress on the
anthropological interpretations of these texts.   A long
citation is merited:

Dinka and Nuer political communities, from the
smallest to the largest, are based upon agnatic
descent groups, which, while always retaining their
distinct identities for themselves, are assimilated
to one and other in relation to opposing groups of
the same kind. Thus those who regard themselves as
members of different lineages at one level of
political action are unified as a single lineage at
a higher genealogical level and in different
political situations. Similarly, in any local
community, groups of different agnatic descent
appear as undifferentiated friends, allies, and
neighbors from some points of view, as members of
their own distinct groups from others.

Total assimilation of one descent group by another
(as with the swallowing and retention of the bead,
had that occurred), or total separation (as it
follows in the myth) would destroy the political
form of the society and the moral basis upon which
it is founded. The myths then represent, between
the resented (but only suspected) ingestion of one
group by another, and the total separation which
becomes its consequence, the logical extremes
between which Dinka and Nuer political process moves
(1975: 230-31).

To become assimilated is to cease to exist altogether. This
conclusion, I believe, though here represented in mythical
form, is an essential phenomenon to bear in mind when
considering the nature of Atuot identity in prehistory and in
the contemporary world.

Up to this point, this chapter has been concerned with
early references in print concerning the Atuot-speaking
peoples and some general observations on Nilotic ethnology and
myths of origin or what might equally be termed legends of
creation and separation. Some summary observations may be
offered in the latter regard before addressing some of the
ways in which British colonial rule affected and changed
pastoral Nilotic societies.
There is little ambiguity in the ethnological import of
the texts as presented. They simply point to the fact that
the Atuot evidence confirms an especially close relationship
at some point in the past with the Nuer, as Atuot share in
common a quasi-historical account of their migration from Nuer
territories. There is on the other hand considerable
discrepancy in the more numerous tales which explain the
origin of each of the six Atuot sections as well as clans
within sections. These have been summarized elsewhere (see
Burton 1981a), and convey the impression that the Atuot, or
for that matter the Nuer, did not happen within a short time
span (see also Johnson 1979). As noted, the Apak section
includes clans that claim agnatic heredity from the ancestral
figure Reel, from peoples who migrated into Apak country from
Bor Dinka country to the east of the Nile as well as others
who initially come from Jur country, to the south. An older
man from the Akot section said to me: "Long ago we were Nuer.
One of the sons was killed and the others left Akorlil and
crossed through the Ceic Dinka country. When they came to

Panther they found Luac and Kuek already there. Luac gave
them a daughter to marry and they became in-laws," hence
Atuot. A cursory examination of a map showing named clan and
section distributions throughout the region of pastoral
Nilotic occupation reveals that the common clan names have a
wide distribution.

In consequence, one is inclined to reason that the more
general process of migration and eventual resettlement
entailed a related series of events throughout Nilotic
prehistory. The initial Atuot immigrants exploited resources
of the riverine pastures which extend from Atuot country into
western Nuerland en route south. Successful occupation of
specific territories was achieved either through armed
conflict, peaceable reconciliation, or some variation in
between (see also Kelly 1985). Having established some number
of cattle camps in what is now Atuot country (and reference in
texts to the camp known as Panther might be cited as idiomatic
of this process) indigenous blacksmiths and trappers became
Atuot through intermarriage. In Nuerland, an analogous
circumstance is reported whereby in association with a minor
ritual of sacrifice, Dinka ca naath, or simply "became" Nuer
(see Evans-Pritchard, 1940). In the precolonial era, the
development of cultural, linguistic, and economic forms, which
later came to have a distinctive quality, may have arisen in
association with regional variations in environments. M. H.
Harrison (1955: 21) writes,

> The Dinka [a nomenclature which in this account also
> includes the Atuot] of the Bahr-el-Ghazal in the
> rains have refuge from the flood region on the
> fringes of the division. Here, on ironstone soils,
> they graze their cattle, cultivate crops and have
> their villages. In this they are far more fortunate
> than the Nilotes of the Upper Nile Province (i.e.,
> the Nuer) who have far worse rainy season
> conditions. Grazing and cropping [in the Bahr-el-
> Ghazal] are much better than in the flood region.

In areas of western Dinkaland where human and bovine
populations are the highest for the pastoral Nilotic Sudan,
one finds that the indigenous institution and political
authority of the spear master is most developed. By contrast,
ordered anarchy, as Evans-Pritchard phrased it, reigns in the
much more sparsely populated areas of eastern Nuerland, where
he carried out most of his studies. Into this spectrum of
variation one would place the Atuot betwixt and between these
poles as their own gwan riang, or possessors of a centrally
important spiritual power (see Chapter 4), were analogous to
Dinka spear masters in their ritual functions while possessing
only a limited degree of actual political power, and thus more
like the Nuer leopard-skin chief.

An essential prerequisite in considering pastoral Nilotic
ethnology is the recognition of the arbitrary and contextual
features of ethnic boundaries, a point made with
characteristic clarity by Evans-Pritchard in the epigraph for
this chapter. Just as the Nuer are Naath to themselves, the
Dinka Jieng, and the Atuot Reel, so too are they all
pastoralists who occupy particular, named territories. Since
as many as half of the Lau Nuer, the largest section, are of
Dinka descent, the evident maxim seems to be when in Nuerland,

do as the Nuer. In a brief appraisal of my doctoral
dissertation, a study that was primarily concerned with an
understanding of traditional Atuot cosmology and ritual, the
leading authority on Nilotic studies remarked that the Atuot
seemed to be neither Nuer nor Dinka, but in a sense, both.
The brief review of Nilotic ethnology attempted here would
imply that no different conclusion might even be expected.

BRITISH RULE IN THE NILOTIC SUDAN

To the Atuot the first cadre of British administrators may
have appeared as yet another collection of transient aliens
who would claim to govern them but would disappear, as had the
Turks, Egyptians, Mahdists and others. Surely the eventual
demise of British colonialism was inevitable, yet this
remained beyond the ken of any individual Atuot at the turn of
the century. Few material vestiges of British presence in the
southern Sudan have weathered the past half-century and in
many regards the first years of their presence in the region
were likewise of no lasting significance. Colonial rule in
the southern Sudan was experienced more as an aftershock, with
its reverberations severing the facade of national unity in
the course of a seventeen-year-long civil war, erupting on the
eve of Sudanese independence in 1955.
     Here I wish to discuss two clearly related phases of
colonial rule in the Nilotic Sudan and the manner in which
Dinka, Nuer, and Atuot responded to this alien presence. The
first era was characterized most of all by a general lack of
administrative policy. The second was one in which the
British were more neglectful than mindful of the
responsibilities they had declared as their mission.
Correspondingly, one can discern two rather different
types of response by the pastoral peoples toward foreign
domination.
     At the international level, British policy in this region
of Africa was oriented primarily toward maintaining control
over and access to the White Nile. It was argued in Whitehall
that if the French were able to establish a transcontinental
dominance on an east-west axis, the enormous British
investment in Egypt might evaporate with the Nile (see Brown
1969). This particular problem was gingerly settled in the
course of the "Fashoda Incident," wherein the French absconded
from a military confrontation over control of the southern
Sudan in exchange for free colonial rein in Chad (Collins
1962). The immediate problem the British inherited was
finding the people who inhabited the southern regions of the
country, who proved to be infinitely less predictable than the
seasonal Nile floods.
     Due to ecological and geomorphological features of the
country they occupy, the pastoral mode of adaptation
necessitates seasonal migrations with their herds between
well-defined territories. Long before the arrival of the
British, Atuot had by necessity learned to protect their herds
from raids by neighboring peoples and had gained considerable
experience in the same exercise during the years of the ivory
and slave trade. In the early years, the British found time
and again that the people they claimed to govern simply could
not be found; on the other hand, if local people were
contacted, their cattle were often some distance off in

temporary care of political allies. When word spread that a
British patrol was in the area, Atuot took to the forest to
scatter their cattle and to take cover for their own well-
being. Unfortunately, few records exist describing the
initial encounter between the mounted soldier with a rifle and
the barefoot pastoralist with a spear. The history that has
survived consists in the main of British accounts of their own
efforts aimed at military subjugation.

District headquarters were established in small towns
which had served as staging grounds for the ivory and slave
trade. The paramount expressed concerns of the government
were "establishing peace," building rest houses, clearing the
forest to build roads, and collecting tribute in grain, ivory,
and livestock. As a matter of policy, the task of education
was allotted to a variety of mission societies (see Gray 1961;
Beshir 1969; Trimmingham 1948; Henderson 1953; Hill 1965;
Dempsey 1956; Burton 1985a). G. N. Sanderson (1976) argues
that in the early years of administration the small towns were
less the administrative headquarters of provinces than the
rear guard for military patrols against local people,
exercises that were undertaken, according to D. C. Comyn
(1911), to reward someone with a promised brevet. As late as
1920 (twenty-two years after Britain "recaptured" the Sudan)
the legal secretary of the Anglo-Egyptian Sudan government in
Khartoum declared that the administration of the southern
region was an abject failure, evidenced in part by the excess
of expenditures over revenues collected (see Sanderson 1976;
Santandrea 1967; Collins 1971).

Archival sources of this period contain many reports on
the numerous punitive raids conducted against local peoples,
which resulted in the looting of herds and the destruction of
crops, homesteads, and entire villages. On the odd occasion
these operations were aided by the Royal Air Force. The
Foreign Office in London fully endorsed this form of
indiscriminate homicide through the rationale "that in order
to control the savages who inhabit the region, a strong and
direct military presence is essential" (cited in Sanderson
1976). The Atuot, among others, were classified as "wild
folk" by the resident British official in 1924 and in
consequence it was decided that an administrative post should
be built in their country. Those involved in the task were
instructed: "Don't try to capture cattle if there is the
slightest chance of losing them; much better to kill them if
possible. . . . The main point is that the Atuot should lose
them." In the early 1920s one British advance inland from the
Nile into Aliab Dinka country was met by an estimated 1,000
local peoples armed for a defensive confrontation. In the
course of the fray that followed, C. H. Stigand, a charmed
official, met his death along with twenty-four of his
subordinates. The following spring, nearly 1,000 British-led
troops "brought fire and sword to those thousand miles of
Aliabland, supported by gun boats on the Nile equipped with
artillery and the ubiquitous machine guns." At the end of the
so-called Aliab uprising, "Over four hundred Aliab, Atuot and
Mandari had been killed, seven thousand cattle seized, and
every village razed to the ground with the durra stores
destroyed. Peace and famine settled over the Aliab country"
(Collins 1985: 10-11). Such was the nature of the civilizing
mission Britain brought to the southern Sudan in the early
decades of the century.

In the main, colonial administration in the 1920s was confined to riverbanks on the northern and southern fringes of pastoral settlement. In 1924 the district commissioner of the Upper Nile Province confessed that he "rarely saw more than the distant backs of Nuer and then only fleetingly" (Sanderson 1976). When they were encountered, however, the British often proceeded to carry on the tradition of making game of local people; as the Nuer complained to Evans-Pritchard (1940: 11), "you [British] raid us, yet you say we cannot raid the Dinka."

This initial phase of administration showed the British to be adept at alienating the indigenous population and rather inept at governing them. Understandably, the periodic punitive raid was perceived by the pastoralists as an invitation to warfare. Deng (1972: 79) has argued that the presence of armed government soldiers and police effectively encouraged previously unknown levels of physical violence. Thus it appears that the colonial administration was systematically creating a problem it was attempting to resolve. In the process, local peoples were made to suffer for a poorly organized, insufficiently staffed and financed, inadequate part-time government. As late as 1927 there were but five Britons in the southern administration who were considered to be fluent in the local languages--among a population of more than two million.

The guiding principle of indirect rule, as often noted, was riddled with inconsistencies and contradictions. Among the pastoral Nilotes, "chiefs" were to come forward as tribal leaders, yet such offices and individuals did not exist in the traditional context since the very organization of political process in these societies was inconsistent with hierarchical government. R. O. Collins (1971) points out that the baffled Britons tried to force Atuot, Dinka, and Nuer notables into the role of Arab sheikh or Azande prince (see also Sanderson 1976: 8), a process based not on the local order of society, but on an alien concept of how a tribal society ought to be organized. I have already mentioned that the total number of British officials remained small in the early years of southern administration. Coupled with the inevitable incidence of illness and leaves of absence, it was likely that no more than six British officials would be in a province at any given time (Santandrea 1967). As a result, the intermediary positions were filled by northern Sudanese and Egyptian ma'murs, peoples whose collective history demonstrated a most profound disregard for Black Africans of the southern region since they had been thought of as slaves by the northern Sudanese for centuries. This problem was critical in the eyes of an Aliab Dinka man, who pleaded with a local missionary,

> We are willing to submit to the government and to pay taxes, but let the government not send non-British ma'murs to rule us nor use Black policemen. Let none but the Englishmen be sent to rule us. If there had been no Arab ma'murs there would have been no fighting (Collins 1967: 82).

The northern Sudanese and Arab functionaries were frequently accused of embezzlement and personal exploitation of local resources, including the consumption and sale of goods collected as tax. Local people sensed that the

government carried out its functions with scant regard for,
and little understanding of, traditional custom and usage.
One could indeed make the argument that direct exploitation
rather than indirect rule characterized the first decades of
"civilized" administration. Punitive expeditions normally
involved one or a number of British officials along with a
regiment of northern Sudanese or Ugandan soldiers,
supplemented by a fluctuating assortment of so-called
friendlies, often members of the "tribe" being fired upon.
The latter category consented to comply with government
directives if they saw it to their own advantage in getting
their own back. In other words, it worked to their advantage
to fight with the protection of British arms in order to seek
revenge in a long-standing feud. Paradoxically, to the
British, payment of tribute in this manner was an indication
of subject status; to individual Atuot, Nuer, or Dinka,
however, it was a way of buying government goodwill and
protection. This afforded indigenous people the chance of
observing benevolent neutrality and, at the same time, the
opportunity to settle their own affairs in their own fashion.
     Beginning in 1930 a notable change in this situation was
heralded by the declaration of a "Southern Policy" for
administration, all the more apparent in retrospect for its
absence during the preceding thirty-two years. Thus began the
virtual elimination of the northern Sudanese ma'murs from
positions of political responsibility, in addition to the
prohibition of social and material artifacts reminiscent of
Islam, in the southern Sudan. Slowly, the lower positions in
the administrative bureaucracy were filled by southern
Sudanese who had gained a primary education in English through
mission societies. This process was paralleled by an implicit
change in attitude toward Nilotic peoples on the part of
British officials. The more or less explicit racism of
previous years was blanketed by an outward expression of care
and paternalistic interest. In their memos to superiors,
commissioners and their assistants began referring to "my
chaps" rather than to "the bloody savages."
     The first article of the memorandum titled "Southern
Policy" stated that the aims of the Anglo-Egyptian government
in the south were to

        build up a series of self-contained racial or tribal
        groups with structure and organization based to
        whatever extent the requirements of equity and good
        judgment permit, upon indigenous customs,
        traditional usage and belief (cited in al-Rahim,
        1969).

This guiding principle did not reflect a very sophisticated
knowledge of local ethnography on the part of the Britons.
With very few exceptions, "self-contained tribal groups" never
existed in the southern Sudan nor elsewhere throughout the
world. Rather, this recourse was an invention of tradition
intended to streamline, if not simply organize, the divide-
and-rule order of the day. Intermarriage across ethnic
boundaries was a commonality in the Nilotic Sudan, a fact that
is positively associated with the pastoral, transhumant manner
of existence. Johnson (1979) provides a detailed review of
what was termed "The Nuer Settlement" of 1929-30, wherein,
among other things, large numbers of Nuer were forcibly

relocated and artificially segregated from neighboring Dinka-
speaking peoples, with whom they previously shared dense
economic and political relations. As Johnson notes (1979: 17)
this attempt to neatly order self-contained tribal groups, in
this case between Nuer and Dinka, "was based on an erroneous
appreciation of those relations." Though the southern policy
was intended to separate one linguistic community from
another, the presence of armed government troops also had the
paradoxical effect of easing relations between neighboring
communities. For example, older Atuot informants suggested
that in the past, one would never seriously consider traveling
too far beyond the periphery of one's country since one's own
well-being could not be presumed. Intermarriage had become
more common in recent years, according to these sources, since
aggressive warfare or raiding was now the exception rather
than an expectation.
     Returning to a central theme of this section with the
comfortable distance historical perspectives allow, it is now
easy to see that the division drawn between the northern and
southern Sudan and the divisions that were imposed within the
south would lead to civil war. As a result of a more readily
profitable source of development (or imperialism) in the
northern Sudan, the north advanced three times as quickly as
the south. On the proverbial eve of independence a great
number of northern Sudanese had acquired a literate education
and had assumed positions of considerable power and influence
in the northern Sudan. Indeed, this pattern of development
had been encouraged in part to avoid a reemergence of
religiously inspired reaction against the British occupation
of the country. The Black African south had never asserted a
comparable united front against the fledgling system of
imperialism, but had instead been temporarily circumvented
from the mainstream of history by such things as the Southern
Policy. It was not that two social classes (in the
Marxist sense) had surfaced but rather that two
different nations had been formed within a single
territorial boundary.
     Against the background of these factors, it is possible
to gain a better appreciation of Atuot responses to colonial
rule. Positive advances toward peaceable administration did
in fact emerge in the latter years of British domination. The
pastoralists realized that advantages could be obtained from
formal facilities for litigation and the sanction of law
behind them. Paul Howell, once an administrator in Nuerland,
observes, "Nuer took kindly to a system which enabled them to
raise disputes which in the past would have had little or no
chance of settlement, at any rate without violence" (n.d.: 3).
Prior to colonial rule and the codification that its policies
sought, legal and political authority were vested in a variety
of ritual and spiritual experts who offered sacred sanctions
to the proceedings of secular affairs.
     In recognition of their martial superiority, the powers
of the British were compared to those of God or Divinity (in
Atuot, Decau); as a class of people the British were called
aceke, from the verb cak, which connotes an ability to create
something that did not exist before. Compared to the
situation in the 1920s a radical change had transpired in the
Atuot perception of the British. Initially perceived as
marauders of a different color, they eventually were seen as
benevolent overlords who advanced Atuot desires for physical

and spiritual well-being. Where seemingly endless controversy
reigned in matters such as the settlement of bridewealth
cattle, compensation for divorce or homicide, Atuot could now
state wadaguk aceke a thil ke dong, "what is written by the
government does not grow old," or what is written down is the
way it will be. Such changes have an enormous influence upon
a social system wherein "law" implied a combination of oral
tradition and consensus.

I was lucky enough to have the opportunity to speak at
some length with older men who had been appointed as chiefs in
the preindependence era. In each case, they recalled their
association with the British in terms that reflected pride and
accomplishment. I remember particularly well an afternoon
conversation with a former chief who showed me his robe of
honor and a sword which he had been awarded by a British
administrator. "These," he said in measured words, "were
given to me by your people, the English, for my work as chief.
I keep them now because the land has changed again." Many of
those who retain clear memories of British rule do so with sad
longing. In 1976, the haunting memories of the war between
northern and southern Sudanese were very much alive. In this
regard F. M. Deng (1978: 158) observes,

> The British are the source of the peace, security
> and dignity that known history has given them. This
> has blinded [the pastoral Nilotes] to the British
> shortcomings whose consequences paradoxically
> plunged the country into a civil war almost as
> grave in magnitude as the upheaval from which the
> British had extricated them in the first place.

SUMMARY

Many years of Nilotic history and a diverse variety of
ethnological, linguistic, and ethnographic topics have
received some attention in this chapter. Still, it is
impossible to say in 1986 who the Dinka are, who the Nuer are,
or who the Atuot are since the peoples referred to are not
now, nor were they at any point in the past, static
ethnographic entities. The accepted knowledge about these
peoples has gone through a number of iridescent
transformations since the Seligmans made a first authentic
ethnographic survey of the region in the first decade of this
century, and styles of "knowing" them anthropologically have
changed repeatedly since that time. A debate has been long
running in one of the premier journals of anthropology about
whether the Nuer are Dinka, the Dinka are Nuer, or they are
simply people. Since the debate has some history one can
imagine it will have some future.

In 1948 A. N. Tucker and M. A. Bryan published a survey
on the distribution of Nilotic languages in the southern
Sudan. According to these authorities Atuot was classified as
a dialect cluster of the Nuer language, and this cluster was
further divided into Apak and Aril (i.e., Reel) dialects. In
Tucker's words (1948: 12) Atuot is spoken by people who call
themselves Atuot, "living in the Lakes District near Yirol, in
an enclave among the Dinka." Just preceding this entry, the
author notes that Nuer is spoken as a second language by many

Dinka who live on the periphery of Nuer settlements. One wants to ask: When are Nuer Dinka, or Dinka Nuer, or are Atuot Dinka or Nuer? Or Atuot? The beginning of one answer would point out that ethnic identity is not always a self-defined outward-looking phenomenon but that it also, and importantly, reflects an externally derived series of stereotypes. As noted earlier, the Ngok Dinka who live some hundreds of miles north and west of Atuot country refer to a particular configuration of ox-horns as Atuot, imagining that these cattle originate there. To the best of my knowledge, few (if any) Ngok Dinka have ever been near Atuot country, and those that might have probably had little interest in ox-horn configurations. In her study of Mandari religion, an authority on southern Sudanese peoples (Buxton 1973: 108) wrote, "The seance as I describe it for the Mandari appears . . . to resemble more closely a Nuer phenomenon and this would suggest perhaps a stronger Atuot influence since Atuot are of Nuer extraction." Throughout his study of Nuer religion, Evans-Pritchard contrasts "true" Nuer custom with usages that have been borrowed from, or incorporated by, Dinka who live among them as Nuer. At a further remove, prior to the colonial period it is unlikely that an individual Dinka had a hint of the enormous territory occupied by his or her people, nor of the number of people who spoke the same language with only minor variation.

Given these considerations, a slippery question also arises here. In the precolonial period, what was the nature of ethnic differentiation in the Nilotic Sudan? Surely, one would like to assume, the geographical range of a linguistic community was dependent upon this differentiation. It is unlikely, at the same time, that it ever assumed the importance some contemporary anthropologists would like to imagine! Linguistic differences aside (and in a sense, these must be peripheral since bilingualism seems to be the norm rather than the exception) concepts of cultural identity paralleled and continue to parallel perceived differences in cultural style, nuance, and geographical range. A number of Atuot families I know of have a considerable history of intermarriage with neighboring Dinka groups while remaining fully Atuot in their own self-perceptions. This too seems to be the rule rather than the exception in pastoral Nilotic history.

Recall Lienhardt's (1975) sage comment on a common Nilotic myth: To merge identity is to image the nightmare of ceasing to exist at all. Since this theme and its narrative expression have such wide currency in the Nilotic Sudan, one can only conclude that it points to the heart of a cultural truth. A more contemporary example might be offered. In the fall of 1984, some time after a renewed civil war had begun in the Sudan, I received a letter from an Atuot friend (who has graduate training in English and American universities) then in Juba, the capital city of the southern Sudan. He reviewed among other things the reemergence of guerrilla fighting. "The Atuot with their usual inability to accept assimilation were the first in the field—in fact, Yirol as a whole was one of the biggest contingents in the movement. Majok (a small rural center in Rorkec) Aluakluak (a small rural center in Apak) and Anual (a small rural center in Kuek) have virtually been liberated zones since last year" (Ambrose Beny, personal communication, October 1984).

Ethnological and historical musings aside, Atuot continue to fight to ensure the persistence of a mode of livelihood and manner of being human which forms the basis of their identity and well-being. This realm of their life is discussed in the next chapter.

A residential section of Yirol

Buying grain from merchants at their shops in Yirol

A homestead in the early rainy season

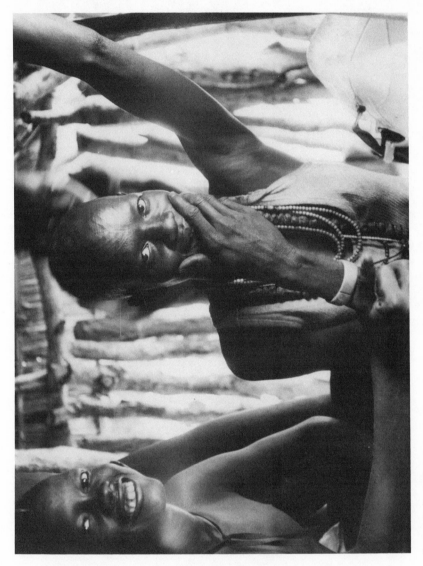

A mother and her son

A family in their cultivation homestead

A diviner at work

Making a new rope under a shelter in a cattle camp

Mid-morning in a wet-season cattle camp

Young children in a cattle camp

Collecting the tethering ropes after the cattle have been driven to pasture

2.
MODES OF EXISTENCE

A contemporary assessment of the geographical distribution of the Atuot-speaking peoples leads to the observation that they might be conceived of historically as a smaller migratory Nuer population which has adopted a number of Dinka usages in a dissimilar manner and degree. In this sense the Apak may be thought of as a population which has most adopted Dinka (particularly Agar) language, and the other five sections may be thought of as peoples who have in contrast retained a Nuer-derived dialect and who have incorporated some of the indigenous peoples into their own social and economic system. This view recognizes both the contextual element of ethnic classification as well as the contemporary localized sense of ethnic distinctiveness.

The choice of the term system in this characterization is intentional and unambiguous. The Atuot system of mixed horticultural production and transhumant pastoralism follows a regular pattern, which is a sophisticated ecological adaptation to regional environmental phenomena. In the course of a 300 to 500 year period (approximate figures at both extremes) separating contemporary Atuot from their migratory ancestors, these adaptive strategies have collectively served to create a sense of their identity. A longer and more detailed survey of the pastoral Nilotic Sudan would no doubt entail a similar observation.

The territory Atuot occupy is located some fifty to sixty miles west of the White Nile, between 6 degrees 30 N. latitude and 30 degrees E. longitude. Today this region is administered within the boundaries of Lakes Province, named for the many shallow basins which dot the countryside. The town of Yirol sits about one mile to the south of Lake Yirol and is the administrative center for the region. Yirol includes a dozen or so shops run by itinerant northern Sudanese merchants, who sell salt, grain, cloth, enameled cookware, and a variety of smaller items. A short distance from these shops is an informal open-air market, where Atuot living near the town sell seasonally available products on a small scale. At varying times throughout the year dried fish, grain, groundnuts, squash, and beans are available. Two elementary schools are also located in the town in addition to army and police stations, the remnants of a small hospital

erected in the colonial period, and the homesteads of
government and associated functionaries. Some seventy miles
to the west at the end of a seasonal, badly rutted dirt road,
is Rumbek, a town many times larger than Yirol. About sixty
miles to the northeast, linked by a road in similar disrepair,
is the small Nile port of Shambe. A track leading south from
Yirol to Atiit in Mandari country terminates at Juba, the
capital of the southern Sudan, approximately 200 miles
distant. Land transport to and from Yirol is drastically
affected by the rainy season, especially when precipitation is
greater than normally expected. This factor of relative
isolation has resulted in the conception that Yirol, like its
immediate environment, is a backwater.

The majority of Atuot wet season villages (cieng), where
gardens are planted, and wet season cattle camps (wuic) are
located on the fringe of the so-called ironstone plateau which
forms a southern perimeter to the swamps of the Upper Nile
basin. Thus Atuot country spans the macroecological zones of
open savannah grassland to the north and increasingly dense
vegetation of tropical forests to the south. The ironstone
plateau lies approximately 435 feet above sea level and
averages some 80 inches of rain per year. Rains typically
commence between March and April and continue on a regular
basis until November or December, when they cease altogether.

From the vantage point of a small aircraft it is easy to
recognize the blending of ecological zones from north to
south. The vegetation observed in regions of true swamp along
the banks and tributaries of the Nile is dominated by papyrus,
the water grass Vossia cuspidata and the tall, reedlike
Echinochloa pyramidalis (Grunnet 1962: 5). In Atuot, Nuer,
and Dinka, the term toic refers to open grasslands that are
more or less permanent and provide crucial grazing resources
at the height of the dry season. The word toic images for
them a particular manner of life and with this certain moral
values, in addition to its use for bovine subsistence.   In
reference to this latter aspect N. Grunnet (1962: 5) notes

> The toic vegetation is strongly influenced by the
> annual [Nile] flood.   The flood period is long
> enough to prevent growth of trees and too short to
> produce swamp vegetation. Through the dry season
> the toic lies as vast meadows of almost pure grass
> stands.

As in many references to the Sudan, the term vast in this
context is not an overstatement. In Lakes Province a toic
stretches from Atuot country on the southern fringe, north to
the east and west as far as Gograil in Dinka country and
Bentiu in Nuerland, some 200 miles distant. In the more
elevated and flood-free savannah forests, Atuot find suitable
sites for establishing gardens as well as resources for
manufacturing many items of their material culture.

Atuot divide the ecological year into twelve months or
moons and further distinguish between the seasons of rains
(deker, when the life-promising rains commence) and the time
of dryness (mai, months when the earth is literally and
figuratively burned).   Rainfall actually occurs in two
intervals, the early rains from March to May and the heavier
rains from July to November, which nourish their staple crops
of sorghum millet and groundnuts. Horticulture is an activity

that consumes human energy in the rainy season, while cattle are moved seasonally between dry season camps in toic environments and wet season camps in the savannah forest. The soils of the ironstone regions are primarily of the laterite catena type. As economic pursuits change from season to season, so too do social relations vary in villages and cattle camps.

The pastoral existence which they enjoy and struggle to preserve is reflected in an alphabetic inventory of Atuot culture and values, a fact that will appear and reappear throughout this study. Interested readers can consult Grunnet's (1962) essay for specific characteristics of their herds. N. R. Joshni and others (1957: 178-79) offer a number of interesting comments also. In regard to Nilotic cattle:

> The cattle type appears to be of great antiquity and is generally supposed to have resulted from an intermixture of the original wild longhorned cattle of Africa (Bos africanus) with later incursions of Asiatic zebus (Bos indicus) . . . local differences in conformation and size as exist appear to be largely of environmental origin. . . . Nilotic cattle are of an undifferentiated type which has developed as a result of a form of natural selection under the difficult conditions imposed by an environment dominated by seasonal and prolonged flooding and the prevalence of insect pests. . . . Trypanosomiasis is widespread, particularly in the Bahr-el-Ghazal where the cattle graze in the wooded ironstone country during the rains.

In view of the genetic characteristics of Nilotic cattle one must assume that pastoralism has been practiced for an extended period of time in this region of Africa. Sophisticated adaptations to this environment (now aided by western-derived veterinary science), as evidenced by the enormity of their herds, further indicate the antiquity of pastoral transhumance in the southern Sudan.

Grunnet contributes a number of related observations. "Wading or half swimming, they are capable of existing on the bristly [swamp] grasses over a long period. This is one of their greatest qualities" (1962: 8). Of equal significance is that Nilotic herds "are able to trek 40-50 km per day with only one watering every second day. Such compulsory circumstances can easily arise through fights with fellow tribesmen or a tribe about grazing" (1962: 8). Unlike the Nuer and Dinka, Atuot do not construct cattle byres or shelters for their cows but simply tether them in the camp in open air within an enclosure of thorn and scrub brush. Other herd management practices are discussed later.

Passing through the center of Atuot country is the permanent river they call Payii. Sections of the river are also referred to on the basis of activities carried out along its banks. The river draws its waters in its upper reaches from the Nilo-Congo Divide and when it enters the flat basin of the upper Nile it seasonally floods its banks, transforming scorched dried cotton soils into a seasonal toic. Smaller feeder streams lead to Lakes Yirol and Anyi. Along these banks, especially in the vicinity of abandoned cattle camps, Atuot cultivate tobacco, which requires intensive weeding and

watering to produce leaves that are harvested throughout the
dry season. As the dry season advances and waters recede,
Atuot settlements close to the river and lakes reap large
catches of fish. At the height of the dry season, all but the
old and infirm abandon wet season settlements to live in dry
season cattle camps, and smaller groups move further into the
toic without cattle to settle at temporary fishing camps
(bur). Atuot traditionally fished with the aid of fish spears
(biith), nets (abuoi), and baskets opened at both ends (thoi)
in which game was trapped. Increasingly Atuot use barbed
hooks bought from merchants in Yirol and elsewhere.
     The inland toic is an essential resource for the form of
pastoralism they practice. P. P. Howell (1954: 237) has
commented on the large toic in the region of Lake Nyibor, to
which Luac and Jilek Atuot drive some of their herds in the
dry season.

> In years when the Bahr-el-Jebel [White Nile] toic
> remains inundated and largely inaccessible during
> the dry season, large numbers of Nuong Nuer move
> southward into the Lake Nyibor area. This area is
> fully utilized by the Agar Dinka and the Atuot and
> also in some years by the Ceic [who more commonly
> pasture herds in the area of the White Nile in the
> dry season].   While the Nile remains high,
> congestion and overgrazing along the Lau [the Dinka
> name for the Payii] reaches a climax. Pressure
> between the Nuer and the Dinka increases and trouble
> follows.

Relations of kinship established through marriage among
peoples who share these resources has, on the other hand, an
effect of decreasing the chance of wide-scale raiding and
warfare (see Gluckman 1956). For the Atuot, in addition to
dry season grazing found there, Lake Nyibor is close to salt
licks where cattle are driven for about ten days every season.
Since the Nyibor pastures are some distance away, herdsmen are
ever cautious about the move. This view is expressed most
clearly in a passage of an ox-song composed by a man from the
Luac section.

> I decided to move to the camp, oh Maduol [his bull]
> When people were troubled with their lives
> You the sons of Jilek,
> Do not take the bulls to the side of salt [Lake
>   Nyibor]
> The trouble with Nuer fell on Lau [a Ceic section]
> You, the sons of Nyanyong
> Do not say releasing a bull to graze is an easy
>   thing
> The troubles with Nuer destroyed our land long ago
> You are always insisting to go to the salt
> But later when the raiding of Nuer has come
> You will remain with only the tethering ropes
> Oh this trouble
> You keep it on the left [be ever cautious]

     To reiterate, Atuot share boundaries with the Ceic, Agar,
and Aliab Dinka. To the east an occasionally dense forest
separates them from the Nile. The Luac, Jilek, and Akot who

have settled here make their permanent wet season camps in
this forest and some are able to pasture herds along the Nile
in the dry season because of intermarriage with the Dinka.
This seems especially the case with the Akot (the smallest
Atuot section) whose land merges with that of the Aliab Dinka.
Sectional names in this context are of further interest.   Akot
is cognate with the Dinka _akeu_, meaning border (Nebel 1954:
42) while the name Aliab is cognate with the Atuot term _liab_,
to separate or leave apart.   The Kuek, Rorkec, and Apak make
villages and wet season camps on the southern and western side
of Payii.   Seen from the air in the rainy season the _toic_
alongside both banks of the river appears like an immense
putting green, dotted by the remains of camps long abandoned
in addition to those presently occupied.

Game abounds in both the _toic_ and forest environments
though animals are not systematically hunted.   Rhinoceros,
elephant, buffalo, ostrich, and antelope provide a variety of
resources which Atuot use for making personal ornaments.
Ironsmiths (_adjoung_) ply their craft in the forest and provide
local peoples with fishing spears, fighting spears, and
digging hoes in exchange for smaller stock such as sheep and
goats and, less often, milking cows.   As there is considerable
low-grade ore in their country for smelting, Atuot have never
placed special value on iron products, unlike their distant
kinsmen, the Nuer.   The avian life in this region of Africa is
astounding in its diversity and from these natural species the
Atuot derive many of the color patterns employed in referring
to cattle and smaller stock.

The types of land Atuot exploit are named for their
economic uses, with a primary distinction between the forest
(_gok_ or _yel_) and permanent pastures (_toic_).   Other place names
generally refer to historical events or former sites of
occupation and in this regard physical space itself has a
moral quality.   A particular cattle camp is not simply a place
to tether cows but is also the place where one's grandfathers
and ancestors lived before with the family herds.   With the
first seasonal occupation of a dry or wet season camp, the
move is publicly celebrated with the sacrifice of an ox or
bull, with invocations recalling the agnatic heredity of the
participants.   Concurrently many Atuot cattle camps are named
after the color of an ox or bull that was sacrificed by a
group of settlers to mark, and thereby establish, a particular
territory as their own.

These remarks are importantly related to an understanding
of traditional forms of settlement.   For the Nilotic peoples
the terms _cieng_ (Nuer and Atuot) and _baai_ (Dinka) have
typically been represented in English as "village" or "home"
and settlements where cattle are kept have been termed
"camps."   The distinction that emerges in the English usage
connotes a differing quality of social relations among
residents.   That is, in our manner of thinking a camp seems
necessarily temporary when contrasted with the sense of
permanence associated with the word "village," which also
implies some degree of population density.   For a time in
African studies a village was selected for research on the
premise that it could serve to represent the entire social
universe of a people.

A better understanding of the Atuot usage would be to
think of cattle villages and agricultural camps.   A single wet
season cattle camp often includes as many as 300 individuals

living within the circular confines of an area with a radius
of approximately 200 yards. A typical village is in fact a
dispersed settlement pattern over miles of territory.   In
addition to meaning "home," "land of," "people," and "way of
doing things" the Atuot term cieng can refer to a geographical
area; only when it is named (for example, ciengde, "my home")
does it refer to a specific household in that area. When an
individual says yen a wa cieng, the meaning is often ambiguous
since this can refer to a general area, such as cieng Luac, a
dispersed settlement area, or a particular homestead.
Conversely, the phrase yen a wa wiuc means "I am going home to
such and such a cattle camp."
     A more elusive problem emerges in this context. Seasonal
movement of human and animal populations between two
relatively well-defined and separate types of environment has
often been understood as movement toward villages after herds
have been watered and fed in dry season camps. Here again, we
take village life as the norm and movement from it as a
disruption of normal life. The village is often thought to be
the setting in which social integration is recreated at yearly
intervals.   I began to reason differently in the course of
conversations on quite a different matter.   A man was
relating how at one time he had been moving with his cattle
away from the rising waters of the floods, a usage that is
very common in ox-songs. This suggests an emphasis on the
camp as a permanent enterprise, that is, seasonally
interrupted by high waters. Indeed, horticultural labor is a
seasonal undertaking, while work attending pastoralism is a
perpetual activity.
     Atuot conceptualize the ecological year as a series of
social and economic activities that begin in January, a period
when crops have been harvested and most of the population has
moved to dry season camps to subsist on milk and riverine
resources. This demarcation is consistent with their myths
accounting for creation, which are set in the environment of
dry season camps as well (see also Lienhardt 1961: 195).   In
the songs men compose to record and relate social experience
one of the more common themes is the recitation of cattle
camps where one has lived: it would be inconceivable to sing
laudingly of life in the village setting. A short women's
song expresses a similar sentiment:

     I choose the camp
     The camp where people with beads remain
     Oh our girls, of what do they speak
     They speak of the camp
     I brought the tassels for the horn of Majok
     Our staying in the camp--
     There is no confusion
     I have chosen the camp
     The camp where people with beads remain

The second and last lines of the song make implicit reference
to marriage and the recreation of domestic life.
Traditionally, a young man was given one or a number of bead
necklaces by his agnatic relatives as a sign that he was
mature enough to begin searching in earnest for a wife. The
beads, called tik yang, or beads of cattle, signified, perhaps
more importantly, that he was next in line to make use of
family herds as bridewealth to legitimize marriage. In this

sense the camp images life and social reproduction. An older woman shared her views on what a primordial world might have resembled:

> All the vegetables [adjuaic, "green things"] people now eat were only added to what was. When they tasted food and it did not kill them, the people continued to eat it. Cow is a bad creation. It has been the cause of people being finished. People [long ago] had arguments over the cow. They had a long feud over the cow and the Creator at last allowed the cow to stay with human beings. When a man is speared and he dies--it is because of cows-- because no one accepted to leave the cows. This is why the cow is very important. A man is killed for the sake of cows. The feud of women, like this woman sitting here with you, also kills people. People have these fights over women. Grain and cows were given by the Creator. These are the two things people live on and stay for. Cows and grain stay together.

What Atuot call the hungry months (peth a biath, from buoth, "hunger") are a yearly expectation while their cows are more or less productive throughout the year. In other words, since their horticultural effort is dependent upon rainfall that occurs in an inconsistent pattern, Atuot view their herds as a source of life should all else fail, and thus the cultural value which centers on life in cattle camps.

THE ECOLOGICAL YEAR

The Atuot term ruon refers to a full passage from dry season camp to dry season camp and the natural cycle within which these activities occur is conceptualized through explicit references to changing patterns of rainfall. The first rains in early April are often called kwoth iguong, the rains which "bring out" turtles, iguong. Peth deker are the first full rains which transform the world from an environment of harsh dryness into one of verdant pastures and forests. Then follow peth ba tot, the "big" rains, and finally, peth bau, the time the rainy season is "broken." The months of dryness are also termed mai, which refers to the activity of setting fire to the parched landscape in order to encourage fresh young tufts of grass to grow. Indeed, it has been found that this pattern of open burning is essential in fostering the germination of grasses. One of the more common of these is called mayar, a species which has strong symbolic meaning in Atuot. The mayar grass begins to flourish at the height of the dry season and, as such, is taken as evidence of the return of life and fertility to the countryside. In an obvious sense the entire pastoral and horticultural cycle is dependent upon sufficient and predictable rainfall, though Atuot show little interest in an attempt to control this natural phenomenon. When the first rains have begun to fall in a regular pattern, gwan kwoth, men who possess a power associated with rain may perform a short sacrifice dedicated to this spiritual agent to recognize and welcome, in a sense, the return of rainfall. R. G. Lienhardt likewise observes that for the Dinka,

> those symbolic acts which are regularly performed,
> like the sacrifices made after the harvest, take
> place at a time when people are already beginning to
> experience naturally something of the result which
> the ceremony is intended to bring about, or at least
> may soon expect to do so (1961: 280).

As noted, myths of creation image a world of dry season cattle
camps so that the coming rains have a parallel meaning that is
strongly associated with growth and the nurturance of
life.

In the areas of homestead cultivations on the ironstone
plateau the severity of the dry season is especially evident.
I spent many hours in the company of women who sat through the
night beside deep wells, to recover only small quantities of
muddy water in their buckets. With the coming rains these and
related hardships begin to dissipate. The full rains of the
following months are often preceded by dramatic flourishes of
lightning and thunder. All but the most carefree small
children sit quietly in camps or huts during such moments. In
their view these overwhelming natural elements are symbols of
Divinity's power as well as benevolence. When we shared the
company of their huts at these times, people invariably told
us "you will have a cool and restful sleep." Emerging from a
hut in late afternoon following hours-long torrents of rain,
the clearing horizon, the laughter of children playing in the
mud, the sounds of birds on the move again, and other
experiences have an emotional effect as well. Lienhardt
(1961: 92-93) has noted similar experiences for the Dinka:
"In thunderstorms it is customary to sit quietly and
respectfully, for people are in the immediate presence of
Divinity." Further, "The coming of the first rains in
Dinkaland is the end of a time of great discomfort and
difficulty for many . . . with the rains the periodic attacks
of cerebrospinal meningitis abate. The coming of the rain
thus promises new life in the fullest sense of the
expression." Atuot are grateful not just for the life-giving
rains but also for what they interpret to be evidence of the
continual concern of Divinity for human beings.

On the following table, the ecological year is summarized
according to economic activities and settlement patterns.
Clearly one does not want to confuse a western, linear
conception of time with the Atuot perception of the fluidity
of activities. The events and processes represented here vary
in accordance with the intensity and duration of rainfall. In
years when the rivers flood extensively it may be difficult or
impossible to fire the dry season grasses. Conversely, local
areas may suffer drought and in the past, before there was at
least the hope of government-supplied assistance, very dry
years promised suffering and death.

When the larger portion of the human population begins to
return to higher ground in April and May the crop of durra is
sown. A man with a number of wives is expected to help in the
clearing of the garden of each spouse (see below). Amidst the
first planting of durra women sow pumpkins, millet, sesame,
and a variety of beans. Gourds that will later be fashioned
into bowls, spoons, and food-storage vessels are planted a
distance from each hut. Increasingly Atuot have begun to
cultivate maize. In the southern regions of Atuot country one
also notes small plantings of cassava, which is useful as a

THE ECOLOGICAL YEAR (RUON)

	dry season (mai)							seasons of rain (deker)			
JAN. (hor)	FEB. (kon)	MAR. (nyith)	APR. (kuol)	MAY (akoidit)	JUNE (akoi tot)	JULY (admuong)	AUG. (alathbor)	SEPT. (abothnon)	OCT. (biildito)	NOV. (biiltoto)	DEC. (lal)

dry season camp (wuic)
(cattle camps in the toic)

wet season camp (wiuc)
(cattle camps in the forest)

most people in the camp

settlement in villages (cieng)

fishing

burning grass

first cultivation

second cultivation

hungry months

harvest

hot winds from the north

cool winds from the south

pastoralism

critical staple between the first cultivation and the first
harvest each season.

In homestead settlements the months of July and August
are devoted to weeding the large gardens. With adequate
rainfall the first crop of durra can be harvested by late
August. In mid-July many families begin to dig early maturing
groundnuts which also serve to tide off severe hunger. A
typical meal in early September is made by mixing groundnut
paste with boiled pumpkin, supplemented by durra porridge
(kuen) if available. The harvesting of the main crop of durra
(dieng, the "time" of the harvest and also the verb to
describe the act of breaking the head of the grain from the
stalk) in November coincides with the period in which many
marriages are settled. It also happens that important
sacrifices may be delayed until this time so there will be
sufficient millet beer for the people who gather.

There are minor variations throughout Atuot country in
the actual time of cultivation and harvest, reflecting
differences in soil types and rainfall. Microenvironmental
differences also favor variety in crops. For example, as one
travels south into Aliab country and toward the Nile, the
primary soil type becomes the heavy dark cotton soil. Thus
Aliab plant few groundnuts and are more reliant on durra.
Considerable honey is collected on a seasonal basis in Rorkec
and Kuek territory where the savannah forest is thicker and
more extensive than that to the north. Local peoples here
make a slightly sweet and alcoholic beer from honey as well as
a delicious, highly caloric paste of groundnuts and honey.
Between July and November the wet season cattle camps are
relatively close to the homesteads on the ironstone plateau.
As the season progresses, milk and horticultural products are
exchanged between village and camp with increasing regularity.
A typical pattern which we observed is one in which a father
resides in a cattle camp with his family's herds and looks
after the youngest children in a family. At this time they
consume large quantities of fresh milk, supplemented by durra,
squash, and groundnuts brought to the camp by the child's
mother or older sibling. In turn, women return to cultivation
homesteads carrying gourds filled with milk. As milk is
plentiful at this time of year, younger children will
sometimes make twenty-mile-round-trip visits to Yirol to sell
milk, returning with tobacco, salt, or some other product
purchased in town. In the village settings at this time,
women are largely in control of food production and
preparation. A woman's young children will help weed gardens,
chase off birds from the gardens, and may assist their mother
in domestic chores. Food preparation is entirely a female
domain. In the cattle camps young boys and girls often milk
the cows while adult men control the handling, distribution,
and use of milk. "Leaving milking behind" (pel ngac) is a
central theme in the initiation of boys, as the change in
their economic activities corresponds with changes in their
personal or social status (see Chapter 3). In September,
young men who are actively engaged in the pursuit of affection
from young women temporarily move together to settle in
smaller camps. They bring with them a number of milking cows
and a few oxen that they will slaughter for feasting. In
these camps they begin to harvest the ripening tobacco and
idle hours away drinking milk and conversing with potential
lovers. For both women and men of this age, the expressed

purpose of these two-week sojourns is to become fat, strong,
and attractive.   This period of their life marks the
culmination of their youthful independence and is recalled
with a sense of satisfaction in later years. Howell (1954:
197) writes of a similar custom for the Nuer:

> It appears that nak--the common word meaning "to
> kill," but in this context meaning "a slaughter"--
> was part of the tribal ceremonies concerned with the
> division of age-sets. Age mates of the younger age-
> set would segregate themselves from the rest of the
> community at the cattle byre of one of their number
> and live entirely on the meat of oxen slaughtered
> for the occasion.

The custom is especially notable in that cattle are never
slaughtered for food, except in especially pressing
circumstances. Here, at least for a number of days, the rule
is abandoned so that young men who might have been warriors in
earlier decades of Atuot history feast on the animals which
collectively assure their longevity.

VILLAGES AND CAMPS

We first lived among the Atuot only four years after the first
civil war ended in 1972 so that many communities were just
beginning to reestablish themselves at that time.   The rural
centers such as Yirol, Rumbek, Tonj, Juba, Malakal, and Wau
grew dramatically during the war since they were the only
locations that offered any real sense of personal security and
peace.   In 1976-77 there was a cautious serenity in the rural
countryside which encouraged the resettlement of traditional
homelands.   With these facts in mind we traveled to a village
called Anuol in Kuek country, about forty miles by dirt track
southwest of Yirol.   Northern Sudanese troops had devastated
the village and killed many of its residents in the 1960s, so
what we witnessed was the rebuilding of a community.
     The center of Anuol is defined by a single deep well and
a circular clearing perhaps three hundred yards across.
Scattered around this clearing are the few mud and thatch
buildings which are the locus of government functions: a rest
house, a hut for the single armed policeman in the region, a
primary school, and a dispensary. When we lived in Anuol in
1976, school classes had not met for the last few months as
the teacher had not been paid during that period. No medicine
had been available in the dispensary within recent memory.
Those who live within a radius of five to eight miles of the
well may effectively be called the residents of the village.
     When a plot of land is cleared for the first time with
the intention of creating a homestead and garden nearly all
taller trees save the lulu or shea nut tree (butyuosperum
parkii; in Atuot, arok) are felled.   The vegetation of the
lulu is sparse enough to allow sufficient sunlight to durra
and other plants. The bush and wood collected within the plot
are burned in December, as is much of the open savannah.   The
lulu nuts are collected to be pounded in order to extract oil
which is used for cooking as well as body adornment.   Once
cleared, suitable timber is sought for erecting piles ten- to
twelve-feet tall on which the hut will sit.   The area

underneath the hut is closed off with durra stalks. Here a woman does her cooking and stores her various pots and utensils. Construction of the hut goes on simultaneously with clearing the garden. Many homesteads also consist of one or a number of small huts on the ground where sheep and goats are protected from predators in the evening. The adwil, as it is called, is an extremely solid structure, and with occasional rethatching of the roof will survive the twenty years a garden is expected to be fertile.

After the first rains a family in the process of making a homestead will return to the setting early to plant beans, sesame, and durra, and, in the process, loosen the soil sufficiently so that groundnuts can be planted the following year. Goats and sheep feed off the tall stalks of durra and other leaves, though gardens are not manured with intent. The remaining plant residues are burned that year along with brush collected in the neighboring forest. A second crop of durra, sesame, and millet is planted the following year. The same cycle is repeated in the third and fourth years with the addition of groundnuts and cassava. By the fourth year it is hoped that a large planting of all crops will repay the considerable labor invested. Each year the garden pattern changes slightly, and is smaller or larger depending upon the quantity of seed set apart from the preceding year and, of course, is determined by rainfall patterns. After fifteen to twenty years (according to local friends) mixed cultivation has depleted soils to the extent that additional ash fertilizer helps little.

The savannah forest between homesteads is littered with sunken posts from past adwils, which are frequently accompanied by forked branch shrines that served as the home of a spiritual power (jok) owned by the former residents. When a former garden has become overgrown with trees and brush it is seen as suitable for cultivation again, and a new homestead may incorporate the site of an old adwil within a garden. In this manner, gradually over time, villages occupy slightly different areas within the abundant forest zone. The land is rich and the form of slash and burn horticulture they practice is likewise well-suited to the local environment. As Howell (1954: 365) notes, the Atuot and Ceic Dinka possess a more diversified form of subsistence than is typical in other areas of Nuer and Dinka occupation. The single homestead sits in the middle of cultivated fields. Toward the end of the rainy season when durra stalks reach a height of ten to twelve feet, one has the impression that there is no center to a village such as Anuol other than the common well. Rather, in an area of recent resettlement such as Anuol, larger and smaller tracks of savannah forest separate one household from the next. In one direction or another each homestead within this dispersed form of settlement is connected by a narrow footpath. I estimated that areas under cultivation for homesteads ranged from four to twelve acres, dependent upon the factors outlined.

A newly married man normally builds his own adwil in the same general territory as his father, though it also could be found that the youngest son of a family later came to live in his natal home with his wife. In the cases I knew of this was a common form of postmarital residence when the man's father had died a long time before. Rights to the use of uncultivated land are recognized for any male member of a

family.   The ideal image of residence in localized groups
formed on the basis of common agnatic heredity is explained by
Atuot as a preference related to protection in warfare.
     By way of comparison it can be noted that the typical
Nuer and Dinka homestead consists of a cattle byre and a hut
for each wife of a polygamous union.   Two points are worth
mentioning here.   Among the Atuot, cattle are rarely if ever
brought to homestead settlements.   The exceptions arise when a
social occasion requires an ox, bull, or cow for sacrifice.
Second, while each Atuot wife has her own hut, built by her
husband, often the huts of co-wives may be located as much as
a half-mile apart.   In a fewer number of instances these may
be in entirely different regions of Atuot country.   By their
reasoning,   the separation   of   co-wives' homesteads is a
preferred custom.   Women suggested to me that this ensured
that "people would have respect" between themselves.   An
alternative would be clustering of huts together with gardens
located some short distance away.   However, an adult woman
gains a personal sense of cultural value and achievement by
keeping her yard cleanly swept and noting, as the season
progresses, how well her own garden grows to surround her own
homestead.   Just as the husband controls the distribution of
milk in cattle camps, so too does the adult woman own the
produce of her own labors.   F. M. Deng (1966: 555) reports a
similar circumstance for the Dinka.   For these and related
reasons one can understand how the homestead is part of a
cluster of material and ideational symbols associated with
females in Atuot cosmology.   The Atuot homestead is an
independent unit of production, and is part of a broader
conglomerate of horticultural settlements.   As I hope to show,
wet season cattle camps present a different series of economic
and moral commitments.

     Horticulture may be thought of as a seasonal undertaking.
Though dependable harvests are the expressed intention of
local peoples, given the uncertain and unpredictable nature of
local patterns of rainfall, especially large harvests are the
exception rather than the rule.   In other words, given their
present technology and reliance on natural sources of
nurturance, their gardens are well suited for subsistence
production.   In lean years, families may be forced to exchange
sheep, goats, or cattle for horticultural produce, which
suggests that their cultivated products alone do not provide a
sufficient subsistence base.
     For reasons that are at least in part regulated by the
environment they occupy, pastoralism consumes human energy
throughout the year and, as previous studies of the Sudanese
Nilotes make amply clear, many of their more salient economic
and moral values are focused on their herds.
     Given the range of pastures they exploit during the dry
season, human and bovine populations are dispersed over a wide
area at this time.   In the open toic zones, predatory animals
are scarce so that the herds can be tended with greater
leisure than in the wet season camp areas.   In terms of
cultural adaptation this allows for an intensive exploitation
of riverine resources so that in the dry season cattle camps a
considerable effort is put into setting traps and fishing for
the many species found in the river Payii and the Lake Nyibor
and Lake Yirol environments, as well as smaller feeder streams
of the Nile.   Small quantities of grain are carried from wet

season settlements to dry season camps, though in the main the
common diet in dry season camps consists of fish, milk, and,
when the need for a sacrifice arises, the flesh of a
slaughtered animal.   On an inconsistent basis these foods are
supplemented by game Atuot hunt with spears and traps, such as
thiang, gazelle, and, less often, giraffe, elephant, and
buffalo.   The general tempo of life seems slow and monotonous
in dry season camps, at least to a foreigner.   E. E. Evans-
Pritchard (1936) suggests that this is in part due to the less
substantial diet common at this time and is also a consequence
of the fact that the need for constant human labor lessens in
dry season camps.   Shelters erected for sleeping and shade are
manufactured in a casual manner from dried reeds and elephant
grass, and they are abandoned any number of times during the
dry months as people follow their senses and knowledge in
search for pasture.   The wide dispersal of the human
population at this time also allows for opportunities to meet
and engage the company of potential lovers or spouses.
Another factor worthy of note is that like other pastoral
peoples, Atuot have a true devotion to their herds, so that a
man thinks little of walking many miles in the scorching sun
to find adequate grazing for his cattle.   Indeed, this is a
matter of pride and self-esteem.   Perhaps the clearest
indication of these sentiments figure in their sung poetry, or
ox-songs.   In this cultural form a man recounts his past
travels, his agnatic heredity, and boasts of his prowess as
herdsman and lover.   As one man sings,

     I moved with my ox to the pasture of Akam and Payic
     This pasture is the garden of the ox
     The stomach of Magon [his ox] hangs like the belly
          of a buffalo
     The ox ate the pasture of Nuer
     Magon, even if I have to carry three children
     I can still keep them and take you to pasture
     I must take the chief [his ox] to the land of Nuer
     This is the grazing of my fathers long ago
     I follow the animal until I am exhausted

     The rising waters from the first rains slowly drive
herders and herds away from the rivers and herald the slow
retracing of miles back toward higher ground on the ironstone
plateau and the more permanent cattle camps in the savannah
forest.   Tethering ropes and pegs, bundles of dried fish,
sleeping hides, and cooking utensils are wrapped in bundles to
be carried back to cultivation settlements and camps.
Settlement patterns and economic activities in the wet season
camps differ significantly from those in the dry season.
     Wet season cattle camps dot the forested countryside and
are usually located no more than a day's trek away from
cultivation sites.   During the rainy season the division of
labor by sex is most marked.   As noted earlier, in the wet
season cattle camps human population densities reach their
highest in the cycle of the ecological year, and it follows
that a fundamental ethic in these settings is cooperation.   A
large wet season camp not only connotes a high degree of
prestige for its members but is also less likely to suffer
raids by other camps.   Any wet season camp is known as the
camp of a named descent group, though people related through
marriage often tether their herds in a common camp.   We lived

for a time in a wet season camp known as Wunarok, in Atuot terms, "a camp of Luac." There we slept in the shelter of our fictive uncle Maker. To our right in the camp was the shelter of Igai, the brother of a wife of Maker's from the Jilek section. The shelter closest to ours on the left belonged to Cep, the husband of Alak, the sister of Maker's wife, also from Jilek. On the far side of the camp were a number of men from the Ceic Dinka who had married women of the Luac. In other words, while the idiom of camp residence and settlement reflects agnatic values and is at least conceptually formed on the basis of such principles, observed patterns evidence a liberal interpretation of these rules. Thus, while Luac or Kuek men will say, for example, that such and such camp is the camp of _cieng_ Rorkec, it is so in principle but not necessarily in actual composition.

What I have referred to as "shelters" in the wet season camps Atuot call _adhang_. From a distance they resemble giant mushrooms but are in fact substantial structures built with ten or twelve posts and rafters, covered with a thick layer of thatch. With occasional rethatching, the _adhang_ will weather many seasons. The _adhang_ creates a small roof over large conical mounds of dried, ever-burning cattle dung, called _gol_. The smoke produced is very effective in repelling biting insects and flies which would otherwise have an adverse effect on both the human and bovine populations, especially in the wet season. Atuot use the fine greyish-white ash produced by burning for a number of purposes. One might better say that the dung ash has a number of meanings.

In ox-songs as well as at public sacrificial gatherings Atuot commonly refer to their herds as the ancestral herds of their grandfathers. Clearly, they do not intend this to mean that their living herds are literally the same as those tended by past generations. Reference is made instead to the fact that their own manner of being and basis for prosperity is their inheritance. As Evans-Pritchard (1956: 258) wrote,

> Nuer conceive of the ancestor of a clan, and likewise the ancestors of its component lineages, as having possessed a herd, the descendants of which have had, and continue to have, though distributed among different families, a constant relationship with the descendants of their original owners and are still thought of as one herd . . . conceptually [the herd] is an enduring collectivity.

An Atuot singer makes reference to this notion in more figurative terms:

> The spirit of my father let the bull remain with us
> The bull makes the name of my father known by all
> Every man is proud of his father
> A man's name is made by his father and his cows
> This is the animal that remains with testicles

The burnt dung ash likewise symbolizes this continuity, fictive though it may be. When a man acquires cattle through marriage and leads them to his camp to be tethered, one of the first things he will do is sift through the _gol_ to find clean ashes which he then spreads over the back, loins and head of each animal. Through this simple act they then "become" part

of the same ancestral herd.   One of the first cosmetic chores
each morning in the camp is to spread warm ashes over one's
own body, an act which accomplishes a similar end.   When
sacrifices are enacted in camps invocations are made while
scattering ash over the back of the victim, indicating that
the sacrifice is intended to benefit not only the living but
also the ancestors, who are given new life with each act of
animal sacrifice.

     This brief digression is intended to highlight the moral
value with which Atuot imbue the physical space of wet season
camps.   Another common usage in ox-songs is the line "The
ashes of the dung fire in my camp are so very deep,"
suggesting that the singer is a descendant of an ancient
ancestor whose people have occupied the same space for
uncountable years.   This also points to wider, collective
associations which are the result of, and reproduce, local
political communities.   It was noted earlier that the
clustering of agnates and kin in local communities reflects a
sentiment that connotes physical security.   In this regard, it
is interesting to consider the observations of Andrew Acijok
Yak, a man from Kuek country who was acting commissioner of
local government in 1977.   As he noted in his official
records, "The increased sense of security given by the
presence of government has greatly modified their original
habit of herding cattle within a comparatively few, large
cattle camps, in favor of the present practice of a great
number of smaller camps."   A related example comes from Howell
(1954: 185), who observes, "During the period of invasion and
occupation of Dinka country there were periods when the Nuer
lived in cattle camps of concentrated form, a circle
of huts or shelters, and did so for several years at
a time."

     The number of gols in any camp is a variable that results
from changing climatic factors, the local availability of
pastures, and, less directly, relations between agnatic kin
through marriage.   An additional circumstance that affects the
seasonal composition of wet season camps is the physical
distribution of family herds.   A personal anecdote will
introduce the significance of the latter factor.   When he
learned that we were living in the camp called Wunarok,
Maker's mother's brother's son, in an act of friendship and
good wishes, decided to tether two of his own oxen among the
cattle of our fictive gol.   In this sense the presence of his
cattle among our own symbolized his own presence as well as
his moral sentiments, though this was hardly a novel idea.
Indeed, there are sound reasons for distributing one's herds
over a wide area in a number of different camps.   On the one
hand, this offers some assurance that if there is a localized
outbreak of one or another cattle diseases, at least some
portion of one's own herd will remain healthy.   Closely
related to this, though perhaps more so in former days, a
localized feud or cattle raid would also result in a minor
loss of family herds.   In a broader ethnographic summary of
this phenomenon P. T. Baxter (1972: 176) points out "Men
distribute their stock to spread their risks, partly to meet
differing grazing needs of different types of stock, and
partly to create social links."   The Atuot manner of herd
distribution also reflects a more common Nilotic theme: To
successfully manage as a pastoralist, one must call upon a
wide range of kin.   No single individual can manage a herd.

Conversely, one also wants to limit the degree to which one must reciprocate such favors and moral demands.

Returning now to an earlier point, wet season camps show some variation in size. Local estimates offered by herdsmen figured that an average camp would include as many as thirty to forty gols and anywhere from 1,000 to 1,500 head of cattle. Our own survey indicated that within any single gol one could expect to find an adult male, often in the company of a younger brother, and typically two or three children, ranging in age from three years to early teens. In the older male group one finds elders who remain in these camps for much of the rainy season, somewhat younger men who have been married, and finally representatives of the age category called awuot, men who range in age from twenty to thirty who carry out the better part of daily herding, eager to gain the approval of their fathers and uncles to use herds for arranging their own marriages. Throughout Atuot country there are notable disparities in the size of family herds; in the main, however, it is fair to observe that such differences show considerable variation over time. A camp with a large number of cattle is likely to have a smaller number in a short time since one of its members is probably preparing for a marriage; the death of a family member calls for the sacrifice of cattle at the gravesite and additional sacrifices months later to appease the ghost of the deceased; cattle may be given to more distant agnatic kin to formalize a marriage; and so on. In our experience an average herd tethered around the circular space defined by a gol consisted of one or two bulls, between five and eight milking cows, and as many as ten oxen in addition to a smaller number of calves.

In addition to the cultural usages just mentioned, herds are culled or at least limited in growth by what might be characterized as an aggressive policy of castration. Stud bulls are not only more difficult to control but they have a perceived tendency to create chaos within a grazing herd. Castrated animals are more easily kept in herd and are often the required victim in a wide range of sacrificial rites. Castration occurs when the animals are approximately eighteen months old. N. Grunnet (1962: 12) writes,

> The scrotum is grasped with one hand and an incision is made over one testicle. It is pulled out of the incision and uncovered, together with the spermatic cord, by cutting and scraping of the covering sheath . . . the procedure is repeated on the other testicle. Some people fill the incisions with baking hot cattle dung. . . . It is common to bury the testicles at the tethering pole in order that the animal shall not lose strength or get ill.

Of the milking cows in each gol it is customary that each child is assured the yield of one or two milkings daily, with an average milk yield of two-and-one-half liters per day. In the morning when they wake, a father will ask his daughter or son if they are hungry and want milk. The patent response is gore cak guar! or "Yes indeed, Father!" "Where is your cow?" he will ask, and even by the age of two, the young child knows which cow will be milked to provide the morning meal. As noted, young uninitiated boys and girls and occasionally married women milk the cows, careful to leave a sufficient feeding for calves. During the rainy season some surplus milk is normally assured. This is preserved by mixing fresh milk with small quantities of cow urine. When tightly sealed in a milk gourd, the milk will curdle and can be stored for as long as two months before consumption. Cattle are also bled on an irregular basis by shooting a small arrow into a prominent vein in the neck. The blood thus drawn is often mixed with fresh milk as a meal during this season. Cattle suffer little disability from the minor operation.

Cattle are tethered around each gol in a manner that images the organization of society itself. The bulls of a man's herd are tethered facing the center of the cattle camp. When reflecting on the organization of their social world, men draw attention to the significance of agnatic heredity. Closer to the small shelters are the cows, which are essential for the perpetuation of family and lineage. Closer still to the adhang itself are the young calves, often under the watchful eye of children. Mirroring now more specific kin relations, each animal tethered in a camp has its own tethering rope. When the awuot leave with the cattle in mid-morning it is time for younger boys to collect the ropes, still secured to tethering pegs. Together in each gol, these are hung from a post sunk in the ground for this sole purpose. To our eyes, one rope looks nearly identical to the next, yet each young boy knows exactly which rope belongs to each animal. In the evening, if some animals have not returned to the camp with the herd, it is easy for these young herdsboys to call by name the absent animals by noting which ropes remain on the hanging post. In learning the ancestry of herds they are at the same time learning the details of their own agnatic heredity. This fact is reflected in local knowledge. One afternoon as we sat under an adhang in Wunarok my friend Maker asked who might read what I was writing. I replied that anyone might read it but that the purpose of writing was to make the information known to others who would live after my own death. Maker remarked, "This is the same with our ropes. Every cow has its own rope and each rope is our writing. The writing of our ancestors are these cows in the camp."

The locus of a political community in the pastoral Nilotic world is identified idiomatically by reference to cattle camps rather than wet season cultivation settlements. By exploiting affinal and agnatic relationships individuals opt to tether their cattle in specific locations, which result in public declarations about their moral, political, and personal alliances. Membership within a particular cattle camp presumes a common sense of community, which in turn is manifested in territorial values. Within each camp one finds a hierarchical ranking of genealogical time. The center of the circular clearing (thar wuic, "the head of the camp") is typically more elevated land and thus receives better drainage. Those who can assert closer agnatic ties with the founders of the cattle camp tether their cattle here. The Dinka likewise associate physical space and the political community with wet season camps. As Lienhardt (1961: 19) writes, "The nuclear sub-clans of the tribes, and the nuclear lineages of sub-tribes, are spoken of as the 'people of the center of the camp,' since they have first established the cattle camps and occupy central positions on the sites." In these usages it is clear that the idiom of centrality is physically manifested in settlement patterns, appropriately enough, at the center of the herds which in turn are symbolic of the local polity.

ECOLOGY AND COSMOLOGY

The preceding observations have indicated some of the ways in which ecology and settlement patterns are reflected in Atuot values and morality. The physical world they occupy provides the basis for a series of related symbolic references.

Traditionally Atuot conceive of the world as a vast flat plain, where the sky (nhial) is seen to be in permanent juxtaposition above the land (piny). On a heavily overcast day, common in the rainy season, it appears as though the sky has moved closer to the human realm and at this time Atuot imagine that Divinity has also come near to humans. The perpetual separation of night and day also figures in their conception of life and well-being. The common greeting exchanged by individuals on a daily basis is the question ci ker?, a phrase that literally means "has it separated?" and implicitly refers to the Atuot variation of a common Nilotic myth. Long ago, when heaven and earth were connected by a rope, human beings could travel freely between the two worlds. Death was unknown and people satisfied their hunger with a single grain of millet. The creation of the world as they now know it occurred when the rope was severed, in some versions by the durra bird and in others by the fox. A related theme is that when a young wife was pounding grain into flour for the evening meal, she struck Divinity with her pestle. In anger, Divinity decided that all living things would thenceforth die. Thus, where cosmic unity had once existed, a radical distinction--now impossible for human beings to bridge physically--had been created. Human life begins with this separation. The darkness of night temporarily obliterates once again this otherwise clear distinction between heavenly and earthly abodes. In this manner, the morning greeting ci ker? implies "has life returned?" The following question in the Atuot sequential formula of greeting, ci yi tei?, "have you remained?," does not deny the obvious fact of physical presence but is instead intended to mean "has Divinity given back life?"

Atuot associate the light of the new day with the return of life. An individual reposed in sleep is prone to the evil intentions of his or her enemies through the medium of earthly powers (see Chapter 4) or by the activities of sorcerers, witches, and potentially malignant ghosts of the recently deceased. If one is already suffering ill health, night is an even less propitious time. One friend related that his father, who had killed a number of men in his lifetime, slept surrounded by his spears in order to protect himself from the angry ghosts of men he had killed. It follows logically for them that one should not disturb another's sleep nor waken a person suddenly, for that person will "awaken before the jok [power that protects an individual's life] that goes off at night has returned." The third common question in greeting underscores this notion. When Atuot then ask ci nien e gau?, "have you slept well?," they imply, "have you slept untroubled by malignancy?." It is the common idea that Divinity or the Creator "has given us sleeping and waking. When we wake in

the morning it is because of the Creator." To their understanding the ultimate source of human life lies in the
unpredictable sentiments of the Creator, a being that can only
be petitioned through sacrifice. I once asked what would
happen if a person died at night, after I was told that human
beings normally only die during the day. One response, by an
older woman, was offered with a pronounced air of
indignation: "We do not die at night. Only witches die at
night!"

One primary distinction in Atuot cosmology can thus be
noted in the form of a binary opposition between things of
"above" and "below," a contrast that implies a divergence
between the divine and human realms. A related contrast is
that which involves the association between daylight and
health, and between darkness and death. As young children
learn in one folktale, "morning comes with a person alive/
evening comes with the hatred of an animal." By analogical
association these divisions imply a congruence between
daylight, strength, masculinity, and knowledge and a converse
symbolic identity between darkness, weakness, femininity, and
uncertainty.

The Atuot term for east, the direction from which life is
thought to emanate, is "right" or thang cuic, "the right
side." West connotes the inverse moral associations as the
left side, thang cam. In physical space this results in the
orientation of individuals facing toward the east and the
light of the new day, with their back toward what is behind
them. For example, in the course of sacrifices intended to
assure human well-being, the individual leading the
invocations will face east while he speaks. This physical
association bears a close association with their precepts of
lineal descent. Simply stated, deceased forebears are
"behind" one. The first child of the marital union enjoys a
slightly elevated status since he or she is the one who is
said to "open the way" for other children, and implicitly
portends the formation of a new lineage. Morally those things
which are "behind" a person are nonetheless a perpetual aspect
of social experience as indicated by the proverb "every person
has his back." Among other things, the proverb implies that
the antecedent experience of his or her own life, as well as
that of deceased lineal kin, are factors influencing the
ongoing behavior of specific individuals. Long-deceased
ancestors are imbued with very strong moral evaluation and
they are in a figurative sense closer to Divinity. The fiery
winds which blow at the zenith of the dry season originate "on
the left side" and Atuot recognize that during this season
they are most subject to the possibility of contracting
cerebrospinal meningitis. The cool air (alier) of rain-filled
skies is said to originate from the "right side" of the
physical world. In light of these ideas and figurative
analogies, it is significant that the Atuot term for the
season of rains, de ker (as noted above, the division of the
wet from the dry season) is cognate with the morning greeting
ci ker?, "has the world separated?" As is obvious to those
who have traveled in the Nilotic Sudan, the dry season lends
to human capabilities the greatest test in surviving harsh
conditions. It is a time when people speak of being "killed
by the sun." Indeed, the foreigner may be astonished by the
dramatic transformation of the parched dusty environment into
a lush green world following the early rains. Of this

phenomenon Atuot say "now with the coming of de ker, life has
returned" (na de ker ben, yei ce ke jao ben). I would suggest
then that the right/left system of symbolic gender and moral
associations can also be observed in the classification of
physical space.
    While these ideas are voiced within a particular dialect
they are not uncommon in the Nilotic Sudan.   Evans-Pritchard
(1956: 148) writes that Nuer consider the west to be the side
of death and the east the side of life.   Thus, left is spoken
of as kwi giakni, "the side of badness" or evil.   In the
course of Nuer sacrifice, the animal "should fall
well . . . falling well means falling cleanly on its side,
preferably on its right side" (1956: 211).   The right hand is
symbolic of strength, vitality, and virtue as well as patrikin
and the patrilineage (1956: 233).   Summarizing this theme of
lateral symbolism Evans-Pritchard (1956: 234) writes, "Thus we
have here two opposites, the one comprising the left side,
weakness, femininity and evil, and the other comprising the
right side, strength, masculinity and goodness."   Similar
concepts figure in Dinka thought.   For these peoples, "East is
the direction of new life, associated with the rising sun"
(Lienhardt 1961: 188).   Following the act of immolation in
sacrifice, animals are left "to lie for a short time pointing
to the east" (1961: 267), a custom expressing the underlying
expectation that the life of the victim will be accepted by
Divinity in order that human beings might remain healthy.   It
is customary in all three societies to bury adult women to the
left of the cooking windscreen in the cultivation homesteads,
and for men to be buried to the right side of a cattle byre or
shelter in a particular cattle camp.   This practice in a sense
defines the ultimate association between women, homesteads,
and cultivation, and that between men, cattle camps, and
pastoralism.   The analogy is plainly evident in the course of
burials for Dinka chiefs, where "milk is poured into his right
hand, millet placed in his left hand" (Lienhardt 1961: 308).

SUMMARY

Some readers may wonder why a description of symbolic usages
is included in a discussion of subsistence activities.   In
some recent anthropological literature, for example, it has
become fashionable to adopt the analytic style of neo-Marxism.
In essence, this method presumes that the ways in which human
beings produce their livelihood largely determines the manner
in which people conceive of their existence, so that
ideological experience is secondary to an explanation of
material and economic production.   In this Nilotic world, I
think that an analytic method such as this artificially
represents the "facts" as observed and experienced.
    This chapter began with the statement that the Atuot mode
of horticultural and pastoral production is systematic, that
one part of this process is densely interrelated with all
others, and is best understood in this manner.   An important
part of this system is reflected in the ways Atuot conceive of
space, time, production, and experience.   Cultural values draw
special attention to cattle even while horticultural products,
in particular millet and durra, provide the essential staple
of the common diet.   However, meaning is given to productive
labor through a series of symbolic usages which are

systematically _related_ _to_ productive activities. As a consequence of this it would be an artificial exercise to draw out one part of this system for exclusive discussion. I can't imagine that any individual Atuot would. It is rather an artifact of western experience that allows for such an easy distinction to be drawn between conception and production.

I would argue that the entire system of production (and perhaps more particularly, pastoral transhumance) is for them an engrossing, meaningful, and satisfying experience and, indeed, is the essence of their own cultural identity. Settling in a wet season camp for the first time in a year or planting the first seeds of produce each year are activities which are accompanied by small rituals--the sacrifice of an ox or the blessing of the seed. On the whole, though, Atuot do not engage in an elaborate series of ritualized festivities or celebrations. As I understand their world, the broader pattern of transhumance is _itself_ ceremonial. An analogous case that comes to mind is that of the nomadic Basseri, in what is now Iran. Fredrik Barth (1961: 152-153) writes that,

> the poverty which seemed to characterize Basseri ritual life is an artifact of the descriptive categories I have employed, and that it depends essentially on the naive assumption that _because_ certain activities are of fundamental practical economic importance, they cannot _also_ be vested with supreme ritual value. If one grants this possibility, on the other hand, it becomes very reasonable to expect the activities connected with migration to have a number of meanings to the nomads, and to be vested with value to the extent of making the whole migration the central rite of nomadic society. It is, admittedly, a methodological problem to demonstrate the value that is placed on a migration, when this value is not, in fact, expressed by means of technically unnecessary symbolic acts and exotic paraphernalia. . . . The Basseri differ from many people in that they seem to vest their central values in, and express them through, the very activities most central to their ecologic adaptation.

The manner in which production is embedded in the person is most clearly evident in the cultural form of ox-songs, a subject addressed more completely in Chapter 5. As Barth notes, it is problematic to externally verify inner experience, to demonstrate that value is placed on migration. In the following passage of an ox-song composed by Maker Iwer, of the Luac section of Atuot, I think the attempt is made:

> A man who has cows but cannot sing of an ox
> [Is a man] who can never be known--
> He will never be known anywhere
> Abilduk [the ox-name of the singer's paternal
>   grandfather] is walking with a fire in his heart
>   [though he is long deceased, the memory of him
>   is much alive]
> The sons of Jilouth capture the pasture of Panther
> My Manguak [a bull] of the camp of Ithoiny,
> I listen to the sound of my bull

I went to Akot to buy the bull [he received the
    animal in the marriage of his sister by the
    Akot]
The camp where people of words settled
You, Manguak, the people of a small camp cannot
    speak the words of men
Manguak travels without sleep in search of sweet
    grass [Manguak here represents the singer
    himself]
Manguak left for pasture
Without the cows of his father a person may as well
    be an orphan
The cow of my grandfather Abilduk
This is a cow that does not die
Ajuot, there is a word I do not understand
It is because of the cows that I am hated
Or is it the curse of people like the Dinka?
Or simply my way of doing things?
Oh, the bull of my grandfathers
I will never abandon the camp.

3.
THE SOCIAL REPRODUCTION OF SOCIETY

The preceding comments have given some indication of the central economic and social value of cattle in this Nilotic world. I should perhaps emphasize once more that horticultural products provide much of the daily fare, even while the possession of herds per se commands greater cultural value: Cattle are the focus for many additional interests. The exchange of cattle in the form of bridewealth is one of their primary definitions of marriage, an institution which recreates social relations each generation by redefining patterns of inheritance and residence.

As E. E. Evans-Pritchard (1940) long ago wrote of the Nuer, the social idiom is a bovine idiom, a remark that characterizes Atuot and Dinka communities as well. The key notion to appreciate is _idiom_, or a characteristic mode of expression. Thus adult Atuot speak of their herds as the cattle of their ancestors, creating an image of a single consistent line of agnatic descent and inheritance through time. In this chapter, following a review of some data concerned with age categories, marriage, and relations between the sexes, I will try to underscore the imaginary nature of such timeless descent groups. Whereas local peoples speak of their communities as structured upon clear and consistent patterns of agnatic descent, the process of social life belies the idiom employed. The reader should recall the earlier observation that cultivation homesteads (associated with women) and cattle camps (associated with men) are interconnected by small footpaths. Tracing these paths on the ground is, in a sense, like tracing the relations of agnation and affiliation between the residents of each type of settlement. Paths between homesteads are in effect paths created by marriage, and those between homesteads and cattle camps, frail outlines of agnatic heredity. By necessity and convention, all paths overlap in time and space. The central matrix in which local life is reproduced is marriage, and marriage is a primary goal in the adult life of all Atuot women and men. The following section is concerned with an understanding of the relationship between age status and this central cultural goal.

AGE CATEGORIES AND MARRIAGE

I had thought that an obvious technique to use in assessing
the age of nonliterate Atuot was to pose the question "How
many years do you have?" (teke yin ruon na di?) but realized
my error when the common response was "I've really no idea at
all." Age classification among the Atuot as in many other
societies is a matter of social prescription. Age categories
and modes of classification are manifested in the course of
daily life by divergent economic and symbolic attributes which
accrue to distinctive categories. The Atuot term ric could be
translated as "age grade" or age set. This would imply a
homology with "warrior age set," a phrase often used in
reference to a similar phenomenon in other pastoral societies
of eastern Africa. However, when I asked Atuot friends if ric
were organized for the purpose of raiding or fighting, a
common reply was "of course not. When there is a fight,
everyone takes up the spear." Lacking any specific military
function, then, the purpose of Atuot ric might be sought
elsewhere. It seems that a more instructive gloss of the term
would be "marriage class" or "marriage set." This usage
suggests a group of persons who, because of their social and
physical maturity, are considered responsible enough by elders
to enter into marriage. F. M. Deng (1971: 130) also observes
that "The most important aspects of the solidarity of age sets
is their close association with the marriage of every age mate
and with other male-female social activities."
    Among the Atuot relative age has no positive evaluation
per se though a person who has survived the physical
discomforts and very real dangers of existence as they know it
has proven to have acquired an acute knowledge of the social,
spiritual, and physical world. For economy of presentation
basic Atuot age categories can be summarized schematically:

Female

gat nyal: baby girl
nyal: small girl, prepubescent
nyal ce kaai: from the verb kai, "to have power, to
    ripen or mature," hence a girl who has reached
    pubescence
nyal awuot: young woman of marriageable age and
    status
cek: wife (of)
cek me dong: older woman
madong: grandmother, living or dead

Male

gat: baby boy
dhol: small boy, prepubescent
acot: an adolescent boy who has been initiated.
    Atuot say, "his testes have fallen"
awuot: man of marriageable age
cou: husband (of)
cou me dong: older man
gwadong: grandfather or ancestor

I am not aware of a separate term for the plural of husband,
other than a variant in the possessive suffix, such as coudan,

"our husbands" or <u>couken,</u> "their husbands." In Atuot theory,
men can marry as many women as they have cattle readily at
hand for bridewealth. The term for mature, adult woman (<u>cek,</u>
pl. <u>men</u>) implicitly means "wife (of)" or "married woman" and
is symbolized in public most strongly by the triangular skirt
she wears, often made from goat hide. Just as every man hopes
to marry at least one woman to raise children in his name, so
too do women expect and hope to be married. Among the
neighboring Dinka, either sex "is quite happy to accept any
one of a range of mates not deformed, ancient or notorious for
greed, anger and licentiousness" (Lienhardt 1963: 85).

Pride in being a wife is a common theme of Atuot women's
songs, as in this extract:

Their hearts are filled with envy
My skirt is given in the cattle camp of Loguany
[i.e., the bridewealth cattle of her marriage
were exchanged in this setting]
I am the lady of the skirt of Loguany
Such a beautiful skirt--
<u>Majiim</u> [small metal rings] adorn the hem of the
skirt
I will dance with any wife
I will dance with the beautiful skirt
Women who compare their skirts to our own--
Only envy is in their hearts
I searched for a good skirt
And found it [i.e., the husband] in the camp
My sister says "come and admire the skirt"
They sing, let us come near and admire the skirt

In the same manner that a man's spear is a prized personal
possession and an important artifact almost always by his
side, so does a woman's skirt represent her own status as well
as authority over juniors of her own sex. Another short
passage from a woman's song draws an implicit association
between the bride's skirt as a material symbol of the social
relations created through a marriage:

The skirt is made by Nyangyang
The women worked so long on the skirt
That they forgot to tend the cooking fire
The women worked while the fire died
To whom does the skirt belong?
It is the skirt of the daughter of Darceng
Which is the family that owns the skirt?
It is the people of Dundok
It is the skirt of the daughter of Darceng
The <u>ric</u> made the skirt

One thinks here of Evans-Pritchard's (1940: 89) comment:

I risk being accused of speaking idly when I suggest
that a very simple material culture narrows social
ties. . . . Technology from one point of view is an
ecological process: an adaptation of human behaviour
to natural circumstances. From another point of
view material culture may be regarded as part of
social relations, for material objects are chains
along which social relationships run, and the more

simple is a material culture the more numerous are
the relationships expressed through it. . . . Thus
people not only create their material culture and
attach themselves to it, but also build up their
relationships through it and see them in terms of
it. As Nuer have very few kinds of material objects
and very few specimens of each kind, their social
value is increased by their having to serve as the
media of many relationships and they are, in
consequence, often invested with ritual functions.

After a marriage has been settled (see below) it is
customary for the new bride to return to her natal village or
homestead, where she remains throughout pregnancy to deliver
her firstborn. Mother and child remain here, under normal
circumstances, until the baby is weaned. Atuot mothers often
nurse their children for as long as three or four years. As a
result, an early period of intensive social contact for a
young child is with maternal kin. One Atuot woman typified
common sentiments regarding this pattern of postmarital
residence with these words:

Why do we go home to deliver? You were only born
yesterday. You grow up and you are married but you
have never delivered once. It is because you fear
you will kill the child or that you will not bring
it out well. You are taken to your mother and
father who were given cows [as bridewealth]. They
see to it that all goes well. If you delivered
badly and killed the child of those people [who
contributed the bridewealth] they will find this out
and want the cows returned to them. It is because
of the child--that is why they look for a wife. If
you deliver in the place where you were not born in,
people will fear you. They will watch you suffer
and the child will die. When the wife has known
delivery, she can stay in the other home the next
time.

Their own emphasis on the value of exchange in marriage, the
notion that the wealth of one family will later be that of
another, seems to invite little additional comment. What is
desired in all marriages is an equivalence of exchange between
dintinct kin-based communities, which, with the passage of
time and the birth of additional children, creates a single
larger community. A corollary to this is the important ethic
stressing the complementarity of economic tasks expected of
women and men respectively. Throughout childhood and even
into the early years of adolescence, young females and males
contribute to household production in essentially the same
manner. Their change in age classification is marked by the
onset of distinct productive tasks. Teenage girls become more
directly involved with their mothers in horticultural
production while their male age-mates are given new
responsibilies in tending smaller stock as well as cattle.
    Physiological maturity in females marks the occasion for
their initiation into age categories in a short ritual called
tuol nyal, derived from the verb tuol, "to emerge." Freely
translated, the phrase suggests a public marking of entry into
a new social status. Some time after reaching puberty young

males likewise enter a new social status following the ritual
known as pel ngac, "leaving milking behind." Earlier in
childhood many children will have already experienced the rite
called nak in which the lower incisors are extracted. This is
primarily a cosmetic rite having little to do with a change in
social or sexual status. As each is held with his or her back
to the ground, the heated point of a fishing spear is inserted
into the mouth in order to pry the teeth apart and remove
them. I learned that these teeth, which have grown in after
the milk teeth, are most difficult to remove. Some friends
referred to them as juel nar, the teeth of the maternal uncle,
who may be summoned to attend the ceremony in order to spit
into the mouth of his sister's child as an act of blessing,
thereby easing the task and lessening the pain. (As already
noted, it is common for the first child of a union to be
raised in the mother's natal home. Though no individual ever
made the suggestion to me, the rite may be thought of, in one
sense, as symbolic of a division or "extraction" from one
social environment to another. The child is later returned to
the husband's homestead where he or she must then come to
know, and become a member of, the father's agnatically defined
social universe.) At roughly the same period of physical
development, both sexes may receive gar or head scarification
in the manner described by Evans-Pritchard (1940) for the Nuer
and Deng (1972) for the Dinka. There was a consensus among
all elders with whom I spoke that gar was not a long-standing
tradition among the Atuot. In the contemporary world, as an
increasing number of youths have expectations of leaving their
land of birth after achieving formal education, fewer elect to
be decorated in this manner.

When a boy's "testes have fallen," as Atuot say, "it is
time for his head to be shaven," an act that symbolizes his
entry into the age category acot, a term that also means
"without horns" when applied to cattle (see Burton 1974). A
group of males who are always kin in one manner or another,
and who are also close in age, are then subjected to a period
of training which stresses in the main the need to pay strict
deference to all males who are their seniors. The new
initiates are abused and insulted by those older than they,
and in addition to performing menial and sometimes humiliating
tasks, the young boys are forced to drink large quantities of
milk. By itself this is most enjoyable. However, they are
only permitted to urinate once in the course of a day. A
number of friends expressed the severity of the pain they felt
holding their bladders while being cajoled into drinking yet
another full gourd of milk. Should one boy try to "sneak a
pee" as it were and be caught in the act, the result is a
painful whack across the head by an older man keeping watch.
This exaggerated form of control by age over youth continues
for about one month after which the young boys are loiny raar,
or "untethered," a phrase that also describes the untethering
of cattle to graze each morning. From that time forward they
are known collectively as a ric, an age or marriage class,
whose name is derived from either a notable event that was
roughly contemporaneous with their training, or from the
dominant color of the bead girdle that they are now allowed to
wear (see also Buxton 1975). Unlike many eastern African
initiation cycles, there is not among the Atuot a fixed
pattern of age grades through which the ric advances, nor is
there any further ceremony performed for the group in order to

advance to a senior status. This, rather, is marked by individuals' marriage. The principle at work entails seniority rather than gerontocracy. Throughout the years of his later adolescence a young man is given additional adornments by elder brothers and uncles. The greatest gift, however, is that of his own ox, a custom described in greater detail in Chapter 5. An immediate change in his individual being--namely his relationship to cattle, or cows in particular--is also marked at this time. Instead of milking the cows each morning and gathering their dung to dry for the _gol_ fire, he now actively assumes herding responsibilities.

The _acot_ then become self-consciously aware of social etiquette deemed proper for young adult males, notably in regard to culinary habits. The _ric_ collectively visit in turn the homesteads and cattle camps of each member and demand large portions of millet porridge served with sauces of milk, dried fish, and groundnut paste. In the camps, oxen are slaughtered for the occasion so that the young men can fatten themselves in order to appear handsome and strong to potential female suitors. There is an element of ritual and license to these occasions since a short while later, as individuals, they will never think of asking for food--behavior that is typical of and expected only of small children. Nor would they divulge in public hunger or thirst since this too evidences lack of control over physical needs.

In passing, I think it is worthwhile to consider a wider social function of age categories. Kulang Takpiny, a man who became a trusted and close friend, offered these comments:

> We know _ric_ according to _pel ngac_. You will never be in the same _ric_ as the brother ahead of you [i.e., one's older brother] because you have not gone through _pel ngac_ together. If that were to happen, then you could claim the same rights when it is time to marry. When we are in the cattle camp together we send a younger _ric_ to look after the cattle while we sit and talk. The _ric_ is for marriage and this is so for two reasons. Any older _ric_ speaks before the younger one. People of the older _ric_ are the first to be given cows for marriage. Then, it works this way: If the people of your _ric_ have been married and you have not, you go to your father and bring a word that it is now your time for marriage too.

These observations offer evidence of the fact that age categories have a great deal to do with access to, and manipulation of, cattle wealth, which is both acquired and regenerated through the institutions of marriage and bridewealth exchange. In this regard, the activities associated with _pel ngac_ may be thought of as marking a social and individual transition from the domestic to the jural domain.

The initiation of Atuot girls is more directly related toward the public recognition of their pubescence than a rite to emphasize dramatically a change in economic role. Soon after their first menstruation a number of girls are collected by their mothers in a single homestead. I was present for such a ceremony on two occasions and here combine these observations with a number of verbal accounts.

When the blood has come for the first time the girls are collected to sit near the windscreen [akel] of the hut. Three stones are placed in front of this so that a broken clay pot can be placed atop them. If there are five girls for whom this is done then five boys must also be present because when a girl becomes a wife later, she should give birth to both males and females. The children should not be one sex alone. The girl sits on the lap of her mother who faces the windscreen. Apuo [ocher-colored ashes from burnt cow dung] is placed in the broken pot. Three pieces of straw are taken by the women. At the end of each a triangle is formed and this is placed in the ash. A fire is lit under the shard and the women then pass one straw to the next woman [clockwise] until each straw has been passed around the pot three times. When this is completed the women jump to their feet and smash the pot and extinguish the fire by stamping their feet. Then they make dainy [as a generic term this refers to "women's dances"]. The neck and chest of each girl is smeared with clarified butter and they are told to run off.

This is a brief ceremony, though women suggested that unless it was performed "the girl would go for one year without menstruating." The girls shortly return to the homestead and are instructed to remain secluded while menstruating (i.e., to avoid contact with males) and never to milk cows or walk upon the burnt cow dung ash in the cattle camp when they have their periods. The young girls are then referred to as nyal awuot, women of marriageable age. As with their male counterparts, they now expect to receive decorative and cosmetic paraphernalia, such as iron bracelets, beads, and perhaps an ivory armband from the husband of an elder sister, who in turn expects eventually to receive a portion of her bridewealth when she is later married. A number of women said when I asked that the recurring reference to three in the rite stood for the fact that in order to become a "good wife" (cek me gau) a woman should bear at least three children.

In the light of this brief description and in consequence of extended discussions with Atuot women on the topic of tuol nyal, I would suggest that at a conscious level of experience for them, the girls thus emerge as a marriage class. They are not immediately expected to perform new economic tasks but instead are informed of their eventual responsibilities toward men as wives. Clearly, the formality of the rite for young girls achieves no great moment since they have been observing sisters, mothers, and aunts perform these tasks all their lives. Those who pass through the rite together are often visited as a group by a ric group of males in the courting behavior Atuot call gorniin, which I discuss below.

In summary to this point: A principle of seniority in accordance with the institution of ric determines the order of marriage for Atuot men. Men speak of marriages being performed for the brother who is "ahead" or next in line. When a son has proven himself capable of assuming the

responsibilities incurring from marriage, his father, an elder
brother, or a paternal uncle will give him (or more correctly,
let him wear) a string of beads called tik yang, the bead of
the cow, which symbolizes and announces his right to access to
cattle for marriage. All who see him wearing these beads
recognize that he is a matured individual, or awuot, seeking a
wife. In their manner of thinking, ca awuot me gor puthe, he
has become a gentleman who will look for marriage.

GORNIIN

The Atuot term gorniin is a compound of the words gor, to
seek, look for, or want and nien, to sleep, and thus connotes
for them the search for a sleeping place. This is a custom
that entails highly formalized rules of behavior and that
Atuot think of as distinctively their own. Indeed, many
important values of their culture are expressed in procedures
leading to marriage; on this account, some who had traveled
more widely than others in the southern Sudan contrasted their
traditions with those of Dinka neighbors. Parenthetically one
should add that these sentiments are in part an accurate
representation, and at the same time an expression, of
cultural pride. In eastern Dinka groups such as the Ceic and
Aliab, a similar custom called korniin, obviously cognate, is
practiced.
Walking along a path through the forest during the rainy
season the traveler in their country may encounter a number of
age mates, their bodies glistening with oil, their hair dyed
rusty orange, and their spears scattering reflected moonlight.
Their spears serve the obvious function of self-protection
since lions and other predatory beasts frequent the forests in
the rainy season, but on occasions such as these, special care
is taken to oil the shafts and hone and polish the blades.
Wako gorniin, "we are going to look for a sleeping place," is
the expected response to a question regarding their
destination. They are headed for one or another homestead to
seek the company of suitors to spend the evening in
conversation, with the hope of eventually sleeping with them.
They are intent upon the evening's adventure as a means toward
the end of marriage. Though deeply resentful if their
advances are rebuked or simply ignored (as custom allows),
Atuot awuot expressed to me strong pride in their women, as
they put it, since they view them as free to converse and
socialize with whomever they wish, independent of mind, and
able to make their own choices for amorous company.
A phase of life centered around the youthful activities
of the cattle camp and the custom of gorniin are two of the
most highly valued experiences in a young man's life. Among
other things, it is a period of relative freedom as well as
increasing social status for the individual. Young men take
pride in developing conversational styles that reveal both wit
and insight: When conversing with the young women, only a fine
line separates their implicit self-boasting from cultivated
smooth style. As noted, men of this age category are actively
involved in tending cattle, which is an arduous undertaking
especially during the rainy season, when thunder and evening
showers often frighten herds in the darkened forest on the
return from pastures. Yet for them this period of life in
camps is thought of as the best of all possible worlds. It

culminates for them when, along with those of their marriage
class, bridewealth cattle are exchanged to legitimize
marriage.

An interesting "just-so" text suggests both the origin as
well as a contemporary function of the practice known as
gorniin:

> We learned long ago that there was once no thing
> called gorniin. People [i.e., men] never courted
> girls. There was pregnancy because women were able
> to do this by themselves. There was a man who
> protected his daughter very much. He watched after
> her so much that he did not even let her go to fetch
> water by herself. One day the daughter chanced to
> meet an awuot and she pointed toward the direction
> of her hut and told him to go and wait for her in
> the back of the homestead. When he later went there
> she said he should put his penis through a hole in
> the wall. In the meanwhile, she returned to her
> home, unnoticed in her absence, and entered the hut.
> She then pressed herself against the wall of the hut
> and felt the man's penis against her. Soon she
> became erect [tar ke tier, the clitoris became
> erect]. When she became more excited she told her
> father that he should push her against the wall.
> Because he did not know what was actually happening,
> he did as she asked. She met the man several times
> and eventually she became pregnant. The father was
> very surprised to learn of this until the daughter
> explained the hole in the wall. Then the father
> decided that instead of being angry with the girl,
> it was better that she should decide who would meet
> with her. "This is good too," he said, "because now
> I will be able to see the ones who court her."

Atuot cite the practice of gorniin as the reason why elopement
is infrequent. J. Buxton (1963) notes in her discussion of a
similar custom of courting among the neighboring Mandari that
Mandari women view Atuot suitors as self-assertive to the
point of rudeness in violating their norms of courting
behavior and etiquette. It was my impression from living in
Anuol, a village in Kuek not far from Mandari country, that
Atuot awuot deliberately show disrespect for Mandari women
almost for the fun of it. One man from Kuek explained his
behavior and that of his ric toward Mandari women with a
boastful air of ethnic pride: "Mandari have only begun to
learn what the cow is. We fight with the Nuer in the toic!"
What was intended was an insult both to Mandari men because of
the small size of their herds, and to Mandari women, who are
still willing to become the men's wives.

When a young man has decided upon a woman who to some
degree suits his fancy, he does not approach her himself.
Instead, he will draw aside one or another age mate and reveal
his choice to him. When the occasion presents itself his
comrade will approach the young woman and say ca yi dom e ko,
"we have caught you" to speak of gorniin. She casually
enquires: "Who is the awuot among you that courts me? Let him
go to my house to visit." Two or three days later he will
appear at the homestead in the company of his friends. With
luck, he will receive the reply "the girl you are seeking has

taken a liking to you," the formal invitation to enter the household. The woman should have also invited a number of her own age mates to gather that evening so that the two groups eventually converge in the upper portion of the adwil. Her younger siblings are encouraged to spend the night elsewhere, since to be in the vicinity when amorous affairs are in the making invites an association with incest. The evening is spent in conversation, with the males holding forth most of the time. They share freshly harvested tobacco while boasting about the size of their family herds, the beauty of their personal ox, the fearlessness they show in battle, and so forth.

Young women do enjoy a great measure of freedom in opting for one mate over another, and will probably visit with a dozen or more men in gorniin while teenagers. Often a number of awuot appear at the edge of the homestead on a particular night so it is inevitable that some of them will be informed thil wan wene, "there is no place for you here." As one friend put it, she may also say, "well, I should like to see you but you are third on my priority. As it is, Mayan has been selected before you" (Mayan be yin mac: The verb mac means to choose or set aside, to reserve. Amac also means "to rope," as one ropes or tethers an animal). The analogy with herds can be more fully understood in this context by pointing out that in a cattle camp, bulls are often seen or figured as jostling for the opportunity to mount a cow. Indeed, it is a common custom to sharpen the horns of a stud bull, and its owner takes pride in the manner in which it fights with other bulls. This image is a common theme in ox-songs, as in this example:

> My bull is tethered in the middle of the camp
> The bull with the horns is tethered
> The animal that mounts the cows of Anyong
> My bull mounts the cows of the clan
> The bull is bending the tethering peg
> The bull is snapping the ropes

In open-ended conversation with male and female friends, it was always asserted that a couple would only sleep together and engage in casual petting. The greater my skepticism on this matter, the more adamant was their insistence that sexual intercourse was not the purpose of gorniin, yet it was my impression that many marriages were settled after a woman was already pregnant or had delivered a child.

ENGAGEMENT

The next stage of life centers around a more determined effort to find a wife, designated by the term muon, which refers to a formal arrangement of initial cattle transactions which precedes the announcement of a marriage. Adult women and men characterize gorniin as "a thing of children" in contrast to muon, which in their eyes is a far more serious undertaking. As other members of his ric become involved in this process a young man senses that he now also has the right to approach paternal relatives to discuss the formation of bridewealth cattle for his own marriage. Since he is actively involved in tending family herds he knows how many animals each relative

might be able to contribute in the exchange, though there is
always the possibility that a half-brother, a paternal uncle
or cousin, or even his own father may have eyes on herds to
arrange marriages of their own. When he senses the moment is
right, he will approach his seniors in a cattle camp to
discuss the girl he has in mind and, for the elders gathered,
to discuss the reputation of the family of the potential
bride. I found a number of common reasons elders would cite
in rejecting his initial request. They include the suspicion
that the family of the woman may be witches or that one or
another member of the family possesses the evil eye. Elders
would argue as a result that only misfortune could ensue from
the union of the two families. Another common reason for
denial is the accusation that the family has a reputation for
stealing cattle, that is, never making good their promises to
hand over cattle that are legitimately requested. The bride's
family, in particular, may fear there could be an
unnecessarily long delay in bridewealth exchange. Others
suggested the idea that while certain families may be wealthy
in cattle, they are also poor in heart. Finally, if there is
any history of physical or moral hostility between the
families or lineages of the potential spouses, there is little
reason to expect that anything fruitful could ever result from
a marriage. It may also happen that even though one son has
the full right to make requests for cattle for his marriage,
the bridewealth given in the marriage of an elder brother may
have depleted herds, which take a considerable period to
naturally increase.

The prospective groom suffers the most anxiety in the
whole procedure for he is dependent upon his kin for providing
bridewealth cattle. By contrast, a young woman enjoys some
freedom since if she learns that her family has arranged a
marriage with a man not to her liking, she may either
encourage pregnancy with the man of her choosing or leave her
homestead to live with kin elsewhere. On the other hand, the
parents of the prospective groom may inform the woman's family
that it was not in fact his turn for marriage. Had the young
woman become pregnant in the meanwhile, the man's family would
have to compensate her with a cow calf. However, a woman in
this circumstance will probably end up as a second or third
wife, a status to which few aspire. Extracts from two women's
songs lament this circumstance:

Oh women, the vagina moves between the thighs
The vagina has become a problem
What gave me a vagina?
The vagina that made me walk [leave her homestead to
     marry]
The vagina has brought me shame among my age set
The vagina has smacked me and poked me in the eye
This is what I tell the son of my father--
When I told the vagina to find a good place for me
It only left me lying in the grass

The age set that grew up
The age set that grew up and waited for the beads
The age set that finally reached the camp
I am told the house has no akol [sleeping hide; the
     singer intimates that she is being married into

a family that is so poor there is no place to
sleep]
How can this insult have come to me?
The walls of the hut are unplastered
Oh my brother, give it up [do not force the
marriage]
There is not even a broom to sweep the yard

THE CATTLE OF MARRIAGE

Atuot distinguish any single marriage (acop) from the
associated institution focused on yok puthe, "exchanging the
cattle of marriage." Another translation of the phrase could
mean "sharing the marriage cattle" since the Atuot word puth
can mean in certain contexts "to have in common," and in this
way may be cognate with the Nuer term for agnatic
relationship, buth. Bridewealth is the single most important
factor in legitimizing marriages; ideally the cattle exchanged
should include sufficient herds, a nucleus around which a herd
can reproduce itself and hence increase. It should be
stressed that this image is an ideal. Adult women and men
suggested that the number of animals exchanged as bridewealth
should number between thirty and forty, though I found
considerable variation in actual practice. On the one hand
one man I knew well was only able to offer his bride's family
two goats and a mosquito net, which was accepted at the time
in the hope that he would be able to offer a cow and perhaps
some oxen at some point in the future. The other extreme was
represented by a marriage in which 160 cattle were exchanged
between the groom's and bride's relatives. As I understand
their views, what is critical is that something is given at
marriage rather than the gross number of cattle actually
mustered for the occasion.
     Common opinion suggested that in the past the exchange of
marriage cattle took place in the cattle camp of the groom's
family, and that the animals given in exchange for the wife's
procreative ability were actually driven off the same day by
the recipients. Today discussions concerning the settlement
of bridewealth are more often centered in the village areas.
In either case the two parties to the marriage are collected
together. The discussions are undertaken in a standardized
and formal manner.
     In one exchange where I was present the future affines of
the bride sat about one hundred yards from the groom's family,
whose elders sat together under the shade of a tree. Those
who will receive the girl in marriage are given neither food
nor water until the fundamental purpose of their gathering--
the exchange of rights of ownership over cattle--has been
concluded. Representing each group of kin are two older men
called gwan acop, whose role is to officiate in the
discussions, acting as representative spokesmen for the two
groups. In his turn, each man of the bride's side who has a
claim to make for a number of cattle will address the gwan
acop who then "brings the word" to the cattle givers. He then
addresses the other party, saying "we have heard your word and
agree to your claim," "this will take more consideration," or
"we reject this outright." As noted, there is a degree of
formality to all of this and a respectful social as well as
physical distance is maintained between the two groups

throughout the proceedings, which may be settled in a day or
continue for a week or more. Indeed, it seems as though the
participants agree to disagree as part of the process.

Pieces of straw that represent cows, oxen, and bulls are
given to the rightful recipient. Ideally the elder brother of
the bride should receive ten cows, the next eldest five, and
the younger brother two or three. The bride's father asserts
a claim of ten to fifteen and the maternal uncle, five to ten
cows. Invariably, additional close agnatic relatives of the
bride will assert their own claims. If their niece is being
married into a family that has a wide reputation for owning
unusually large herds, the pleas of this latter category are
likely to be accepted. This of course benefits both parties:
The recipients will gain cattle they might not have expected
to in some other case, while the cattle givers will later take
pride in their generosity, boasting of their wealth in songs
that will be composed to remember the marriage settlement.
Bridewealth is given by the groom's kin to members of the
wife's family on the principle of status equivalence. For
example, the elder brother of the groom gives the elder
brother of the bride a number of cattle, and the bride's
father receives cattle which, in theory, are selected from the
groom's father's herd. Likewise among the Nuer, "Movements of
cattle from kraal to kraal are equivalent to lines on a
genealogical chart" (Evans-Pritchard 1940: 18).

In traditional usage, Atuot maintain that a man can marry
a woman but that a woman cannot marry a man. Among other
things this implies that a central notion of marriage as they
conceive of it is an exchange of cattle for women rather than
the inverse situation. In the course of observing these
transactions one afternoon a friend explained, "We are putting
down the cattle as the cattle of marriage," yok nane piny na
yok puthe. That is, they do not say they are giving cattle
for the woman since this verb buol, to give, has altogether
different connotations. Nor do they use the term "to buy" (ba
yoic) as they would when speaking of a piece of cloth in a
merchant's shop. Cattle are exchanged in the place of
children who will carry on generations of the groom's agnatic
heritage. Thus, patrilineal kin of his own generation or
marriage class (and less commonly senior males of his family)
will address the groom's wife as cek cang, "my wife of the
daytime." Just as a herd of cattle cannot be said to be owned
by any single individual so too are the products of a wife's
labor shared by her husband's agnatic kin. The usage implies
that while her first priorities should be centered on her own
domestic sphere, her husband's agnatic kin expect she will be
generous to them as well.

Once all those who have claims to receive cattle have
spoken and those who must procure them have promised to
fulfill their debts, the father of the bride signals to the
gwan acop to ask publicly if a consensus has been reached.
Normally by this point, after people have stalled, bargained,
and haggled, the answer is obvious and it is confirmed that
"the marriage has been made" (ca acap luoi). Preparations for
the public celebration of the marriage then begin. Women brew
pots of millet beer (kung) and cook quantities of porridge
with vegetable or meat sauces. Young women and men visit
local cattle camps to collect calabashes full of fresh milk.
A senior member representing each family offers a bull from
his camp to the other party as a gift (buol) to be slaughtered

and consumed in the course of festivities. This first act of
commonsality is a symbol of the reciprocity they ought to now
evidence toward each other as kin. With the feasting and
dancing completed, the bride is accompanied by her age mates
to her new homestead. En route, while carrying cooking
utensils and gourds of milk, the party sings

>The girl is taken to her husband
>The husband is proud--
>What troubles do you have with us?
>We, the age set of Acol
>You--those who look for marriage
>Give me a fat bull to eat

Another song includes the lines,

>The women are eager
>The women of the marriage are eager
>The women who want the skirts
>Like the skirt of Iding
>All the day we have talked about the skirt of Anyang
>And the skirt has become mine
>We are the women with the skirts

In their ox-songs, men often include lines or passages
concerning the matrix of agnation, marriage, and bridewealth
cattle. A standard usage makes reference to "the bull that
was brought with my sister," as in this illustration:

>The day of the girl is good
>I brought the animal from a distant land
>Oh, to remain alone is a bad thing
>I ignore the words of women
>This is why we remain peacefully
>The settlement of the marriage of a girl--
>It is a thing made with the words of elders
>A man with a sister is always lucky
>This is how my bull has come
>I brought the bull with a beautiful girl

On the evening after her arrival in her new homestead a
ram (amel cieng nyal, "the ram of the homestead of the girl")
is held to the ground in front of the doorway of the hut where
the married couple will sleep. Each spouse steps over the
animal when entering the hut and once again when they step
outside, an act which I was told made it possible for them to
have sexual intercourse with full moral sanction. A number of
related rites are enacted during the following days. The wife
is given a "cow for the cooking pot" (yang that) which she
later prepares for her in-laws, and this also allows for the
new spouses to eat from a common pot, though not yet in each
other's company. The husband gives her a goat or sheep which
she cooks to signify that she may then eat whatever food
remains after her husband has satisfied his hunger (tuer
atuok, literally, "so she can scrape out the food remaining in
the bowl"). Until a child is born and weaned it is deemed
improper for the husband to eat any food prepared by his new
affines, which was explained to be a way of "respecting" them.
When a second child is born, his in-laws give the husband yang
mieth, "a cow for eating," to signify that the prohibition on

their commensality has ceased. Atuot suggest that "with many children the marriage is tied" (teke gaat na ca puth yien), a common idea in pastoral Nilotic societies (see Lienhardt 1963; Evans-Pritchard 1951; Deng 1972). Marriage is thus best understood as a process rather than a single event. It is hoped that relations between the new wife and her husband's kin will become increasingly intimate just as it is hoped that the husband's family will make good on their promises of bridewealth cattle. The increased sense of moral and economic unity promised by the initial bridewealth exchange is revealed in the course of a later series of cattle exchanges, which I review next.

COMPLIMENTARY PRESTATION

In a family composed of many sons but only a single daughter, bridewealth transactions can virtually devastate family herds. Evans-Pritchard observed this among the Nuer in writing that the exchange of bridewealth "changes a man's fortune in a very material way. The bridegroom's family is impoverished, sometimes to the point of privation" (1951: 89). Some measure of material security is offered by the institution known as thuik in Nuer, arueth in Dinka, and thio in Atuot. Paul Howell (1954: 113) translates the Nuer thuik as "cattle given by the bride's family to her husband" and notes, "The payment [sic] is accompanied by ritual which symbolizes the removal of the taboo on the two families eating and drinking together. . . . I have heard Nuer say that they used to be paid on a larger scale in the old days when 'people married with many cattle'." Deng (1971: 390) defines the Dinka term arueth as "reverse payment [sic] of cattle made by the bride's kin to the bridegroom's kin. It approximates one-third of the bridewealth cattle paid [sic] by the bridegroom's kin." Assuming an idealized bridewealth exchange of forty animals, the value of arueth is significant. Deng (1971: 262) also writes that the Dinka

> do not use any fixed proportion, but they will readily give the corresponding reverse value of any amount of bridewealth given them as an example. Thus, they say that forty corresponds to one hundred and six to forty, though it is not explained how these figures are arrived at. . . . Reverse payment is compulsory. Indeed, a great deal of litigation concerns failure to discharge the obligation.

An important point to underscore is the fact that arueth cattle offered by the bride's kin are collected "from their own cattle, and not from the cattle given them by the bridegroom's kin" (1971: 262). In the contemporary Nilotic Sudan the exchange of arueth has been made standard and codified as one right accruing to the husband through marriage "at the rate of three cows for every ten cows paid as bridewealth" (Dinka Customary Law, n.d.).

Atuot suggested that within some years of the counting of the marriage cattle, thio (from the verb thiok, "to close," thus suggesting the closing or sealing of the marriage) is made to the family of the husband. Though equally vague about the formula employed, friends stated that for every ten cows exchanged as bridewealth, the husband's people should later receive two cows and one bull as thio. In the situation of a man's successful plea for divorce (see below) he will in principle receive back all the cattle (and their progeny) initially exchanged and must, on his part, return thio received from his bride's kin. On a more positive note the practice of counter-prestation marks the fact that two previously distinct families and agnatic groups become a single community through the transmission of debts, prestations, and complimentary prestations.

SOME FORMS OF MARRIAGE

In the preceding discussion I have tried to point out an association between age categories or ric and processes leading toward marriage. It also seems clear that age categories are explicitly related to the acquisition and management of bovine resources, which ultimately remain the affair of elder males. Children in Atuot communities, as among the Dinka and Nuer, learn early on in life that the ultimate purpose of sexual relationships is marriage and the birth of children. Among the values that it represents to them, marriage promises a degree of adult independence, the possibility of increasing the size of family herds, and, of equal importance, the chance to produce children whose children will carry on the living memory of deceased generations. My shorter experience in Atuot communities is reflected in R. G. Lienhardt's (1963: 79) observation that "In travelling extensively through Dinkaland for nearly two and a half years, I never met a middle-aged man or woman who was not, or had not at some time been, married."

As is common in this region of Africa the ideology of descent is patrilineally biased and postmarital residence favors patrilocality. Marriage occurs among the Atuot in diverse forms, each of which is possible only in recognition of rules of incest (rual). In passing I confess that incest was a topic I found few willing to discuss, and on occasion I felt suspect for broaching the subject. The more common alleged instance I did learn of was the father-daughter type, and those who volunteered information considered sibling or mother-son forms virtually inconceivable. The following brief text was recorded a number of times in nearly identical form, so one has the feeling it represents a standardized image:

> A woman had intercourse with a man and she bore a girl. Later, when the girl had grown, the same man had sex with her and she also became pregnant. But when she delivered, her uterus burst open and she died, as did the man.

In their eyes, individuals who would actively seek out such a relation would probably die immediately. Disapproved sexual liaisons occasionally do occur and when incest is alleged, a sacrifice called riet ruale is called for. The carcass of the sacrificial victim is severed completely in half from head to tail. Incestuous congress may also be cited as the source of complications during childbirth. A related notion is that if spouses respect (thek) different totemic or clan emblems (wet) they ought to respect each other's different emblem as they would their own.

Before discussing some of the forms in which marriages occur one may consider certain results from a marriage survey conducted between 1976 and 1977. Of 120 extant marriages examined, 87 percent were ethnically endogamous. Fifty percent of adult males had one wife, roughly 33 percent were married to two women, 6 percent were married to three women, approximately 5 percent had four wives, while the remaining 6 percent indicated having five or more wives. The mean (estimated) age at the time of first marriage for males was in the area of thirty years, though older people suggested that the age of first marriage had decreased within living memory. There was no significant correlation found between advanced age and a greater number of wives and in the majority of cases bridewealth exchanged in the first marriage was not superseded in subsequent marriages. As noted, ideal figures were offered for the number and composition of bridewealth cattle even though the sample collected evidenced wide variation in this regard.

The most common type of marriage is the simple legal union between a woman and a man. Often they have been engaged, though the marriage is not complete until the exchange of bridewealth. This exchange is intended to compensate the bride's family for her productive labor and reproductive capabilities. This is the form of marriage (see Evans-Pritchard 1951) Atuot have in mind when offering general observations on the topic. Those who gather to settle yok puthe are commonly termed ji puthe, or the people of the marriage. The survey I conducted indicated that another common traditional form of marriage is called cuong, or "ghost marriage."

Ghost marriage traditionally took place in the name of a man who died without having been married or for a man who died lacking a son to "carry his name." In effect ghost marriage is identical to the simple legal union of two spouses since bridewealth cattle are exchanged between the family of the deceased and the agnatic kin of the bride in the standard fashion. Those individuals who would have been expected to contribute livestock for the marriage of the deceased bear the responsibility of arranging a marriage in his name. The selection of a suitor to actually cohabit with the bride is largely a matter of her own discretion, made in accord with the proscriptive norms of incest. The children born of this union are known as the children of the ghost of the deceased (jaat atip). When asked to explain why marriages are arranged in this manner the common response is "this is done so a man's name will be heard tomorrow," that is, so that a form of social immortality is promised.

The word cuong, which designates a ghost marriage, has a number of other meanings in different contexts. When leading a dance, for example, a singer may reprimand the dancers to kuong cuong, to make a straight line. Anxious to voice their opinions in a heated argument a man or woman may exclaim kuong cuong, analogous to the English usage "now you just hold it a minute!" Thus, the central notion expressed through ghost marriage is the intention to "hold the name of a man straight" so he will "stand" or be remembered in the future. A precise record of the incidence of ghost marriages could only be

derived from a prolonged residence in all communities which
share the perception of common ancestry. Even in such ideal
circumstances the task would be difficult. As Evans-Pritchard
long ago noted for the Nuer, lineal genealogies are at one
point condensed or "telescoped," thereby obfuscating the
possibility of documenting actual relationships and patterns
of descent. I take some refuge in the caveat expressed by
Evans-Pritchard who wrote, "Indeed, I know of no more
difficult task among Nilotic peoples than that of obtaining
correct genealogies" (1945: 29). It is also likely that some
people are ignorant of the fact that a particular marriage was
performed in the name of a ghost. I have also known children
of ghost marriages to deny the information (even while it was
confirmed by others), seeking instead to be known as the
direct descendant of an individual, for political or economic
ends. There is a psychological parameter involved here too,
for one who lives among them gains the impression that "the
child of a ghost" is an expression intimating the status of an
orphan, a fate Atuot lament. Genealogies I obtained indicated
that in the generation of contemporary elders roughly 30
percent of marriages were made in the name of a ghost, that
is, for a dead man.

As I already noted, seniority of age determines the order
of marriage among sons of a single father. Hence the eldest
son is given first priority to use cattle for bridewealth,
followed in order by the second, third, and fourth sons of a
man's family. This proscription not uncommonly results in
open hostility between half brothers of different mothers, who
may be close enough in age for each to consider his own
demands above the other. Indeed, the few cases of fratricide
of which I learned were explained to me as being the result of
similar confrontations. Since a ghost marriage was arranged
when, for example, an elder brother died before having
married, the marriage of the next son would have been delayed
for a considerable time. The cattle which would have been
allocated for his marriage would be used to marry a woman in
the name of the deceased elder brother. The ideological
sanctions for this custom are clearly expressed in Atuot
notions concerning ghostly vengeance and the curse of the
dead. In the odd instance where a son made a case to delay
his debt to a deceased brother in this circumstance, he would
be allowed to marry, though only to a woman from a poor
family, which would accept a token bridewealth in expectation
of better days. However, fear of the curse of the deceased
has a powerful impact on actual usage. For example, people
suggested to me that the reason one man had no surviving
children even after many years of marriage was because he had
failed to marry a woman to the ghost of his deceased brother.
In anger and vengeance, the ghost had cursed the living to
remain childless forever.

There are a number of reasons to surmise that violent
death through warfare or feuding accounted in part for a
higher frequency of ghost marriages in the past. Those
herding cattle--young men who were of the age deemed proper
for their first marriage--were the same individuals who died
in cattle raids and violent confrontations. Thus if 30
percent of marriages are ghost marriages (and this may be an
underestimate), a significant proportion of the male
population inherited an obligation to use their bridewealth
cattle for the marriage of a deceased kinsman. Clearly, the

institution of ghost marriage would have been an important
facet of Atuot economic and social organization. Comparative
data is provided by Evans-Pritchard on the Nuer. "The number
of widow concubines and of old women without mates (who are
also widows) suggests a very high mortality rate among males.
This is partly due to the constant fighting that used to go
on, and still to a lesser extent goes on between Nuer" (1945:
7-8). He observes further,

> They [ghost marriages] must be almost as numerous as
> simple legal families. Not only do many youths die
> before marriage--and this was yet more the case
> before the government restricted fighting--but for
> one reason or another married men do not always have
> male children to continue their line. A man's
> children may die. He and his wife may die. His
> widow may have no children or go back to her own
> people and be married to another man. He may beget
> only daughters (1945: 7-8).

This digression into the topic of ghost marriage is
warranted because of its social and ideological significance
in the reproduction of social life. In addition to simple
legal unions and ghost marriages, Atuot also practice
additional forms. Less common is what they term puth ke cek,
or woman-woman marriage. In extreme circumstances, a young
woman may be the sole individual who survives within a family.
If she is socially classified as an adult, she will use the
family cattle to marry a woman whose children will be counted
as direct agnatic descendents of her father's lineage. Women
who offered information on this subject expressed indignation
over the possibility of becoming a wife in this fashion. The
true levirate is also practiced and is called wa yot or
"coming into the brother's hut." The younger brother cohabits
with the dead brother's wife and if children had been born
before the death, no cattle are exchanged as bridewealth.
Some friends described the levirate to me as lau (from the
verb lak, to wash), an act to wash away the sorrows of the
wife. In this instance, if a brother or some other
appropriate agnate is unavailable, the wife is permitted to
reside with a suitor of her own choice. If she becomes
pregnant and bears a child, her lover's family will compensate
her with a number of cattle. I might also add that while
there is considerable freedom in selecting a suitor, most
women prefer to find a permanent mate for their own comfort,
as well as to avoid insult about being of easy virtue. A
further variation of ghost and leviratic marriage is called
amuom. A husband may choose not to divorce a barren wife and
yet may marry another woman. The first male child of the
second wife is supposed to marry a woman in the name of the
father, and she is called the wife of the barren woman. This
is performed "for the son who was not born" from the first
marriage.
    A number of other customs exist to resolve the problem of
impotency. "Entering the hut of the wife of your father" (wa
yot cio guar) refers to a situation in which an impotent man
with two or more wives asks a son to sleep with a stepmother,
with the result that the son becomes the biological father of
his brother or sister. In the same dilemma, the maternal
uncle can request that his sister's son provide the same

service.   The phrase <u>guel</u> <u>yot</u> can be glossed as "sororate" but
suggests in literal translation "replacing the hut." Here the
sister of a deceased wife leaves her natal home to assume
marital status.   As with the levirate, no cattle are
exchanged.   The children born are conceived of as the children
of the dead woman.

These forms of marriage, as noted, do not occur with the
same regularity but are all in principle concerned with
addressing two central values: the birth of children and the
establishment of their legitimacy through bridewealth
exchange.   In light of the variegate conditions of traditional
livelihood in this region of Africa, it is not really
surprising that so many alternative strategies exist in order
to continue a family name and to maintain jural access to
valued property.   I have already made reference to the idea
that with the birth of two or three children, Atuot think of
the marriage as "tied" or secure and after this time, the
groom's family begins to lose track of the use and
distribution of the bridewealth given to the wife's family
(see Evans-Pritchard 1951).   At roughly the same time, the
husband may then begin to actively seek a second wife to
increase the size of his own progeny as well as to decrease
the amount of domestic labor for his first wife.   Indeed, the
relationship between the spouses begins to take a new
direction at this point.   On the one hand, after she has given
birth to three or four children, a woman has the explicit
right to refuse sexual companionship with him.   The Atuot
speak of such a woman as <u>cek</u> <u>ce</u> <u>pel</u> <u>ngoth,</u> a wife who has left
intercourse behind.   She may also encourage her husband to
marry another woman who, as a junior wife, would assume a
greater portion of domestic labor.   Should a husband later
marry once more, the senior wife commands considerable
authority over her younger co-wives and also takes on a
greater role in the affairs of her husband's larger agnatic
kin group.

A life history along these lines is what characterizes
Atuot values attending the institution of marriage, yet they
represent ideals which are not always realized.

THE DISSOLUTION OF MARRIAGE

Unlike the typical expectation in many western societies,
barrenness rather than adultery is the most common argument
for divorce among the Atuot.   As one might imagine for a
pastoral society, divorce, like marriage, is conceived of
through the idiom of cattle.   Hence divorce is referred to as
<u>dao</u> <u>puthe,</u> dividing or untethering the bridewealth cattle.

The most common and socially sanctioned ground for
divorce from the husband's perspective is his wife's alleged
barrenness.   In the past this condition was not necessarily
associated with a physiological malady.   Instead a diviner was
consulted to establish the identity of the individual who has
cursed the woman with a malignant power.   A variety of rituals
were performed in the attempt to exorcise this power with the
eventual hope of restoring her full health.   Answers to my
questions suggested that the maternal uncle of the woman is
frequently the first suspect, especially if he has made it
public knowledge that he was dissatisfied with his share of
bridewealth at the time of her marriage, or if these animals

had become unhealthy. Less often, a woman is said simply to be cursed and thus unable to reproduce. If in addition to her barrenness a woman was often criticized for her cooking, was often accused of adultery, and made little attempt to befriend herself to her husband's family, divorce would be the common expectation. Assuming all these failures Atuot would say <u>loic cek ce lieu</u>, that the heart of the wife had died. Thus would begin the difficult task of reclaiming cattle exchanged as bridewealth earlier on.

On the death of a wife the marriage is immediately absolved. By contrast, the woman remains married to the husband even after his death. Traditional custom has been codified and standardized throughout the region in association with a brief entitled <u>Dinka Customary Law</u>, a handbook adopted by governmental authorities in the mid-1970s. Within this document the grounds for divorce are enumerated thus: (1) Barrenness of the wife; (2) Impotence of the husband; (3) Death of the children of the spouses; (4) Incest; (5) Gross misconduct by the wife; (6) Cruelty by the husband or his relatives to the wife; (7) Infection with venereal disease passed to the complaining spouse; (8) Serious deterioration of relations between relatives. In this form certain traditional values have been reserved and some measure of protest by the wife is promised at least partial hearing. However, the codified form continues to protest marriage as an institution with self-expressed interests in maintaining and promoting a somewhat patriarchal society (see Johnson 1986).

WOMEN AND MEN IN MARRIAGE

Having offered an outline of the general features and forms of marriage and some of the reasons for its demise, it may be of some value to consider a variety of texts illustrating how, in their own words, Atuot conceive of the marital relationship. The initial question I posed was "What are the relations of a wife and husband?" (<u>kue kam den</u>?, "what is it between them?") and "how do they come to quarrel?" (<u>ku guac thuke thok</u>?, "what makes their words go in opposite directions?" or contradict). By way of introduction something can be said of common themes which emerge from the accounts. The first and most obvious is the enormous attention given to reproduction, which is not surprising given that they see this as the fundamental purpose of marriage. A second theme concerns the formal respect each spouse ought to evidence for the other. The feeling is that each person's sense of self should not be compromised, that though they are married they remain individuals. Closely related to this is the fact that time makes one bolder, seen for instance in the fact that a woman can refuse her husband's sexual advances if she has already fulfilled cultural expectations by giving birth to a number of healthy children. One's initial and, it should be stressed, superficial impression of the qualitative facet of Atuot marriage is that an element of romantic fascination is absent. However, as any anthropologist would find with the passage of time, one comes to be treated less as a stranger and more like a kinsman and at that point it becomes clear that there is a very strong sense of intimacy between the spouses. It is an intimacy, stemming from their pronounced stance of public respect toward each other, that is reserved for the privacy of each other's company.

Text I. Alak Angui, mother of five children, presently widowed:

The reason a girl is married is to get cows. Your father says that you are to be married to so and so and you are taken there to stay. You stay like a guest, almost hiding away. When you see the face of your husband, you run and hide. You stay in the hut without doing anything. In the daytime you are taken to the forest so you can urinate and defecate and when you return you go right back in the hut and stay. You stay with the husband respecting each other and you do not have quarrels. You only talk together by night when you are alone together away from other people and in the daytime you do not see each other. You stay, and when the Creator gives you a child, you are taken back to your mother's home. There you stay and give birth to the child and nurse it. Then you are given yoal, the sling made from the goat's hide to carry the child. After that you are taken back to the husband's home and the child is seen by your mother-in-law and your father-in-law. When the child comes to know itself and is able to drink some of the cow's milk it is taken to your mother and brother in the cattle camp. Then you return to your husband's home and when you arrive you begin to cook and bake your foods. You pound millet, distribute the food and treat all the relatives well because you are the wife of their son. The brother of your husband (cou cang: husband of the daytime) must also be fed well because he gave cows for the marriage yesterday.

The wife comes to be yang [kue ben ke be wa yang: she enters the household of the husband to offer the services that the cows gave beforehand]. She cooks well and all become satisfied. When she has the next child it is taken care of by the mother-in-law. When she speaks to you, you say nothing and it is the same with your father-in-law. By night you tell your husband what has been told to you by so and so, and even if the word you hear is not good, you do not talk back and make a quarrel. When you treat your in-laws poorly, your husband will ask, what is it? And his brother will say, only yesterday I exchanged my cows for you and now you mistreat us. He will beat you. If you have no heart, things will go in a different way. He will beat you daily. People will ask, why is this woman beaten daily? It is because of your bad ways. If you are divorced, people will always remember it was because of these things. It is what your husband told you--but you failed to listen. It is the husband who talks and the wife who listens. You accept his word. You, the wife--if you think something is bad--then you speak only to the husband. This is how we stay in our homes.

Text II: Mayan Akuot, father of six children:

We keep cows. You keep your father's cows that are given to you. Your father married your mother who bore you.

You grow . . . you find your woman and you engage her.
Your fathers all come and make the marriage. You put a
skirt on her, and she is given to you. The song is heard
by the whole village, that the son of so and so is being
given the daughter of so and so. It is said like that.
The wife is brought and taken into the hut. Women are
given an ox to eat, and when they have finished they
return to their homes. Then you go into the hut and bear
children. When she is pregnant there is milk in the
cattle camp for her food . . . she is taken back to her
mother's village and stays there for all her pregnancy.
She delivers and nurses the child and when he is big and
strong he stops taking milk from his mother. The woman
is then returned to you and is given the things of the
house and begins to cook for her husband. This is how
people stay in the home.

They stay in the hut and respect each other. You do
not call the name of the woman and she does not call you
by name. They respect themselves. The children can go
to five or six, like with my wife Ayor. I am coming back
from the work of cattle and when I arrive tomorrow she
will not greet me, because she has borne me five children
so we only say hello. If the woman has no mind, if she
is a lame person with no heart, then she will call the
name of the husband. A husband is taught by the wife.
If she is not a base person and not a rogue, the house
will be good. It is the wife who teaches the husband. I
am now with my wife Ayor and there is good respect
between us. She does not just call out my name. I think
she will bear children up to ten and we will never beat
each other. If I have gone for a journey and I come back
and sit, she will give me food that she has cooked. I
will ask her, mother of my children, how did you stay
with the land? Have you kept the house well? That is
our conversing. Too many words make a husband and wife
quarrel.

In our land, it is for a woman to give birth to
children. Women are not good or bad--they are in
between. Their badness is that even if you are married
with one hundred cows, she may still leave. Even if you
cultivate much grain, she may still leave you. This is
because some women have no heart. If it is a good woman
she will bear many children. If there were not women,
how would all the people be here? She is the one who
created the land. There is the wife of the black people,
of the animals, of the cows, of the fish--all of them
have this land. If it were not for women, how would
people be so many? Women are good--they make children
and food and beer. The woman has the land. If a man
stays in this land without a woman, he will not go ahead
[i.e., his progeny will never be realized].

Text III: Acol Ijuong, mother of six children:

In our home, Atuotland, marriage is made to give birth to
children. A woman's work is so much that she is always
exhausted. Cultivating--that is the work of women, along
with drawing water. You keep the house and bear
children. If the Creator gives you children, you will

have ten. And then, tomorrow, you will have a name. One
child will look after the cows and one will go to school
and become a child of the government. When your daughter
is married you are given wealth, and you tell her to hold
her house properly and to cook well for the people. You
never speak loudly to your mother-in-law and father-in-
law. He is like the father who bore you and she is like
your own mother. You cannot invent your own ways of
staying [in your husband's home]. In our land when
people have respect between themselves it means you can
not talk to a husband when he has not said anything to
you. You can give birth to four children and never have
a word with him. If nothing bad happens you will stay in
your home well because you were brought there with his
wealth.

Text IV: Kulang Takpiny, father of ten children:

The best in marriage was your mother who was chosen among
the other girls and was married to your father. You were
born, you stop breast feeding, you become a young man,
you are initiated and then you mature. When your father
has cows and your sister has been married then you go to
look for a girl you like, and when you find her you will
go tell this to your father. He will ask whose daughter
she is and if she has a good family.

    When it is tuek (the last months of the rainy season)
you go to the camp and you call for your marriage to be
made. You stay with her, and the Creator gives you a
child. She goes to live with her mother and you spend a
great deal of time collecting milk in your cattle camp
for her food. She stays like that for one year and then
comes to stay in your home. During that year, if there
is hunger like there is now, you see to it that she has
food. When the first rains come you go and cultivate if
she is still with her mother. When she comes to your
home she will cook a very big meal for all your
relatives. This is her first cooking for you. All the
old people of the family will gather together for this
meal and then go back to their own homes. If the first
child is a boy, he stays with your wife's brother until
he has gone through initiation and if it is a girl she
stays until she has had her first menstruation. At
first, when the wife has a child, she stays like an
unrelated guest, but later she becomes one of us, and
even if you are away in the cattle camp, she will cook
food for guests and give them tobacco.

Text V: Anan Luk, divorcee, no children:

There is a man and there is a woman and the thing that
makes their staying together good is a child. The child
is the one who holds them together. When a woman has no
child and her relations with her husband are bad, she
will leave. If there is a child, she keeps on until she
is old. Cows are already given and you do not yet know
what they will bring [i.e., what will become of the
marriage]. If there are no children, there is no
marriage.

Aii, with no husband life is so hard. You are married
and given a skirt and you have this so you will give
birth. When the child is small you never leave the home.
Even if I am beaten and no grain is cultivated, and the
husband does not build me a good house, I have to stay
because of the child. The child I bore died and my
husband beat me. Our words were bad and I left. But you
cannot stay alone since you know that you can still give
birth and your hands are strong. You can still make food
for another man and Creator will give you a child. A
person who has been divorced should be married again.
Another person can also bear children with you and you
stay in his place until you get old. If you are divorced
you can marry another husband. It is not good to come
and stay in your house and never marry again. In our
land women do not leave only because their husbands beat
them. But without children, marriage is hard--this is
why there is sometimes divorce.

Text VI: Iwer Deng, grandmother, and mother of nine
children:

When you marry you give cows to the relatives of the wife
and you are given a girl. She pounds and cooks millet.
She brings a child, and to all this work, she adds a good
tongue. Any girl who does not work well and speaks with
a bad tongue is divorced. A man who found a good woman
will always have food to give his relatives. This is how
the house is made well. The husband cultivates and makes
the hut and puts on the roof. The walls are plastered
with mud by the women. If a man has two wives, if they
both have hearts coming with them into the marriage, they
will stay like sisters. If they have hatred among
themselves, they have come with bad hearts. Each has her
own hut where she cooks. They should respect themselves.
If the heart of a wife dies, if she no longer does the
things she ought to do, then she has become bitter and
the marriage is separated.

Text VII: Akutei Muokjok, grandfather, and father of
seven children:

When you marry in our land you are in the front of the
line. You make your home and build your house, and you
stay, the two of you together. If you do not keep her
well, she will be angry. She will say "this is a husband
who does not keep me well. He does not fill my stomach
and so I had better leave." If you do not know your
stomach, your words will end on the sleeping hide. This
is what was created by Creator. It was created long ago
that a man and woman should stay together as one in one
house to bear children. People do not stay in the house
with two tongues. If there is a quarrel, you keep it
inside, between the two of you. And then, after that,
you come outside as husband and wife. But when we first
joined with women it was the waves of the river that were
the husbands. It was women who had cows. Then man found
the vagina. That is what gave us a quarrel with women,
the vagina.

Text VIII: Alak Bilieu, grandmother, and mother of seven
children:

A woman stays with her husband well, each with their own
sleeping hides. She prepares the food for the husband
and together they bear children. They stay in the house
until they are old, and when the husband speaks, a woman
keeps quiet without giving an answer to his word. The
husband looks after the concerns of the family so that
his wife will have food and she will be healthy. This is
how they will stay without quarreling, so they will have
a name tomorrow.

SOCIAL AND MORAL SPACE

In the concluding section of this chapter, attention is
focused on a series of relationships or entailments involving
notions of descent, relations based on common kinship and
forms of residence. An underlying concern involves the manner
in which physical space per se is imbued with social and moral
connotations.

To begin, one can recall a common theme in pastoral
Nilotic ethnology that reveals an epic notion of ethnogenesis
(see Lienhardt 1975). At the most general level genealogies
of common agnatic identification lead ultimately to quasi-
mythical apical ancestors, who are spoken of in the
contemporary world as the first people who "made the land" of
founded local communities. Among the Nuer, for example, so-
called aristocrats are those who assert pure agnatic descent
from the first "true" Nuer who settled a new territory.
Evans-Pritchard (1945) describes some of the ways in which
local peoples transform their genealogies in the attempt to
conform to this cultural ideal. The simple fact of common
residence over a number of generations seems to offer
sufficient evidence of this putative relationship. Elsewhere
(Evans-Pritchard 1951: 174) he cites the local observation "He
has lived so long among us that I call him 'son of my father'
(gat gwar)." By an analogous manner in Dinka communities,
highly regarded ritual experts all claim agnatic descent from
an original culture hero named Awiel Longar. Collectively,
Atuot speak of their territory as cieng Reel, the home or land
of Atuot-speaking peoples, comprised of cieng Apak, cieng
Luac, cieng Akot, cieng Jilek, cieng Rorkec, and cieng Kuek.
In this sense the name of each people is the place of each
people. Oral traditions (see Burton 1981a) in certain cases
posit an apical ancestor of a named territory. Jilek, for
example, means "People (ji) descended from Lek," a man who is
said to have "come from up the river." Kec, in these same
texts, was the "owner of the land" now called Rorkec. Luac
and Kuek traditions consistently make reference to man called
Cuonga, who is figured as having led their initial migrations
into what became cieng Luac and cieng Kuek.

It is convenient to speak of these six named territories
as sections, which are physically discernable in physical
space though internally based on dissimilar or even
contradictory traditions and origins (see below re Apak).
Each section is composed of a differing number of
"birthgroups" known as dieth dor, and at the time of field
research these were as follows:

Luac, consisting of:
1. Adjong Perio
2. Yol
3. Gumrou
4. Aruol
5. Againy
6. Pirpiu
7. Kuol

Rorkec, consisting of:
1. Thiang
2. Yuom
3. Pariak
4. Paleu
5. Nyang

Kuek, consisting of:
1. Nyanying
2. Nyang
3. Gwarang
4. Jilouth
5. Jikaliep
6. Nyuei
7. Ajong Karam
8. Balang

Akot, consisting of:
1. Diel
2. Riair

Jilek, consisting of:
1. Awen
2. Piir
3. Maker
4. Aciri
5. Alik

Apak, consisting of:
1. Awen
2. Aper
3. Acok
4. Palual
5. Riir
6. Aperer
7. Pakuac
8. Atoc

Each birth group is defined in part through identification
with a common emblem or "totem" (wet). In local theory each
named group consists of larger or smaller numbers of gol and
in the initial situation the dieth dor have increased in size
over many generations through the birth of children. As noted
earlier, the term gol refers in context to the mud and
thatched roof shelters in cattle camps. In the present
context it is understood as Atuot speak of it, as "a man and
his increase." The phrase ji gol de connotes the living
generations of a family whose elder males share the perception
of agnatic heredity with deceased members of a particular
dieth dor. Paralleling this usage is the custom whereby
children of a common father inherit the respect (thek) of

their father's _wet_ so that by analogy, when tracing agnatic heredity, the mother's relations have no significance. During the colonial era, "chiefs" were selected to represent each of the six named sections and "subchiefs" were recruited to represent the government to each subsection or _dieth dor_.

It is difficult to assert with any certainty that _dieth dor_ ever acted corporately as one might imagine if the Atuot phrase was translated by the English term "clan" and even more unlikely that a named section (e.g., Kuek, or Akot) acted in concert. Lienhardt (1958) has noted that among the Dinka, in principle, common membership in a tribe or subtribe indicates a moral obligation to maintain peace with its members, yet two different tribal segments which share a common boundary are likely to be more closely integrated than sections of the same tribe living many miles distant. It has also been noted that for the Nuer social cohesion "increases as the size of the community narrows" (Evans-Pritchard 1940: 162).

Birth groups conceive of their identity in association with common territory, common herds, and the abstracted framework of a common agnatic heredity while in fact the lineage, _any_ lineage, truly begins with women and their offspring. Support of this assertion is provided by customary and polite usages of relationship terms which are discussed more fully below. At this point, however, it is interesting to consider the text of a myth that has wide currency in Atuot communities. The story images a period in the past, long before any human memory of the experience, when women and men lived in quite separate worlds. In this imaginary setting men lived among themselves in their own camp in the forest but the animals they kept tethered were buffalo rather than cattle. To satisfy their sexual desires they kept vaginas tied to their arms which they would use and then refasten as need be. Women also lived in a camp by themselves in a riverside setting, tending herds of cattle, cultivating millet, and fishing.

> One day a buffalo calf strayed away from the other animals and did not return that evening. The next morning a man followed its trail which led to the camp of women. Until this time when women desired sex they went to the riverside and splashed the foam of the waves between their legs, giving birth to females only. When the man asked if his calf had come into the camp a woman answered "no," and while he was satisfied with this reply, he soon took interest in another matter, asking the woman what the separation was between her legs. She answered, "This is vagina" and asked in turn what might be the thing dangling between his legs. He said, "This is penis" and then said to the woman, "You bring that here and let me see if it is sweet." When he later said it was very very good, all the other women of the camp rushed upon him and they fucked him so much he died. He died completely.

> A short while later the women said among themselves, "Now it is time to look after the cows" but each avoided the responsibility, saying, "It is now time to dry the millet so it can be pounded into flour." Then men from the other camp arrived in search of

their friend. The women insulted them for thinking
that their buffaloes were like cows and went on
pounding their grain. Seeing that the women
appeared to take no interest in the cows, the men
stole them. Later in the day each woman sought out
a man of her liking and remained with him that
evening. The next day, when each man wanted to
marry a woman, the senior woman of the camp said,
"You have given up your buffaloes and that is good.
But if you want to marry my daughters then you must
give cows to replace them."

The text offers sufficient background for understanding the
Atuot proverb, "The feud of the cow and the feud of the vagina
are one" but perhaps it also offers something of more concrete
value in understanding the seeming paradox between the
overreaching principle of agnatic descent and the relative
absence of "pure" agnatic groups in village and cattle camp
settlements. (Evans-Pritchard [1940: 49] offers a different
explanation of the proverb: "Nuer say that it is cattle that
destroy people, for 'more people have died for the sake of a
cow than for any other cause.' They have a story which tells
how, when the beasts broke up their community and each went
its own way and lived its own life, Man slew the mother of Cow
and Buffalo. Buffalo said she would avenge her mother by
attacking them in the bush, but Cow said that she would remain
in the habitations of men and avenge her mother by causing
endless disputes about debts, bridewealth, and adultery, which
would lead to fighting and death among the people" [see also
Lienhardt 1961: 27].)
     The process of social reproduction in Atuot communities
entails the productive and reproductive contributions of
women. No stronger moral tie exists than that between
children borne by the same mother. As they mature, men become
more fully cognizant of their dependence on women for social
continuity. The first hints of this dependence come about
fairly early in childhood. Members of the immediate family or
cieng, homestead (recall that each wife in a polygynous union
has her own gardens and hut), are spoken of in Atuot as ji
mac, or "people of the cooking fire." This idiom points to
the fact that commensality is a marker of agnatic relations,
which are in practice created by women. (The extreme example
of this is provided by the woman-woman form of marriage).
While they are members of different elementary families in
village settlements children sired by a single male are
members of a common gol in the cattle camp. The relationship
term gat jiede, "child of my insides," consciously underscores
the fact that two individuals were borne by the same mother,
and I cannot think of a more endearing term for reference in
Atuot than the phrase gat e mar, "child of my mother," which
is reserved for individuals who truly fit the classification.
     The practice of polygyny, which men value as a means of
increasing the labor pool to tend herds of cattle and
promoting their social immortality, in practice works against
the principle of agnatic unity. Here, the significance of the
uterine relationship is most apparent. It is only through
social fabrication that half brothers are members of the same
birth group. At the time of their first marriage half
brothers may be in direct competition for access to
bridewealth cattle, even though each in his turn can expect

some small contribution from the respective mother's brother.
And since they have different mothers, they have different
kinship communities beyond their father's family so that the
moral unity of this family is inherently fragile (see Gluckman
1956).   By definition, a similar situation cannot arise
between uterine brothers since age categories determine rights
to the use of cattle as bridewealth.

Virtually identical conditions prevail in Nuer and Dinka
communities. Economic and moral ties are especially strong
between opposite sex siblings. As Lienhardt (1963: 83)
observes,

> The children of any mother have superior rights in
> certain cattle accruing from marriages of their
> girls. . . . The earliest and most intimate co-
> operation between the sexes then is that between a
> mother and her sons and daughters. . . . The
> services of their sisters to them are exchanged, on
> marriage, for the services of a wife, and in the
> actual marriage transactions of the Dinka sisters
> are viewed as the providers, by means of their
> bridewealth, of wives for their brothers.

Among the Nuer, according to Evans-Pritchard (1951: 127), as
boys grow up

> they attach themselves more and more to the [cattle]
> byre, but each remains, both in sentiment and by
> social alignment, also a member of his mother's hut.
> Hence one may distinguish between full brothers and
> paternal half brothers by saying that the first
> brothers are kwi dweil, on the side of the hut,
> while the second are kwi luak, on the side of the
> byre.

Elsewhere he writes,

> Maternal descent does not count within the lineage and
> therefore ought not to count within the family, for by
> the agnatic principle in Nuer social life the family
> derives from the father. Hence, Nuer say, if your
> uterine brother and your paternal half-brother quarrel
> you must not enter the dispute on your uterine brother's
> side, because by doing so you divide the family. You
> split, as it were, the father.

But people do take sides, and histories of families I recorded
often indicated that disputes between half brothers, or at
least those expressed this way idiomatically, led to the
division of an idealized agnatic unity in the effort of each
to create his own gol or, in their usage, "to increase his
number."

Whereas agnatic principles explicitly exclude reference
to women, it is they who create the birth group. Before
saying something additional about the way in which
relationship terms reflect the dialectical tension between
maternal and paternal relations I would like to note that on a
number of occasions I heard Atuot refer to the female genitals
as wa thok, a phrase that can also mean "the opening of the
door" or simply doorway. Beyond this, wa thok can also refer

to river banks, more specifically, places where it appears that the land "opens up" to the river. It is interesting to surmise, given the strong association between women, femininity, and rivers, that rivers per se provide a physical image of social continuity, especially that provided by women, flowing across space and time with unseen yet constant energy. In the text cited earlier women were impregnated by drawing the waves and foam of rivers into their vaginas. (In Atuot country the names of many small streams and lakes bear the feminine prefix **nya** or **nyi**, as in Lake Nyirol and Lake Nyibor. D. Zahan has recently remarked on the commonality of the association involving women, rivers, and the generation of life more widely accepted in Africa. He writes (1979: 21), "Junod remarks that the word which designates water among the Thonga, as well as many of the names of streams among the Bantu of Southeast Africa, possess the feminine suffix **ti**, which seems to show that long ago water was considered a feminine principle. The connection between fecundity and flowing water is also found elsewhere in Africa. For example, the section of the Niger river flowing through Bambara territory is given the same meaning. This part of the river is regarded as the body of **Faro**, who is associated with the multiplication and proliferation of things.") The broader symbolic universe of Atuot women conjoins horticultural production, village homesteads, and the recreation of domestic life. These spacial and moral environments provide a complementary contrast to the value of agnatic heredity and its equally strong association with men and the world of cattle camps.

As noted, the Atuot phrase **gat e mar**, "child of my mother," is precise and suggests a moral bond stronger than any other. By contrast, **gat e gwa**, "child of my father," is ambiguous as it implies a less specified degree of relation even while it is a polite mode of address between appropriately aged individuals. Those who share common resources within an agnatically defined group may refer to each other as **gat gwalen**, "child of my father's brother," a usage that recognizes some degree of political and economic solidarity while still polite, rather than intimate. Indeed, ambiguous terms seem to be the norm rather than the exception beyond the domestic field and this makes good sense when one is trying to further economic adaptation. In other words, when one is attempting to maximize economic interests, especially as these relate to the use of pastures or camps, imprecision in terms of address is the rule, as suggested by the phrase **yin**, **gat wuicde**, "you, the child of my cattle camp." The focus here is on a field of agnatic relatives rather than on specific individuals with whom one is in contact on a daily basis. Conversely, in situations where formal distinctions must be emphasized, such as in the settlement of bridewealth or in the situation of sacrifice, relational precision is the common expectation. Atuot usage here is once again paralleled by that noted for the Nuer. Evans-Pritchard (1951: 178) writes,

Kinship values and political values based on locality are interdependent. All who live together express their relations to one another in terms of the kinship system. . . . Hence it is that individuals stress whatever category of kinship is

most significant in the particular circumstances of
residence in which at any time they find themselves.

Another way of underscoring the nature of local usage is to
observe that kith are kin because relationship terms are
idioms for space, which takes on a moral value in relation to
specific residence.   The proximity suggested by differing
usages of relationship terminology parallels or reflects
territorial and hence economic contiguity.   Still another
means of perceiving this fact is to regard the traditional
boundaries of residence as manifestations of spacial and
temporal proximity.   Wet season cattle camps in Atuot country
are circular in shape.   The ancestral cattle of the apical
founders of cattle camps are tethered in the center, now the
property of the central members of cattle camps.   The
homestead too is defined by the circular walls of a hut which
is   surrounded by a woman's garden.   The center of the hut is
the location of the cooking fire.   These circles of social
recreation, homesteads, and cattle camps are interconnected by
footpaths.   As suggested earlier, tracing the paths on the
ground is in a sense like tracing the lines of agnation and
affiliation between the residents of each form of settlement.
Given the need for mobility in order to exploit
productive pastures as well as garden plots in the forested
areas, the contextual use of kin terms which either encourage
or deter degrees of relatedness are a significant index for
assessing social relations.   I do not wish to imply, however,
that terms for address reflect only economic interests.   In a
strict sense, Atuot have no system of land tenure apart from
the terms at their disposal to address agnates and kin.   In
other words, since no individual owns a herd of cattle or a
parcel of land, kinship usage clearly refers to more than
property relations.   The use of relationship terms refers to
more than property relations.   The use of relationship terms
refers to the possibility of using, not owning, productive
resources.   The we/they dichotomy which results from the
contextual usage of these modes of address creates the moral
distinction, in spacial terms, between "here" and "there."
Still, to suggest that residence is the result of a moral
evaluation of space is not to deny the obvious economic
necessity of maintaining access to land.   Given the wide range
of possible terms for reference one can conclude that the use
of one term over another indicates, on the part of any
individual, attentive reflection on space and time, that is,
on where they are and why they are.

SUMMARY

An implicit fact I have had in mind in the course of these
observations is that while Atuot stress the value of agnatic
heredity when accounting for their social history and patterns
of daily subsistence, their form of mixed horticultural and
transhumant pastoral economy demands considerable flexibility
in the interpretation and use of norms regarding descent and
residence.   While cieng Luac is the "homeland" of the Luac,
many who were born in different sections live here.   The
contextual interpretation of social identity is most apparent
to an observer of their world through the record of
relationship terms which individuals use for significant

others. On the basis of my understanding, it can be said that
the relationships of descent are spoken of in terms of common
rights to the use and distribution of herds, and since this
element of their productive system is largely in the hands of
adult males, lineages are conceived of in the masculine idiom.
In any given circumstance, however, the social composition of
named territories reflect patterns of reciprocity which are
established through marriage. The perpetual dialectic that
ensues creates a situation in which any individual seeks to
maximize the size of this egocentrically defined social
environment when seeking matrimonial or political alliances;
conversely, when similar sentiments are reciprocated, putative
agnatic relations may come into public question.

The Atuot, like other Nilotic pastoralists, cherish the
image of a peaceable world since in their view the cultural
ideal is one in which herds increase, crops are bountiful, and
families increase their number. Thus the cattle camp is the
community that provides public evidence of this ideal. Given
the cultural value of cattle, it is not surprising that moral
and productive sentiments meet in a herd. However, disputes
which inevitably arise between members of communal territories
are recalled in words that emphasize disputes over cattle.
Disputes over cattle, in turn, are often the consequence of
marriage and bridewealth. A family herd increases and
decreases as a function of marriage. As the myth cited
earlier intimates, if men want wives, they must surrender
cattle. In that circumstance, they seek to gain cattle
through the marriage of a daughter or must transfer rights to
ownership to ensure the progeny of a son. The social
reproduction of this world is founded upon these exchanges.

4.
A MORAL ORDER
OF SOCIETY

> If a man wishes to be in the right with God he must
> be in the right with men (Evans-Pritchard 1956:
> 18).

Though their language does not include a term for "religion"
that closely corresponds to western usage, the Atuot can be
characterized as a deeply religious people. That is, their
ideas, sentiments, and experiences in the course of secular
life are densely interrelated with received truths regarding
suprahuman agencies, and many of these secular activities are
enacted or defined by association with blood sacrifice, their
central religious act. The purpose of this chapter is to
offer an outline of Atuot cosmology and indicate a number of
ways in which religious sentiments condition moral values.

DIVINITY

To their understanding, Decau is the being or Divinity who
alone has the puissance of creation. The material world and
all it includes is said to have been created by the Creator
long ago (muon kuonon ce cak e Decau nemei). In the Atuot
language, "to create" means to bring into existence something
that never existed before. A woman and man give birth to a
child (ce gat dieth) while it is the Creator who creates the
human being in the womb and gives it life (ce gat cak Decau).
In an analogous manner, a woman forms (luoi) a pot from the
clay she finds by the riverside while Creator brought into
existence the water and soil from which it is formed. This
division in their world, between manifestations of human
agency and the limits of human knowledge and effort, is an
underlying orientation in all sacrificial contexts. Human
beings can do just so much to better their lives and seek
satisfactions while ultimately it is Decau who makes these
ends more or less an experiential reality in their lives.
    Depending on the context, the Creator may be addressed as
Decau, as in the phrase era Decau, "it is only the Creator
that could do such things," or nhial Decau, "Creator of the
heavens." Confronted with a problem for which there seems to
be no immediate or utile recourse a man or woman may say Nhial

guar lueke, "Creator my father, help me." In prayer and
sacrificial invocation Atuot idiomatically refer to themselves
as acuek Decau, tiny black ants created by Divinity, and in
this manner contrast their insignificance with the omnipotence
of the Creator.
     As noted, while we typically categorize forms of social
life using terms that delineate spheres of activity, such as
politics, economics, or religion, Atuot do not make such
distinctions. When speaking of philosophical truths that stem
from social experience Atuot do, however, use the phrase ruaic
Decau, which can be translated as "the words and deeds of the
Creator." Likewise I do not think there is a single term
which can be translated as "belief" though some quality of
this inner state is an element of their religious experience.
The word tak, to think or expect, suggests a high probability
of something being or existing. This quality of mind differs
from that one can know, ngac. While an outsider traveling
through their country may ask the awkward question "Do you
know Divinity?" (ce ngac e yin Decau?), the response I was
offered suggested "we have God and he is the same as your God,
for he created all things and all people." From their view,
the reality of Divinity is unquestioned. To translate their
sentiments as a kind of "belief" would belittle them since, in
common usage, belief allows for the possibility of disinterest
or disbelief. In the traditional world, there was no such
possibility. These brief comments are significant in
understanding the absence of formalized liturgy in traditional
usage. In their sacrifices, they hope that Divinity will
recognize their plight and eventually help to reconcile their
suffering, and this is why they dedicate the life of a
sacrificial being to him. At the same time, they know they
will later cook the flesh of the victim in a festive mood.
Seen in combination, these factors suggest that a separate
word to describe an attitude of strictly religious sentiment
would be redundant where experience itself points in the
direction of a reality for Atuot that we refer to with the
qualifying term "belief." Religious experience is at one
level an internal or intuitive phenomenon. If a man knowingly
transgresses his social rights or responsibilities, Atuot
suggest that Divinity will "see" or "know" this to be the case
(a be juic Decau). Yet the problems of an individual
necessarily affect the well-being of his or her family, if not
a larger group of kin. Thus, while each person may offer his
or her own invocation in the course of a sacrifice, the import
of collective sentiment is deemed of equal or greater
importance for efficacious benefits. A sinner cannot profit
from the misfortunes of others. The inevitability of
individual assertiveness and pressure to conform to social
ideals is reflected, then, in the forms of communication they
seek between humanity and Divinity.
     All sacrifices that are intended to benefit human well-
being are ultimately dedicated to Divinity. In their view, it
is Divinity that brings the gift (buol) of life so that when
death has occurred, or when a sacrifice has been enacted, life
returns to Divinity once more. Though this concept of
Divinity assumes his omnipotence, he is in another sense
distant from the world of human beings. Divinity may enter
their lives directly, as Atuot explain the occurrence of birth
defects, twin birth, abundant rains, or drought as a direct
manifestation of his power, though in another sense he is

distant from the world of human beings. More commonly, Atuot interpret spiritual power through manifestations of Decau, and Atuot speak of these "refractions" of Divinity as "powers of the above" (jao nhial) and "powers of the earth" (jao piny). The powers of the above are imagined to partake more directly of Divinity, to be in a sense closer to him, and the powers of the earth, which are more numerous, are more directly related to the social world of human affairs. The single term jok (pl. jao) subsumes both categories, however, offering one indication of a polythetic mode of classification in Atuot cosmology (see Needham 1975). Any single translation of the word jok is in some way unsatisfactory, though its most frequent referent approaches the meaning of terms such as power, divinity, or spiritual agent. Here I adopt the phrase "power (of Divinity)" to convey the Atuot intention. The concept jok is idiomatic in Atuot religion to the same degree that a bovine idiom communicates information about social relationships.

Collectively, the powers of the above or "heavenly powers" (jao nhial) are termed gaat Decau, or "sons of the Creator." These are considered to be the first powers created by Divinity, in part, I think, because the human experience of them has greater social magnitude than is the case with earthly powers. Following the suggested analogy with kinship, heavenly powers are inherited across time by agnatic descent. The most important of these powers, col wic, kulang, kwoth, and ring are emblems or mediums of rain, lightning, twin birth, and the essence of corporeal existence. The jao piny, or powers of the earth, are said to have become more numerous within living memory; many are said to have originated with peoples surrounding Atuot country. They include mathiang gook, thong alal, makao, mabier, agok, payenya, abiel, and koro. An earthly power is commonly said to travel in the company of a "wife." Rather than being solely inherited by males, earthly powers can be bought and sold by women and men. In each case, earthly powers are manifested in physical symptoms of illness, such as tuberculosis, forms of dysentery, meningitis, and a variety of other maladies common in environments of this latitude. The heavenly powers are in the main imbued with positive value since they are associated with forces which benefit the lives of all human beings, while earthly powers have negative social and moral connotations. The symbolic attributes of persons credited with the control of each class of power parallel this moral disparity. As indicated, a man cannot buy the power to call rain (often referred to by its ox name awumkuai). Rather, it is maintained that Divinity chooses particular individuals to fill their psychic and physical selves with the power. The person who incorporates the power of "life" or "flesh" (ring) is called a gwan riang. The adverb gwan in this usage images a "father" of the power, as he is, by analogy, a creator and genitor of life with the creative power of Divinity. Those who own and communicate with earthly powers are known as tiit (sing. tiet) which is cognate with the Atuot term for hand, tet. As they explain, Divinity chooses individuals to become possessed by heavenly powers. The decision to become a tiet or diviner is made by individuals for personal reasons, when an individual has been afflicted through possession by one or another earthly power and later regained health. Then follows a period of initiation by a seasoned diviner, wherein he instructs the novice concerning the qualities, powers, and methods of dealing with these phenomena.

HEAVENLY AND EARTHLY POWERS

Elsewhere (Burton 1981a: 82-90) a fuller account of heavenly powers is presented. Here, I would like to focus special attention on the power Atuot know as _ring_. In a certain sense _ring_ is the more significant of heavenly powers since it is spoken of as the "eldest" and, as knowledgeable adults told me, before the period of British administration in their country, those possessed by _ring_ carried out both political and religious functions. What follows next is a series of texts offered by senior members of families who carried with them memories of those days.

A person possessed by the power _ring_ is thought to have the ability to guide the lives of people. A person possessed by _ring_ is said to bring things to life and to bring life to people. Literally, _ring_ refers to "flesh," as distinguished from the other elements which form a human being. Atuot say that a _gwan riang_, possessor of _ring_, "has power over the lives of people." His power of life is strongly associated with breath and moving air. In the past, friends maintained, a _gwan riang_ was not allowed to die naturally but was instead suffocated over the grave when death seemed imminent. As I try to explain below, this custom offered a material representation of the way in which a person possessed by _ring_ controlled life. As a preface to this discussion one can consider the following text which describes the ritual functions performed for a woman unable to conceive:

> When there is a woman without a child, a _gwan riang_ is called for and he will make _buong_. A sheep is brought, and it is suffocated, and they do not slaughter it with a knife. This is done this way so that the running of the blood of the woman will not run like the blood when the throat is cut. You try to keep the blood inside the woman, like when they kill the sheep by sitting on it, instead of making the blood run. If they cut the throat of the ram it would mean that the blood of the woman would still run more and she would not have a child. The suffocation keeps the blood inside.

Another text offers a slightly different view of this sacrifice intended to transfer the life of an animal "into" a woman seeking pregnancy:

> _Buong_ is a sacrifice that can be made by any man of _ring_. A very fat sheep is needed. It can begin in the evening when the sheep is tethered in front of the doorway. The man and his wife are inside the hut. Later the sheep is brought inside the hut, and its tail is held over its anus, and its mouth is held closed by the _gwan riang_. Then they [the spouses and _gwan riang_] sit on the ram, facing the door of the hut, and they stay like that until the breath is gone. Then the sheep is cut up and boiled. Very early in the morning the fat is

smeared on the woman. . . . The people making _buong_ stay inside the hut for a number of days, and a pot is brought for them to urinate and defecate into. When the child is born and it is a boy, his name will be Ring, because it is the power _ring_ that brought him to life.

Ring is recognized in a person only after he or she has become a mature adult. The qualities expected of such an individual include the gift of "hearing people's words" with a cool heart, speaking in measured words that encourage people to settle a dispute, in other words, "carrying the lives of people" as Atuot say. Concurrently, in the past, I was told that a _gwan riang_ was asked to bless the efforts of a raiding party. In this instance, he would remain behind in his hut sitting near the corpse of a ram sacrificed prior to the expedition. Holding a small calabash filled with water, he would feign spear thrusts at the imagined enemies seen in the reflection of the water. His word and curse were said to be contingent and causative of real events and their consequences. His political power, then, was manifested in his sanctified words. As one man put it, "The _gwan riang_ only says a simple word and [the deed] is done. If a person does not listen to his word, he can only expect to die." When his own death seemed likely, a large-scale mortuary ceremony was called for. An older man recalled,

> You know when a person of _ring_ is about to die because his body twitches. This is the _ring_ moving inside him. He has become too old to eat and sometimes becomes unconscious. When people become too tired of making him special food, the pestle used by women in pounding grain is brought and he is laid on his back on the ground. The pestle is put across his neck to suffocate him. A dance is made and this goes on for many days. All the men of _ring_ from different Atuot sections come to make sacrifices. After he is buried his son who will carry _ring_ after him takes a ram and holds it by the feet and beats it over the grave until it dies. He will stand on the grave and sing the songs of _ring_. Then the others of _ring_ rush toward him and act as though they are going to spear him. The son then puts a woman's skirt over his head to protect the _ring_ of his father. This is done so that people will remain with life.

Another text, recorded by a man still recognized for his possession by the power _ring_, stated,

> When a man of _ring_ is dead, a sheep is brought and sacrificed over the spot where the grave will be dug. When he is lowered into the grave, another sheep is killed. Every son comes with a sheep to kill on the grave. . . . Then a he-goat is speared and this is eaten by the people who are not related to him. First it is hung up on a forked branch shrine that is put next to the grave. When this is all done his children are gathered and they sit by the grave with a woman's skirt covering their

heads.   Then the eldest son stands over the grave
and sings,

I keep ring properly
Do not leave the power of my father unattended
I bribed it with Malao [an ox sacrificed for ring]
I bribe the power of my father with Mabor
I tether the bull with a rope
The ring of my father will wash my back
The power of my grandfathers--
I will wash your back.

The gwan riang stays, and when the sun comes down
he dies.   He is taken into the hut and washed with
oil.   He became so old he did not know things
anymore.   When people have become too troubled with
trying to feed him, they bring a long heavy log and
press it against his neck, and he dies.   Then ring
has to look for someone, but ring goes slowly.

The final text I cite in this context was recorded in
Anuol, spoken by a former chief in the Kuek section of Atuot.
Before the British appeared in their country, he said,

We had gwan riang.   If you had difficulties, you
came to him, and he would receive you in his gol.
At night, you would tell him what was wrong, if
there was a fight, if you had murdered someone, or
if there was no child in your wife.   When he got so
old that he could not walk or swallow, he was not
allowed to die, but he was killed by suffocation
like a sheep in buong.   They bring a large heavy
wood and lay him down on the ground, and put the
wood across his neck, so there is no air going in.
Sometimes he would just die from the dust of
dancing.   They make a big dance and his bull is
killed and skinned, and the gwan riang is put
inside the hide before he is buried.   All the
people are happy and they sing the songs of fights
and of ring. . . . They dig a shaft and then on the
right side of it they dig out more earth, so there
is a cavity.   Another hide is put down, and then a
platform is made over it, so no dirt will touch
him.   The grave is filled and then a small he-goat
is brought and held by the hind legs and beaten
over the grave until it dies.   Then all the people
take off their clothes and beads for mourning.
Word is sent to his cattle camp not to milk the
cows that evening.   Early the next morning after he
has been buried the eldest son brings a bull and
tethers it next to the grave, and he cuts it in the
face while it is still alive and then it is speared
in the heart.   The sons of the gwan riang then put
the woman's skirt over their heads.   The he-goat is
then hung up from a shrine near the grave.   People
from all Atuot sections come and make sacrifices.
They see the goat and they know there has been a
sacrifice for ring.   Before he died, the gwan riang
gave his walking stick to his son, and then [ring]
would go into him.   When the other Atuot sections

came, they would approach with spears and bows and arrows as though they were going to make a fight, and the people of gwan riang defend it and show that they are keeping the power there. Then the other people come and join the dance. The he-goat is for the ghost [atiep] of the man of ring. It is not cut so that the life will remain with people. In the camp, the cows are led out a short distance, and a cow is sacrificed at the gate of the camp. It is just speared and the meat is for anyone who can grab it. Then the cows are brought back into the camp and they can be milked again.

In light of these texts it should be clear that ring is a spiritual agent that is manifested in the image of life and well-being for political and moral communities. The death and burial of a man possessed by ring is a time for celebration and forceful demonstration of the perpetual life associated with this spirit. Death by suffocation may be understood as a ritual negation of death: by asserting their control over the power ring in this dramatic fashion Atuot create a situation that images their control over life through the power ring (see Lienhardt 1961: 298-319). As suggested elsewhere (Burton 1981g) the power ring has strong affinities with feminine symbols of fertility and procreation. When those possessed by ring are near death, this is most evident in association with the custom of covering the head of the individual who will inherit this power with a woman's skirt. As in the case of marriage cattle, males here assert public control of the means of their agnatic heredity. Recall here the notion that ring is the eldest of powers, an image that accords well with the idiom of agnatic descent.

Earthly powers are on the one hand more numerous than powers associated with the above and are restricted in their distribution to localized fields of social activity. While ring and other heavenly powers are thought to "fill" or "cover" their human agents, earthly powers are sought out as a means of seeking vengeance between parties to a disagreement. They have, in other words, malignant rather than healing and beneficial associations. Ring is a moral and spiritual quality that possesses its human agent. Earthly powers are spiritual agents individuals are possessed by in an act of moral retribution, and they are imagined to have a physical rather than psychic manifestation. Those who are versed in such matters explain that in the course of an exorcism to rid a body of an earthly spirit or power, the tiet or diviner is able to see the power within the human body, sometimes in the form of a cat, a monkey, or a burning spear. As one woman explained,

It was Creator who put something into the eyes of human beings so they could not see the powers. And then he gave us tiit who see them. The people of jok [here intending earthly powers] see jok but the man of ring does not see ring. He is given ring by the Creator. When a person has a big trouble he will go to a man of ring who will make things work in his favor by just saying his word. A tiet sees a power and sucks it out. The man of ring only says his word and then it is done. When there is a

great suffering among many people the man of _ring_
will sacrifice a cow for [to] Creator.

This text might be better understood after relating a
commonly known myth that accounts for the origin of the
powers. One point can be mentioned first in regard to the
analysis attempted here. The initial dispersion of powers
among human beings shares an analogical identity with the
manner in which women are "dispersed" among different social
groups through the institution of marriage. The text just
cited demonstrates clearly enough how Atuot perceive that
heavenly powers affect the lives of all people, whereas
earthly powers are involved in the affairs of particular
individuals. In the words of one man, a widely known diviner,

People were created long ago by _Decau_. _Jok_ was a
different son, and all the people who are now in
the world were different sons. They were all in
one cattle camp and each had their own side. One
time the people went to fish and they caught the
fish that belonged to _abiel_ [one of the earthly
powers] and _abiel_ was angry and went up to the
Divinity and said to him, "The people you have
created and gave the fishing spear to have become
very strong. They have caught our fish." Divinity
listened and said that later in the day he would
send a great wind that would be filled with dust.
He told the [earthly] powers that this would blind
the eyes of the people and allow the powers to go
along with their own things and catch their fish.
[The text at this point reveals that the events are
imagined to have transpired in a dry season fishing
or cattle camp. During the months of January to
March dry dusty winds blow throughout the day, and
it is at this time that people are most likely to
suffer attacks of meningitis.] Divinity told all
the powers to go hide in the ground. A dog [also
called _jok_ in Atuot] happened to be nearby and
overheard the conversation between Divinity and the
power _abiel_. It ran off quickly and unnoticed to
the camp of the people and told them what it had
learned. He told the people that later in the day
when the dusty wind came they should cover their
eyes or else they would be made blind. When people
heard this they became angry with the dog and
kicked it and said, "you dog--you go off with your
lies. When did you speak to Divinity?!."
     In the meanwhile the powers had gone off to
fish and when they returned to the camp the dusty
wind began to blow, so they hid themselves in the
ground. The people at camp sat around and expected
nothing out of the ordinary. The wind blew up
quickly and the dog buried its head in the ground.
When the wind passed the dog could see that all the
people had become blind. Then _abiel_ went to fish
and put some of his catch in the fire to roast.
People smelled the food and said among themselves,
"where is this smell of fish coming from?" _Abiel_
then took up its fishing spear and thrust it into
the left side of a man. The man fell to the ground

and blood streamed from his mouth. The people were
astonished and said, "where is this death coming
from?" Then Divinity saw that the people were
suffering and he said "I will catch one man [the
text reads here be dom e yen nuer me kel; the verb
dom refers to the act of catching or grabbing an
object] and he will have this power. I will open
the eyes of the man and when he goes abiel will
remain in him to help the lives of people." In the
evening abiel returned with more fish and put them
in the fire, realizing that he could not be seen by
the people. He called for the other powers and
they shared the fish. Each one of them went off
with a different family. This is how the [earthly]
powers came to us and why the dog that covered its
eyes can still see the powers at night.

Some versions of this text conclude with the suggestion
that ring, the "oldest" and hence senior of all powers, later
argued with abiel and insulted it for acting so violently
toward human beings and decided in consequence that it would
have nothing to do with the powers of the earth (see Howell
1953: 86-87).

Earthly powers are indeed dispersed throughout the
countryside, as in the majority of homesteads there is a
forked-branch shrine nearby dedicated to the power owned by
the resident family. As noted earlier, ring is conceived of
as "slow" in its manifestations and by this characterization I
think Atuot have in mind the idea that the power of this
spiritual agent is latent within an individual, that it
emerges as a result of knowledge possessed by few. In the
text accounting for the origin of earthly powers, the human
experience of these spiritual agents is represented as fast,
violent, and unpredictable, notions which accord well with
their experience of them. One day a woman is healthy, the
second she is overcome with pain and on the third day she may
be on her deathbed. Thus, when someone is suddenly taken ill
a diviner is consulted and asked to visit the homestead in
order to make initial enquiries about the particular power
that has possessed the person. The primary concerns focus
upon the likely source of spiritual vengeance. In making his
initial diagnosis the diviner recognizes the malignancy as a
manifestation of one or another jok ping. The diviner "sees
it with his eyes," as one man put it, "like you see yourself
in a mirror." Another diviner suggested "The jok comes to
claim its property. The tiet will know the reason because he
can see it. If a man steals a cow, the tiet sees the jok
keeping the cow. The power says this is mine. I am coming
for this and that." An older man who at one point in his life
had practiced divination suggested that the powers of the
earth were like "the policemen of God."

Two additional texts will provide a background for
understanding different contexts of sacrifice, those
concerning possession by earthly powers and those intended to
benefit the well-being of a larger community. The first text
concerns the manner in which an individual becomes a diviner:

Tiet begins with the effects of sickness. When the
family has made many sacrifices for your recovery,
and then you later recover your health, then you

have shown that you have the power over the
jok. It gives you the power to see it, like
when it sits on the roof of a hut. . . . The jok
walks with people like shadows. Then you come to
see and hear the powers, while all the other people
are blind to them. When you first see powers they
are like lizards, and they are not angry or wild
yet. Later you see them like a hairy wolf with
fangs--like when you see agok. When you see them
they are moving. All the powers are male, but
every one also has a wife, and sometimes it is the
wife of the power that brings the sickness because
she wants something, like a goat. The powers of
the earth are the messengers of Divinity, and
sometimes Divinity comes directly to people. Then
people know you have become a tiet.

A text concerned with the same general topic offers a
more detailed description of the "initiation" of a diviner
into his practice.

There are two [kinds of] tiet. There are important
tiet like myself who have a long [rattle] and the
powers stay in the long. The power speaks through
him to the people. When he looks for a power in
the walls of the hut the jok speaks to him through
the rattle. The tiet makes yor yot [rubbing the
rattle along the inside walls of a hut] and the
power enters the rattle and comes out of
the person and into the tiet. There is also the
small tiet. . . . The power does not speak to him.
He can only diagnose the problem but he has no real
relationship with the jok.
Only with the big tiet is the power in the body
of the man. When the power comes into the man it
makes him rock back and forth and shake, and the
power he has tells him to suck out the jok from the
sick person. He pulls out the jok from inside [of
the person] that is making sickness.
A small tiet may sometimes want to become an
important man of powers and he can have the
ceremony nguot long [cutting the rattle, or
"delivering" the rattle]. He goes to look for a
tiet who is known to have control over many powers,
and the man comes to his hut in the afternoon. A
goat is cut in half through the abdomen and the
lower half remains outside the hut and the upper
part with the head is brought up into the adwil.
The small tiet holds the goat, while it is still
alive, in a position as though he was going to
nurse it and while he holds his rattle in
his right hand, the powerful tiet cuts the goat in
half. . . . Inside the hut the smaller tiet sits on
the lap of the man performing the ceremony. He
puts his left arm around the man and with his right
hand he clasps the hand of the smaller tiet and
moves his rattle back and forth against the wall.
Later, the upper part of the goat is eaten by the
new tiet and the other half is given to the
powerful tiet. The new tiet must then remain

inside his hut for six days, never going outside
once. If he even sees the meat of the lower half
he would lose his power immediately. It is always
a goat that is killed in this way because all the
earthly powers favor the meat of goat. And it
always has to be a male goat because it is hotter
and more powerful than a female. Then the new tiet
must give the other man a goat and a spear for
performing the rite. . . . These are the things
that must be done before a man has the power of
divination. This is how a man learns tiet.

Before continuing it may be worthwhile to offer a number
of general observations which emerge through an analysis of
the preceding texts. The earthly powers can be understood as
active agents which are manipulated for personal ends while
the heavenly powers, most important among these ring, are
phenomena Atuot see as manifestations of Divinity. Those
possessed by ring are therefore conceptually "closer" to
Divinity in that they represent creative or life-assuring
power. While the ultimate source of life is Divinity, in
their daily lives it is more commonly diviners who "help them
to have sleep." As they see it, there would be little benefit
in seeking to direct the malignant power of one's jok against
an unknown enemy since there is no basis for alleging
misdeeds. Like the image of Divinity, ring and the other jok
nhial transcend the narrow confines of domestic relationships.
Suffering from the power known as agok, in contrast, is viewed
as the consequence of a breach in social and moral
accountability.
   These observations can be evaluated by comparing
different situations of sacrifice. While Atuot speak of
sacrifice idiomatically as "killing a cow" (nake yang) there
are in fact many differing forms and intentions of the rite
and the victims employed range from wild cucumbers to bulls
(see Burton 1981c).

CONTEXTS OF SACRIFICE

The first sacrifice I describe was performed in a village
called Burtiit in the Luac section of Atuot territory. The
family concerned had recently bought a cow from the Ceic
Dinka, who were said to be dissatisfied with the price
received. As a result, those involved interpreted this to
mean that the Ceic had sent a power (later diagnosed as
mangok) "on the back of the cow." The power had "caught" a
woman of about fifty and caused her to suffer severe stomach
cramps. She had been lying in bed for the past five days,
unable to eat or move. A tiet had been consulted and he told
the family that the power on the back of the cow was demanding
the sacrifice of a goat. When the tiet "saw the power" he
knew it was mangok because "it had blood streaming down its
face." Preparations for the exorcism and sacrifice had begun
three days earlier, and I had attended the seances late at
night when close relatives of the woman made bull jao, "a
dance for the powers," in order that the power would be
entertained and cajoled from the woman's body. On this, the
fourth evening of the ceremony, I arrived while the diviner, a
man named Ijuong from the Jilek section, was walking by

himself around the perimeter of the homestead.   He moved
slowly, pouring small libations of water at the edge of the
yard, into the fire, and across the doorway of the hut.
Ijuong later told me he had done this so that his own power,
mathiang gook, would enter his body and speak, giving him
strength to perform the exorcism.   As he walked he sang a
number of songs that are said to be owned by earthly powers.
The texts of two songs he sang are as follows:

> It is the powers that always burn people
> It is the powers that turn their heads around
> A man who is greedy--
> A man who overlooks me--
> I will agree to the fight
> I will cut the throat of the chief [i.e., if there
>   is a power that ignores the presence of the
>   tiet his own power will overcome it.   Greed and
>   self-assertiveness figure here as the reason a
>   power has possessed the woman]
> So the people will fear for their lives

> I went off into the grass
> I do not want the confusion of the words [i.e., he
>   intends to put an end to the anger between
>   people caused by "the confusion of their
>   words"]
> The words of the ants are confused

After a short while about twenty people had gathered
around the fire outside the woman's hut, and she was carried
from her bed and laid on the ground with her head resting in
her sister's lap.   As Ijuong sang, he often spit onto his
rattle and smeared the saliva across her neck and chest.
About an hour after he had first begun to sing, the people
gathered sang the choruses of songs he introduced and led.
One song leads almost immediately into the next, accompanied
by steady rhythmic clapping.

> The prostitute is causing the troubles
> The mother of Acinbaai sits with her legs open
> Their daughter has a rotten vagina
> The whore who stumbles through the forest
> Like a dog looking for a husband [like a bitch in heat]

> Acol is the father of my power
> The people have gathered before me
> Mayom said the shafts of the spear have been broken
> Mayen, do not break the shafts
> The spears we use to fight in the pastures
> So it is ours forever
> I am troubled with the lives of people
> You my father, son of Nyong
> Help with the lives

> Abuk, my mother, I am left like an orphan
> I carry the hatred of others [In Nilotic mythology
>   Abuk is often figured to be the first woman.
>   The tiet sings that he is left like an orphan,
>   implying that it is his task to look after his

    own life, in this case, the life of the sick
        woman]
I am a man left out
My head spins around with life
The head of a man moves like branches in the wind
Abuk, you come with the lives

My grandfathers, you help the land
A spirit has fallen in the evening
Where did the spirit fall
It has fallen into these lives
You children of Abuk, you help yourselves
We are going to argue [bargain with the power]
The people of long ago fought for this land
I am hated by all the people
My stomach turns inside
Go and bring life into the hut
This is a cow for blood [a sacrifice to promote life]
I pray to Creator like a monkey
I am troubled with the things of the ants
I do not want the annoyance of people
The bad things that come to the ants of Creator

Ijuong now spent more time close to the woman, shaking
the rattle in time with the singing and pausing to massage her
body with it, giving special attention to her neck and lower
back. In retrospect these acts seemed oriented toward a later
stage in the sacrifice and exorcism during which he sucked at
the same places to draw away the badness into his own body.
Followed by four older men, including the woman's husband and
father-in-law, Ijuong led a goat around the perimeter of the
homestead three times, and as they walked, the men sang the
choruses to these songs:

I am praying for the lives of everyone
I pray for the lives of people
I pray for the lives of Atuot
I pray for the lives of Nuer
I pray for the lives of Rek [a Dinka section]
I pray for the lives of Agar [another Dinka section]

If there is no one here
If the owner of the hut is away
The words of the tiet are away
The words of a great man are absent
There is no need for lives
Who is to do it if I do not come
No man can come in my place
My father, my Creator
Give me strength in my heart
Strength to take away the hatreds
Make mine a strong heart for the work
My mother, Abuk, wash my heart
To take away the hatreds of these people

Separate and untie the hatred of witches
I am overcome by a great thing
I hear the word of a power and I come
Disperse these hatreds of people
My father Awumkuai, make the thunder again

> Scatter the hatred of witches
> I find a man helpless in his life
> This is a man known to everyone
> This is a man struck down

Unless there is a large enough gathering to sing the songs of the powers, Atuot expect that little can be done to heal the afflicted person. Indeed, it is a fundamental social obligation to demonstrate one's concern for a kinsperson by being present in such circumstances, since failure to participate may lead others to suggest one is guilty of witchcraft or simply longing for the things that properly belong to someone else. In this, the exorcism is not just the work of the diviner but is a collective enterprise among a circumscribed group of kin. One might also add that by gathering together on such an occasion they are in a sense asserting their own collective well-being, recreating in a fashion the local moral community.

Soon after these songs were completed Ijuong sat close to the woman and began to shake violently, a sign that he was in communication with the world of powers. Possession would not be an entirely accurate description of his state, for his _jok_ is latent within him at all times. Instead, his power now became an active agent within him while he served as a mouthpiece for the power thought to be in possession of the woman. He rose quickly and called for a chicken to be brought to him from inside the hut. Ijuong then stopped shaking as suddenly as he had begun and stood above the woman so that her outstretched legs lay on the ground beneath him. He held the chicken in his right hand, spat on it a number of times to "invoke his _jok_ onto it" and then drew it around the woman's head and body whispering, "you Creator, see the life given to you. Take the cow for the woman." The same act was repeated for the woman's two sisters, her husband, and small child. The chicken was then set on the ground, and, oddly enough, sat without moving in front of her. The next moment the singing resumed as though precisely choreographed. The woman's younger sister shrieked in a deep gutteral voice and began rising up and down on her knees in double time to the rhythm of singing and clapping. With every movement she repeated the same growling scream. In the meanwhile Ijuong had stood up and began running back and forth between the woman and the edge of the homestead, brandishing his rattle and spear in his right hand. This continued for about fifteen minutes, at which point the sister stood up and, as though hit solidly on the back with a heavy club, screeched once more and fell limp to the ground. Ijuong began hopping and dancing on one foot, nearly on top of the woman, and then back to the tethered goat. The violence of his movements in such close quarters made the presence of his _jok_ all the more apparent. He later told me that his power animated his movements in order to force _mangok_ to leave the woman's body. He also said that the reason why the woman's sister became possessed was because his power "was speaking so quickly it had to seek another person to speak through as well." It was a moment, he said, "when there were so many powers rushing in."

Ijuong sat momentarily to regain his calm and then began slowly undressing, at the same time crawling toward the woman on hands and knees, quite like an animal stalking prey. Just as he was about to touch her, he began shaking violently once more and dipped his head to bring it against the woman's stomach. He then lunged toward her chest and began to "suck out the power" while she was held securely by her family. Then Ijuong jumped to his feet and ran off to the edge of the yard to "spit out the badness." This was repeated a number of times, concentrating in turn on her lower back, shoulders and neck. The woman's sister shouted loudly, ordering the others to sing with more vigor to draw out the _jok_. In the middle of her remonstration Ijuong recoiled from her body and screamed as he shook violently. In the next instance he became rigid and corpselike, falling on top of the woman. Two men rose to carry him to the edge of the homestead and returned to the woman's side without the _tiet_.

Ijuong later told me something others had emphasized before: When the _jok_ comes out of the person and enters the _tiet_, it burns like fire. About ten minutes passed before he returned to the gathering and the singing ceased for the first time in more than two hours. He placed his mouth quite delicately against the woman's neck, and taking hold of his rattle once more, rubbed this against her body in the same places at which he had sucked at before. Following this, the goat was untethered and led to where the woman lay prostrate. Its head was brought up against hers while Ijuong drew his left hand across her head from the back to the temple and then onto the head and back of the goat. With this done, the power was placed "on the back of the goat." Looking rather exhausted (more than five hours had passed since the first songs were sung) Ijuong turned toward the people sitting around the fire and said "the work of exorcism is finished, the badness has gone" (_teet e ce thu, tuiny ce wei_). The goat was then held to the ground, its throat severed by Ijuong and its flesh butchered. The blood from the carcass was collected in a small calabash bowl and placed inside the hut next to the corpse in order that "_mangok_ could sit on the animal and drink its blood," that is, take the life it had been given. It was now two o'clock in the morning, seven hours after the ceremony had begun. The immolation of the animal appeared to me to be anticlimactic in relation to the rest of the evening's activities (see also Lienhardt 1961: 236; Evans-Pritchard 1956: 215).

Early the next morning when we returned to the homestead with Ijuong a mince was prepared from the internal organs of the goat, those which Atuot speak of as carrying on the life functions. About half the mixture was placed above the doorway of the woman's hut and the remainder placed next to the fire to be consumed later. I was told that on occasion, when she resumed her normal routine of preparing food, the woman would place small bits of food above the door "for _mangok_ to eat and so the power could see that the family was respecting it." Toward mid-morning Ijuong severed the head from a chicken by the doorway of the hut. The corpse was held aloft as Ijuong uttered a short blessing. Instead of running about the yard aimlessly, the typical and expected reaction of a fowl in this condition, it hobbled directly toward the stake where the goat had been tethered and sacrificed the night before. There it fell dead upon the stake. Understandably, this was immediately interpreted as further evidence that the petition to the power had been accepted and that the exorcism had been successful. Later in the afternoon the woman shared the mince of internal organs with her husband and sister. For

his work in making teet Ijuong was given two Sudanese pounds
(about U.S. $4.00 at the time), the hide of the goat, one hip,
and a leg. The remaining flesh (except for the heart and
lungs which were pilfered by my dog) was prepared for people
who happened to be around the homestead. About a month later
a forked-branch shrine (jath jao, lit. "tree of the power")
was erected on the west side of the hut so that mangok would
remain within the homestead to protect the woman and her
family.

I should note that when I first met the woman and learned
something about her disability, I offered her some capsules of
penicillin and tetracycline in the hope of curing what I
thought was a bout of dysentery. The morning after the
exorcism described here she approached me soon after we had
arrived to visit. She told me that she had vomited the
medicine soon after she swallowed it and added, "that medicine
is good for the diseases of your people. We have different
diseases and you have seen our medicine."

The activities just reviewed can be taken to be
illustrative of virtually all rituals performed in association
with possession. I witnessed, either in the company of my
wife or alone, many other rites of this sort and they follow
this common theme and dramatic pattern. Indeed, as time
passed and I became a regular companion of two diviners who
seemed to appreciate my interest in their work, they would
quiz me on points of detail after observing a ritual. I would
even assert that they expressed a degree of pride in the
growing competence of their student. But my intention here is
not to address my participation but rather what meaning this
has for those who are actively involved. In one sense, these
forms of ritual create models for and models of behavior. It
is the diviner's professed role to offer an explanation for
personal misfortune, and part of his role consists of
suggesting the source of a conscious or unintended breach of
social contract. Since the individual in this circumstance is
not "whole" as is a normal person, the diviner must recreate a
model for recognizing this affliction as well as suggest a
remedial course of action. In this manner of discourse, the
diviner becomes a medium for what one can call psychological
projection. One may distrust another person, a member of a
different family or birth group, because one senses that the
same individual distrusts them. The diviner leads a way
toward that realization by projecting this inner state onto a
public symbol, namely, the animal that both symbolically and
manifestly represents the conflict. R. G. Lienhardt has
addressed this same point more elegantly than I am able. He
writes (1961: 152),

> The diviner . . . vicariously makes a division in
> the experience of suffering and suggests or
> discovers its image, where the patient is not able
> to do so. . . . The diviner is expected also to
> discover a reason for the action of the power, in
> some human sin of omission or commission. . . .
> This reason may be something the patient has half-
> forgotten--one among the many things which are, as
> we should say, 'on his conscience', and which begin
> to become significant for him when he thinks
> himself in danger. . . . When the affective
> condition is imaged in a power, both its grounds

and the reason for it become manifest not only to
him but to those who care for him, and his
experience is represented in a form in which it can
be publicly understood and shared.

Finally, he notes, "The recognition of a formal separation,
within the person of the sufferer, between the self and the
power, is thus followed by the positive enactment, in
dedication and sacrifice, of a material division also. The
'inner' division of experience is sacramentally and externally
confirmed" (1961: 153). Thus, while possession is a decidedly
inner experience it is at the same time symbolic of the
division between one moral community and another.

A second sacrifice I want to briefly describe took place
in a cattle camp called Wunarok several days after we had
first started living there. Early one morning fifteen cows
were collected from the 1500 or so in the camp and tethered
together outside the thorn and scrub brush fence to the east
of the camp. One white cow was tethered alone to the west of
the other animals, and on the ground by its side a bundle of
green leaves had been set afire, which produced wisps of ashen
smoke. These cows were described as **nake Nhial**, suffering
through an act of the Creator. The general complaint was that
they were listless and had been producing less milk than
normally expected. As I approached the gathering a senior
man, who later officiated at the sacrifice, was walking among
the cows, dipping a handful of grass into a milk-filled
calabash, then sprinkling this over the backs of the animals.
A single white ram had been brought from the camp and was
tethered alongside the single cow. A procession of seven
younger men followed in back of the older man as he led the
ram around the perimeter of the herd three times, singing what
Atuot call **dit Nhial**, hymns or songs of the Creator. The ram
was then retethered beside the cow. The invocations made over
its back, punctuated in this case with burnt cow dung ash,
included the petition, "Creator, you see this sickness and
take it away. There is no reason for this sickness of
cattle."

A number of songs were sung while the ram was lifted by
its legs by the elder man, who then pressed the back of the
animal as it was held upside down against the back of the
white cow. This act was repeated three times and then the ram
was held aloft "for Divinity to see." Following this, the ram
was held in the air above the man's head as he stood facing
the east and the pale light of the early morning. Then the
ram was held to the ground on its back between the cattle peg
and the cow, while the elder man slit its throat, drawing his
spear through the abdomen and ending at the hip joint. A
calabash was placed under its neck to collect the flowing
blood. The carcass was next severed completely in two,
creating a left and a right half. The former was carried off
into the bush for it was this half that absorbed the badness
of the disease, while the right half was cooked later and
eaten. The heart and lungs had been cut out of the chest
cavity and placed on the ground next to the calabash filled
with blood. The elder man then took the bundle of grass, and
with this sprinkled the backs of the other cattle with the
blood of the sacrificial ram. In their view, this transferred
the life of the ram as contained in the blood into the sickly

animals. Lastly, the elder man stood beside the cow tethered
apart from the other animals. As he dipped the grass into the
calabash and once again sprinkled blood over its back, he
looked toward the heavens and said, "You Creator, you see this
cow and let the camp remain with sleep [i.e., not be troubled
by illness or disease]. This life is yours and it is yours to
bring or take away."

It has been noted that goats and earthly powers are alike
in that they are conceptually "hot" and unpredictable, while
ring, the heavenly power that represents life and corporeal
existence, is conceptually "cool." Atuot say that in their
sacrifices Divinity and ring want the flesh of a sheep while
earthly powers are thought to be appeased by the flesh of
goats.

The implicit contrast I would like the reader to
appreciate on the basis of these depictions is the contrast
Atuot themselves perceive between sacrifices engendered
through individual misfortune and those which are heralded to
protect the interests of a broader social environment.
Communication with a heavenly power involves sacrifices with a
collective intent since the power or powers therein petitioned
affect the lives of all people. In this sense sacrifice is
its own end since it assumes a moral community. Atuot assert
unequivocally that if a person is struck down by lightning,
associated with the heavenly power col wic, or if there has
been excessive drought or flooding, a phenomenon associated
with the heavenly power kwoth, it has been the work of
Divinity. If a person falls ill and later dies from what we
would diagnose as amoebic dysentery, and what they associate
with an earthly power, they seek out the human agent that sent
the jok that manifests itself in this way.

This may well be a lapse in my field techniques and data:
Even though I attended many ceremonies involving exorcism of
earthly powers, in all the cases which I observed or otherwise
learned of, the victim "caught" by the power was a woman or a
young child. However, I believe this is an accurate depiction
since Atuot say "powers come into the village. It is only
Divinity that comes to the cattle camp." This perception and
sentiment invites further comment. The same phrase was
repeated when I asked if it was a jok that had caused the
cattle to suffer ill health. Recall how one of the earlier
texts states that people are "blind" to the powers. In
physical terms, in the village setting, one cannot in fact
"see" the ways of neighboring peoples, as each homestead is
more or less removed from another. The earthly powers are
also said to be most active at night, when it is often most
difficult to see beyond the dim illumination of the homestead
fire. The villages themselves are located in forested
environments, where diviners find roots and tubers which they
use as medicines, that are "owned" by different jok piny. The
common theme in stories that account for the origin of
different powers (see Burton 1981a) is that they were come
upon "in the forest," a notion with two distinct but related
components. First, the forest symbolizes separation from
one's own kin, those one depends upon in the course of daily
life. By analogy, the forest is seen to be the home of
earthly powers, a world hidden from people. Tiet find powers
in the forest where they are separated from people. This
image is expressed most clearly in song:

The bitter medicine [wal] that kills a man
Where was the medicine found--
It is amidst the grass
I brought the power to help the lives of people
Mathiang gook has spoiled the land of Nuer
Mathiang gook has spoiled the land of Jaang [Dinka]
The strong power of Jur
I dig up the medicine of the power
I work for the power until I am exhausted
I brought the power from Atim Akuei
And I slept away with it.

The last line images living in the forest, away from human
habitations, to learn the ways of the powers. To "see," in
other words, the problems of a local community, the diviner
removes himself from it. The image of blindness noted in the
texts also involves the idea that in the hours of darkness,
the earthly powers attack their victims, causing people to
"remain without sleep." Concurrently, people are said to be
prone to these maladies at night. It follows that sacrifices
for earthly powers are performed at night, when these are
thought to be most active, and hence liable to human control.
It is useful here to think of the earlier discussion focused
on waking and sleeping, and the usage that inhibits someone
from waking another while sleeping. Atuot suggest that while
asleep, one's own power, or the power owned by a family,
wanders off into the night so any individual is in a sense
unprotected at this time. If dreams do indeed offer a
reliable measure of individual psychological experience, it is
not surprising that the source of a spiritual agent is
associated with some individual for whom another harbors
ambiguous feelings. In sleep, then, the psyche wanders off,
as does the tiet in the forest.
    Sacrifices in which Divinity is petitioned directly are
normally enacted in the early hours of morning, a time when
the light of a new day images the creative and life-giving
powers of Divinity.
    Nearly every homestead has on its west side, some
distance from the doorway of the hut, a forked-branch shrine
which is thought of as the home of the earthly power the
family owns. Local common sense advises that it is essential
to own one or a number of powers in order to provide
protection from the potentially evil intentions of others, or
for directing their own toward the same end. Sitting one
afternoon in a cattle camp I asked a friend why there were no
similar shrines there.

There are no shrines of jok in the camp like those
in the village. The powers do not come to the
camp. Here, it is only the Creator. A peg is made
like all the other pegs for tethering cows and it
is driven into the ground. This is a cow that
Divinity has chosen and that peg is used to tether
the cow. When another cow first gives milk we make
clarified butter (ngat yang) and put it on the head
of the cow to give it to Divinity.

The animal thus dedicated becomes a "cow of Divinity."

A division which is authentic with local experience can thus be drawn between religious experience characteristic in village settings and that in cattle camps. If one definition of religion is to equate its ideas and rituals with an "ideology of community" (see Wilson 1973) this would be most evident among the Atuot in the setting of cattle camps. The measure of control which men can assert over experience by religious action is closely associated with the strongly corporate nature of existence in the cattle camp. In a very different manner, earthly powers are used, like the words of witches, in evidence of independence and self-help. Writing generally on the topic of "primitive religion," Lienhardt suggests (1974: 1042)

> The relative lack of centralized coercive secular power in primitive cultures leaves to the gods the important sanctions for correct behavior. . . . When the relations between kin form the fabric of local community this idea of the retributive justice of the gods is a powerful sanction for approved behavior.

Clearly this general observation typifies the data I have been concerned with in this chapter, and underscores the assertion hinted at earlier that those individuals possessed by ring had, in the past, a quality of socially recognized power that was neither strictly secular nor sacred, but rather an admixture of both. As such, the traditional political community was one with the community that recognized the strongest "religious" sentiments, namely, cattle camps.

From another perspective one might suggest that another difference in religious experience between villages and cattle camps reflects the degree of individual as opposed to collective participation and intent, a point analogous to that which M. Mauss (1972) posited between magical and religious ritual. In his view, these differ not so much by way of structure or purpose as in "the circumstances in which these rites occur." An older woman offered an illustration by way of analogy of the differences between powers of the above and earthly powers. She focused attention on a checkered tablecloth on a table in our hut. As she pointed to the individual squares of color she said "These are like the many powers, and they are scattered among the people. The piece of cloth is like the heavenly powers of Creator because it covers everything."

It still remains to offer an interpretation of why women and children are most subject to vengeful retribution, though I am unable to offer any single satisfactory rationale. It can be presumed, however, that this disparity reflects other social institutions. E. E. Evans-Pritchard (1937: 108) wrote in his study of Azande witchcraft that "the curses of an unrelated man can do you no harm." In theory, were it possible to live with no social contact whatsoever, the occasion for vengeance would never arise. There would be no jealousy, there would be no witches, there would be no sense of premeditated violence. There would be no human beings. One of the primary means by which Atuot society exists through time is in the exchange of women between different agnatic groups in marriage. Temporary barrenness (the antithesis of values associated with marriage) is often ascribed to a condition dependent upon the power of Divinity to give and take away life. The intentions of the ritual called buong are an effort to overcome this condition through spiritual blessing. Yet at the more immediate level of face-to-face relationships, spiritual vengeance which may result in barrenness is commonly viewed as a consequence of neglecting to make good one's promises in transferring a number of cattle as bridewealth. In this situation moral sin is redressed and sanctioned by religious ideology. The earthly powers, as noted, become the "policemen of Divinity." The woman who was taken as a bride is made to suffer from her own maternal kin, in their effort to seek retribution from the family that did not complete the bridewealth, from the family that did not complete the cultural expectation of increasing its own heredity by association with a similar community seeking similar ends.

Stated differently, the women are where the cattle are not: By agreeing to a marriage, it is implicit that an equivalence of exchange has been reached. On her part, the bride is expected to bear a number of healthy children, and should she fail in this uncertain task, or leave her husband, spiritual vengeance again offers a sanctioned recourse. Here I would offer the remark that to have suffered some form of physical malignancy is, for them, a psychological projection of a failure to bring to fruition a cultural expectation. One blames one's illness as a consequence of some other, who inhibits this end. Diviners, in this view, function as ad hoc rural sociologists, for if in the course of diagnosis and divination they find little wrong in the affairs involving kin and affines, the sources of suffering or ill health will be attributed to Divinity, the Creator, rather than the ill will of another human being. One might remember that before the days in which one could hope for medical assistance, childbirth was in fact a real threat to both mother and child. To give birth to a healthy child and survive the ordeal was reason for celebration. When a woman failed in this effort, a reason for her misfortune was sought. Thus I would offer the opinion that women and children are most often the locus of spiritual vengeance because it is around them that the very basis of social existence revolves. They are the promise of future generations and it is on them that cultural value is focused. In abstract terms, possession by earthly powers might be understood as a discourse about the recreation of society itself: As an earlier text suggests, "The feud of the cow and the feud of the vagina are one." In fighting for their lives, people inevitably seem to fight among themselves. Possession by earthly powers seems to mirror these events, and data presented here point toward a distinct series of moral values, the one manifested in village settings and the other in cattle camps. These symbolic images also correspond to a distinction between women, horticulture, and individual enterprise on the one hand, and men, pastoralism, and collective effort on the other.

LIVING WITH THE DEAD: GHOSTS AND ANCESTORS

In what might be called typical Nilotic fashion, the origin of death is accounted for in Atuot mythology as the result of a most trifling human error. As a preface to an understanding

of the text accounting for this inevitable circumstance in
Atuot terms, it is important to note that Divinity is said to
have withdrawn from human beings. The story not only offers
an explanation of how people came to know death, but also how
the connection between heavenly and earthly worlds was
severed. As in a number of texts already cited, the pragmatic
behavior of a woman is given special emphasis. With minor
variations, Atuot speak of this circumstance in these terms:

> At one time the sky and earth were very close and
> people traveled back and forth by means of a rope.
> At this time there was no death because Divinity
> would raise the person up to have life again. When
> the people were hungry women took a single grain of
> durra to pound into flour and that was sufficient
> food for all to be satisfied. Once a newly married
> woman said she would work harder and pound more
> grain. When she lifted the pestle to do this she
> struck Divinity, and he became angry. He then said
> to the people, "Before this you were always
> satisfied with this small bit of food, but now you
> will always know hunger, even if you cultivate
> great gardens." Then a bird flew by and severed
> the rope. Later the same day a man died and people
> were stricken with grief. They took ashes from the
> dung fire and covered their bodies.

Having initially reacted in this manner, Divinity is said to
have taken pity on the people he had created when he saw them
in their misery. So even while he had withdrawn from the
world of human beings, he also demonstrated his concern and
benevolence for them since he momentarily considered a
different response.

> The Creator said, "Let me return the dead back to
> life as it was before." He threw a piece of broken
> calabash into the water and it sank, but soon
> floated back to the surface. Divinity said,
> "People will always be like this. First they will
> disappear but then they will come to life again."
> [Here the text alludes to another common theme in
> Nilotic mythology, as crossing or emerging from a
> river is idiomatic of having new life, of being
> created]. The Fox came by and listened to what
> Divinity had said. In disagreement he said, "If
> this were to be so, soon there would not be enough
> pasture for grazing the cows." The Fox threw a
> shard of pottery into the river and it sank
> immediately and stayed on the riverbed. Fox said,
> "People should be like this piece of clay, and when
> they die, remain forever out of sight of the
> living." Divinity replied, "But do you not see?
> The people are suffering in sadness. It would be
> better if I brought them back to life." Then Fox
> tied a small bell onto the tail of Jackal and sent
> him to run off through the cattle camp. When the
> people saw this they began to laugh and soon forgot
> about mourning. When Divinity saw this he was
> satisfied that people should remain with death, for
> they looked happy with life.

The Atuot proverb "Hunger is the oldest of powers" also suggests that human self-assertion, particularly that of women, is the primordial source of suffering. As a result of the actions of a woman, they came to know crucial realities of existence. Though their creative role receives emphasis in certain Atuot rituals, women are rarely recalled as ancestors and hence never achieve even the most limited sense of social immortality. Instead, the ghost of a woman is more often said to be a source of misfortune for the living, for in contrast to the opposite sex, the heart or center of affective emotion is conceptually "hot," unlike the coolness associated with the words and deeds of men. In the text just cited, this is represented by her assertive behavior, the consequences of which men must accept post facto. While she is a medium of life through her physical labors and through childbirth, woman is mythically associated with the origins of death.

As I have noted previously, in Atuot cosmology Divinity is thought to be ultimately responsible for human death, but the immediate cause is more often sought in the workings of a malignant jok or as the consequence of ghostly vengeance. In reflecting upon an extraordinary event Atuot are inclined to assert era Decau apath, or "it is only the Creator who could do such things." Ghosts and powers enter their lives in a more immediate sense, reflecting positive and negative relations between kin, friends and others.

Death (lia) is defined by Atuot as the absence of life (yei) which is especially associated with breath (kwoth). A recurrent euphemism in their oral literature and pedestrian discourse for the phrase "to have died" is the idea of having been "left behind." Another proverb suggests "every man has his back" and intimates that the experiences of one's past are a central element in the local definition of the person: The past is manifest in the present and influences the future. F. M. Deng likewise writes that for the western Dinka "the past is seen in continuous relationship with the present and as influencing the future, a phenomenon which makes the dead perpetually significant" (1973: 88). This temporal continuity is essential to note in reference to the use of the term "soul," a point I address later. Here it is important to note that should a person die with a lingering feeling of hostility toward one or another individual known in life (for them, as for all people, a very likely circumstance) this will be reflected in the affairs of the living.

The breath and life are incorporate in the flesh (ring) and in this state a person is said to have existence (tei). Recall the respectful greeting ce tei?, "have you stayed (with life)?" which does not question the obvious fact of physical existence but is intended to mean "has Divinity given you life?". The human body does not necessarily possess life since the Atuot term nuer refers both to any single individual as well as a human corpse. Everything in the physical world has existence since all things were created by the Creator, but in normal usage, only such things as plants and animals, and of course human beings, could be said to have life. What remains after human death, the ghost, similarly exists though it is problematic to state unambiguously that the ghost has life. This point is discussed later. At death, all life returns to Divinity, the creator of all extant phenomena.

As a public event the situation of death involves women more explicitly than men, for they gather and mourn in high-

pitched wails for a number of days following news of the
death.   Their crying at this time nearly approximates the
behavior of a dance--one woman leads the crying and is
answered by a chorus of women in syncopated rhythm. Brothers,
uncles, and agemates discuss privately among themselves the
consequences of the death in relation to cattle, the birth
group, and the ancestral dead. Atuot characterize this as a
time when the living must "reveal the things in their hearts"
in order to avoid the potentially ill effects of ghostly
vengeance. This is one of the most clearly social aspects of
death. A man might be able to conceal his true feelings from
others, though they maintain that Divinity will always know
what is in the heart of a man. This is primarily a personal
phenomenon. Hence, should a man not confess honest intentions
in this context, he only increases his chances of later
misfortune. The same, of course, applies to women who had
some relationship with the deceased. Divinity will ultimately
condone the curse of the dead upon the living. In this
context, the ancestral dead are also called to mind since
their rights over the use and distribution of cattle must also
be considered, and in this context men also wonder "how the
changed affairs of the living will be seen by the dead."
There are few material possessions that outlast the lifetime
of those who form them. Because rights to village areas and
rights to the use of herds are inherited and passed on
collectively, the legal corporate group in their view
necessarily includes the living and the dead (see also Deng
1966). The sentiments of the recently deceased towards the
living prior to death are as demanding of attention as though
the individual were still alive, a notion central to Atuot
concepts of ghosthood.
     Here I describe the mode of burial Atuot customarily
enact and then the reaction to an encounter with a ghost. In
the course of field work I was present at a number of burials
in which events similar to those described in this text were
witnessed:

> The first reaction of the relatives to the death is
> the weeping and noise of the women. All the
> relatives come to the hut. After they have cried
> the older women must calm them and collect them
> together under the roof of the hut by the mud wind
> screen where the cooking is carried out. The body
> is then carried up into the <u>adwil</u> and the door is
> closed so that no one will enter. After this,
> cooking cannot be done in the hut and all fires
> must be extinguished. If it was a man who died his
> older relatives see to these things and if it was a
> woman or child they are done by women. A man is
> buried on the west side of a hut a short distance
> from the wall. A woman is buried underneath the
> <u>adwil</u> near the place where the food is prepared.
> An old man might also tell his sons that he wants
> to be buried in the cattle camp so he can always
> look after his cows. The hole is dug in the ground
> and for a man three piles of dirt are formed, and
> four if it was a woman. No small children or
> unmarried people can be present. The dirt from the
> grave should not be mixed with the ground because
> this is the earth of the dead. The arms and legs

are broken and he sits in the grave like when he
was born. From now on he will always look toward
the west because that is where death goes. When
the hole is finished an old woman goes into the hut
to shave off all the hair and [she] smears the
corpse with oil. The wife or husband of the dead
do not do anything because if they did, they would
not be respecting the dead. One half of the
sleeping hide is placed at the bottom of the grave
and when the dead is put down, the ears are covered
so no dirt will get in. The eyes must be open so
the dead man can always look after his things.
Then the people who dug the grave squat on their
haunches with their backs toward the grave and push
some of the dirt into the hole, and then turn
around and fill in the grave. A small goat is
brought and pounded over the grave until it dies
and then it is thrown into the forest. All the
bracelets and beads of the dead person are put into
a calabash he used to eat from, and then his spear
and axe are bent because he no longer does the work
of the living. These things are placed on top of
the grave along with some beer for him to drink.
For the next four days no one cooks or sleeps
inside the hut and after this the hut is swept up
and the dirt put into the calabash. A woman
carries this into the forest and places it next to
an anthill. Sometimes a witch will go and steal
these things. Women bring new mud for the floor
and the yard is swept very clean that day. Then
the people who made the burial go to the family of
the dead man or woman and get a goat. A vine is
brought from the forest and placed in the yard and
a fire is lit in the middle of it. Green leaves
are put in the fire to make a lot of smoke. The
smoke from the fire is fanned over the family of
the dead man to take away the death. Then they
each step over the vine three times to leave the
death on the side of the forest. The goat is
killed and eaten by the people who made the burial.

The life is said to return to the Creator while the corpse
remains in the ground. Atuot say that the "shadow" or "ghost"
(tiep) walks with a person throughout life and only leaves at
death. Departing from this world it is said ce wei be nien ke
thuomde, "[the dead] have gone to sleep with our ancestors."
Poetically, Atuot speak of the deceased as having departed to
the "cattle camp of the dead" though this image of a timeless
existence is figurative rather than an imagined reality.
Likewise, ancestors are said to exchange cattle for marriages,
make dances, and cultivate grain to make porridge and beer.
    Some time after the interment, but normally following the
season of rains when sufficient food is available, a sacrifice
called nake yang yuic nuer is carried out in which a "cow is
killed over the head of the person." Invocations made in the
course of the ritual include statements such as "this death is
the bad thing that should not occur again." Addressing the
collectivity of ancestral dead a man says, "Your son has now
come to you. Receive him with this cow that is sacrificed so
he may join you, and let the people remain with sleep," that

is, live untroubled by his ghost. If the sacrifice was not
performed, Atuot suggest, the ancestral dead would not allow
the individual to enter their world. The ghost would be
forced to remain among the living for an indefinite period, a
consequence no one favors. From one analytic perspective it
can thus be suggested that the world of the collective,
nameless dead is analogous to the larger social environment in
which they live. Each living individual, however, is
concerned with a much more limited and personal encounter with
a ghost.

Previous ethnographers in the Nilotic Sudan reported a
degree of reserve in discussing death with local peoples but
this was not my experience in Atuot communities. Indeed, in
the proper context people were quite willing to speak of such
matters, especially if the person recalled had been a dear
friend or close relative. What Atuot do wish to avoid in
conversation and in dreams is mention of or reference to an
individual who died "with an angry heart." An older woman
explained the misfortunes of her family by saying "Mabor died
with a bad heart. This is why the things have gone bad and
people continue to die. Mabor now looks upon us with the
anger of his life." By contrast, the ancestral dead (thuom)
are considered to regard the living with benevolence and also
represent tradition, thereby intimating fundamental moral and
ethical precepts of Atuot society. One may not be certain of
what was lingering in the heart of someone that died recently,
so it is considered best not to mention them, especially in a
public setting. This inclination is manifested in daily life
between spouses who, as noted, should be accorded a formal
degree of respect (thek). A man or woman should never address
the spouse by personal name in public but refers to the other
simply as "my wife" or "my husband." In an analogous manner,
the ghost of a recently deceased person is respected by
avoiding mention of his or her name.

The ghost of a dead man or woman is in a sense still
close to the living, both in psychic and physical forms, for
anyone who shared a relationship with the deceased retains a
graphic image and memory of the dead. In a categorical or
structural sense, this factor of mediality may in part account
for the ambiguity associated with the recently deceased. The
encounter with the "living dead" occurs most frequently in a
dream, when the darkness of night is likened to the lack of
knowledge about the intent of a ghost. When a ghost comes
"crying to you in a dream," it serves as an omen that unless a
sacrifice is made to appease the angered dead, misfortune is
certain to follow. (One can certainly draw a parallel here
between the image of ghostly visitation and the representation
of possession by a jok.) A brief illustration will help in
the interpretation of this event.

Marial Dak, who had once been a prominent chief, died
suddenly and, to the minds of his kin, for no apparent reason.
The burial was elaborate for he had been a man of considerable
renown. Approximately two years after the interment his
eldest son said he had been visited by the ghost of his
father. In the dream, the ghost named a large black bull that
was to be sacrificed over his grave, in his name. A number of
days later his half sister and her child fell ill. A diviner
was consulted and revealed that the malady was caused by the
ghost of Marial Dak, because he was angry that the sacrifice
had been delayed. The diviner said Marial was calling for a

large black bull. For those involved, the concordance between
these separate events offered sufficient evidence of the need
for sacrifice. Before the animal was brought from the cattle
camp a sheep was killed by suffocation (buong) by the sons-
and daughters-in-law of Marial. It was explained to me that
by doing this the power ring that was owned by the family
would travel with the blood of the sacrificial bull to seek
out the initial cause of Marial's death.   Marial's elder
brother Awumkuai did not eat any of the flesh of the
slaughtered bull, for it was an animal he often mentioned in
one of his ox-songs. The sheep was sacrificed by suffocation
to also ensure that in spite of the present ill health of the
woman and child, she would in the future continue to bear
healthy children.
     While anyone can dream of a dead person, the misfortune
imaged by ghostly vengeance can only be experienced by a close
relative of the dead.   Ghostly vengeance (cien) is thus
restricted to people of a single family (ji cieng) and hence
the moral order of this living group is reaffirmed and, in a
sense, recreated in such a circumstance. As Atuot suggest,
"the bringer of the word," that is, the person who had the
dream brought by the ghost, should make the final invocations
over the animal before it is slaughtered. In this, I think,
one can see most clearly how the individual interpretation of
death is a central element of religious experience, and the
way in which moral values are represented in these terms.   The
act of sacrifice demanded by the deceased through the medium
of a ghost, therefore, has a quality of atonement, since
ghostly visitation indicates the occurrence of a breach in
moral norms.   In western terms this might be explained as a
matter of unconscious projection on the part of the dreamer;
however, in Atuot usage, the ghost is the active agent who
comes to an individual. The socially circumscribed nature of
the situation of death is evident in another custom. When it
is recognized that an old person may soon die a natural death,
he or she will summon the immediate family to collect at the
deathbed. It is a solemn occasion for all concerned, not only
because of its emotional quality, but also because life and
death--otherwise radically distinct--are temporarily
contingent. One friend related what his father had said in
this situation.

> You stay with the cattle. It should be done well,
> but if it isn't, I will see you even while I am in
> the ground. Do not let the things of the land go
> bad. Even though I am dying here before you, you
> keep the things of the black people well. When the
> time for marriage has come, you consult me for a
> word. When the rains come, you make a sacrifice.
> You keep the lives and nothing will be bad. So it
> is.

These are the things that a father wills (cien; see Lienhardt
1970) to his family.
     Atuot speak of the curse of one's father as among the
worst things that can befall a person. A father may wish his
son long life but curse him that all his wives and children
will die. The death of a number of cattle may be explained in
these terms. This involves something of a paradox, for the
cattle of his son are also his own, even though he is dead.

If this does not make sound economic sense it does draw into further relief the intense desire for individuality and deference characteristic of Atuot ethics. In this way the curse can be understood as another means of self-assertion, which functions also as an extension of the moral and economic interests which unite (and also divide) a family and kindred. The contrast between an individual's interpretation of the situation of death and its more embracing social aspects are revealed in another text.

> When a person is dead he looks at us as we are staying here. When a man dies and leaves no children behind you must look after the things of the family. When the night comes the ghost walks among his relatives and sees where his children are. The ones who died long ago walk as a group. If there is something that has gone wrong with the cattle or if the dead man did not receive part of the bridewealth, the ghost will come and say, "you, so and so, you tell the people of the family what is wrong. This is the ghost of I, so and so. This is what has gone wrong and this is what must be done to correct it." The ghost comes to you exactly like a person. The ghost comes and sits on your chest when you are sleeping. It does not die.

As far as I understand, when a man dies naturally from old age, or a woman dies in childbirth, the blood is left in the corpse when buried. It has been mentioned that blood and breath are fundamental in the definition of life. The life in the form of breath leaves the body at death.

In most sacrifices the victim is killed by severing the throat with a spear, thereby letting the blood flow out of the corpse with the waning pulsations of the heart. Occasionally it is collected to be boiled and eaten. When a man has been buried, his ox should be brought to the graveside and then speared in the heart. The more typical mode of slaughter is called dhol yang or severing the throat of the cow. When the animal is speared in the heart, conceptually the center of affective experience in human beings, the blood seeps very slowly from the carcass into the earth covering the grave. It is said in this circumstance that the blood of the ox will travel by night and day to seek the cause of death, along with the ghost that summons the sacrifice. Some suggested to me that the ox falls pointing toward the direction from which death originated. What seems essential to emphasize for the purpose of interpretation is that the heart of the beast is singled out, since it is the "heart" of the person that determines his or her relations with others, both when alive and dead. That is, the individuality of a person is represented through his or her words and deeds, which are first of all phenomena that emanate from the emotive and cognitive self. This point emerges from the consideration of another text.

> When a man dies cows are sacrificed for him. He goes down to become one of the people of the ground. People who remain stay up. When a cow is sacrificed over the grave it is not because we want him to come back. This is done so we can have

lives, so we will be protected in our lives by
thuom (ancestors). The cows are sacrificed so he
will go and walk with the ancestors. His ghost
walks after the jok that killed him. All of the
dead are like the people here. If the ancestors
send a power because their hearts are bad there is
no way a man can live even if sacrifices are made
for him. Cuong [ghost marriage] is made for the
dead by the ones who stayed up so people will hear
his name tomorrow. The ghost can kill cows because
his heart is bad. It can destroy the family by the
children of those who remain up. The ghost says
"you have remained with my things but you have not
married a wife for me." If the ghost has a wife
who is alive to cook and give birth to children
then the ancestors will be happy.

Metaphorically, then, the "heart" of the deceased, or in one
sense of the phrase, his social personality, becomes the
ghost. This representation will vary based on individual
memories and experiences of the deceased.
    The term I have translated as ghost has both a single and
a plural form, so that one may name the ghost of one person or
refer to the ghosts of a number of people. The word thuom has
only a plural form and refers to a nameless collectivity of
persons who died before living memory of them. There is never
a confrontation with thuom in dreams, only with individual
ghosts. The English term "ghost" is also appropriate in
conveying a meaning of the Atuot tiep, for in the encounter
with a ghost a person may be haunted (cien) and reminded of
his or her responsibilities toward the dead. Thuom can then
be understood as an imaginative construct, whereas a ghost is
imbued with a mental image and the ability of assertive
action. In this sense the ghost is alive, especially in
association with the human corpse that retains its blood. I
would suggest that the category of ghosthood bridges a gap
between the memory of the recently deceased and the ancestral
dead, the latter forming a nameless collectivity occupying the
dusty archives of birth groups. Ancestors should be respected
and called to mind by name when making sacrifices and
distributing bridewealth cattle. Ghosts are feared, avoided
in conscious recollection, and accorded the deference expected
by any living person. Their presence is imaged by individual
persons, as the text reads, "exactly as they were in life."

    A discussion of a burial and the sacrifices which
followed it will shed further light on the material under
consideration. Reference has already been made to some
general features of mortuary custom, so what follows is a
description of events enacted after one burial I witnessed.
When the corpse had been interred, heavy dark cotton soil was
brought and smeared across the top of the grave. In the
majority of cases no other marking is placed at the site of
burial. Soon after this task was completed a cow of the color
ayan was tethered over the grave and, following a brief
invocation, with one thrust of his spear the elder brother of
the deceased pierced its flesh and struck the heart of the
cow. Since the animal fell dead facing west, this was
interpreted to mean that Divinity had accepted the sacrifice
and taken the death away from the family. The cow, it was

said, "would stay tethered with the ghost." The carcass was butchered and distributed among the relatives of the dead woman, excluding her immediate family, who were prohibited from eating any of it. Meanwhile, on the other side of the hut two additional oxen had been slaughtered for food and women had begun to prepare beer. Over the next four days the mournful cries of women grew less frequent and the general atmosphere changed to one of festivity. Paternal kin of the dead woman from the Ceic Dinka were also present, and made sacrifices of their own. Early in the morning of the fifth day after the burial the family gathered in the homestead of Tuiny, the husband's elder brother. Dominating the center of the yard was a large forked-branch shrine for the power known as _makao_. On the eastern side of the shrine a goat stood tethered. It was a cool and clear morning, an auspicious time for sacrifices when Divinity will be addressed. Tuiny sat close to the goat on his ambatch headrest and by his feet was a small calabash filled with pounded millet. The invocation began as Tuiny rubbed a small handful of flour over the back of the animal after each short phrase he spoke. When the invocations were completed the goat was untethered and led around the hut three times. Most of the others joined in the procession and, while slowly circling the yard, sang these songs.

> I pray to Divinity like a monkey [the image is that
>   of a person sitting on one's haunches with the
>   palms of the hands and the face turned upward
>   to the sky]
> I pray to you my father
> The people are troubled by these things of life
> The bad things have come to the ants
>
> Do not spoil the edge of the spear [i.e., let the
>   sacrifice be made well]
> I pass with the cow _ayan_ in the middle of the camp
> And it is blessed by the people
> Oh, my Creator,
> People all collect together
> The spear has been thrown
> The people of long ago fought for this land
> Take the life of this cow to give us lives
> Go and bring life into the hut
> This is a cow for blood
> I pray to you my great father
>
> You bring a fat cow for blood
> Give me the fat animal to exchange for lives
> Bring the bull of Wunjier for blood
> Oh Creator, take the blood
> [You] take the blood for the bad things
> Give us lives and take the blood

The he-goat was retethered when Tuiny began another invocation, at which point the animal urinated. The urine was collected in a calabash and sprinkled over the heads of the family members. (When an animal urinates in the course of an invocation, it is suggested that Divinity has heard the words and intentions of the people, and will thus accept the sacrifice.) Following this the rope was untied and thrown onto the roof of the hut. The animal was held on its back against the ground and killed by severing its throat. The spear used in killing the animal was passed around in order that they could lick some of the blood, an act which identifies people with the intent of the sacrifice as well as demonstrating that none of them were in any way responsible for the death. Here again, the association between blood and life is manifest.

The atmosphere grew quiet, and all one could hear was the crackling of a fire that had been lit to provide warmth in the chill of the early morning. People began to talk among themselves in whispers and relit their pipes as a white ram was brought out of the hut. The same acts were repeated before it was slaughtered near the shrine for makao. A short dance began, accompanied by fight songs (yaai) praising their cleverness and success in warfare and their cunning in seeing after their affairs as well as recalling the names of their ancestors. One can surmise that these songs in some manner reinstill in the living a sense of their own achievements in the past, which do not lose their quality of valor and persistence, even in this humbling circumstance. The dance continued for about a quarter of an hour, and then the people were reseated and a similar stillness was observed. Refraining from conversation at this time was said to be a way of showing respect to Divinity, who would see their hearts and witness the sincerity of their sacrificial intent. It was also necessary to remain quiet so that "makao could walk in secret to find the death." Now, in retrospect this short dance and the songs that accompany it appear to me as a representative or symbolic fight against death (see Lienhardt 1961: 281).

Tuiny then washed the faces of all the women with water from a calabash in order to "cleanse them of the death," and gathered small bits of urine-soaked mud to smear across the foreheads of all those collected. In addition to the demonstration of their identification with the sacrifice, this act also perhaps recalled the notion in Atuot religion that when a person dies, he or she returns once again to earth. Rather than washing the faces of all the men present it was agreed that if the face of the ram was washed, this would represent their own cleansing.

The premise on which further representational action is based is viewed in relation to a power which brought about the death, and as in the case of ghostly visitation, a single individual is held responsible for its occurrence. Tuiny later told me,

> The wife had been married from the Ceic Dinka and we of the family of Againy have taken their women as wives before. We are now troubled by these marriages. We have always fulfilled our debts of cattle, but then this woman, like others before her, dies after she has only given us three or four children. Those of Ceic say this is not a problem of theirs. Instead, they say it is a problem of the hatred among the Luac in the old feud over the chiefship brought by the English.

Although the dead woman was too young to have been personally involved in this dispute, in part, the cause of death was seen as the result of "the bad things in people's hearts from long ago." There is also a history of accusations of witchcraft between members of this larger birth group. Tuiny continued,

> When the Ceic killed an ox at the site of the grave they said to it "you take this death away. You go down and tell thuom and the ghost, 'I am the ox killed to take away the death from the people. If the cause of death is with us, let it not happen again.'" Ceic have said to us you are fighting among yourselves, that we have not said openly what is really in our hearts. But anyway, we cannot go on marrying their women if they only die like this one. This is the time when everyone should clear their hearts and make their words good so that people can stay without suspicion. Now too many people have died with anger in their hearts.

Six days after the interment a final sacrifice was made in the homestead of the husband. The short invocation over the back of the bull, punctuated with thrusts of his spear toward the animal, was made by a senior member of the family. He said,

> Our family has been broken. The death has now started with the younger people. If it is the Creator who has taken her life then it is a good thing. The ghost of the woman will be pleased and the people will have sleep. If she is killed by another human being, you Manger [the bull] see to it properly. Let him die also with the woman of this family . . . this bad thing . . . what has gone wrong? We have built new huts and sacrificed cows and still this death comes. You, Athildor [the husband of the deceased] do not give it up. Creator, you take this cow for the lives of the people.

After he spoke, the bull was thrown to the ground and slaughtered and its flesh meted out among the same people who had been excluded from eating the first animal sacrificed after the burial days before. Since the masculine idiom designates the unity of those who share economic and moral interests in a herd of cattle, the scrotum and pestle of the bull was given to be eaten by the eldest members of cieng Dak. Members of this birth group will explain that it was "Dak who bore them all with his penis." This practice represents the unity of the sacrificing group--a unity that is hoped for, in this case, rather than established in fact. A perpetual theme in contexts such as these is that those who survive the death should speak their hearts openly and honestly, a usage that invites further reflection on the dialectical relation between unity and individuality. In other words, while sacrifice offers a public expression of the collective interests of a group, this is ever threatened by social ethics that give value to individual dignity and identity, which are in turn represented in local images of ghosts and the effects of the dead upon the living.

The individual, then, is defined in relation to a moral community, publicly defined and recognized in the course of religious ritual. Concurrently, for the Atuot, the personal

identity of an individual (nuer keu ro) is defined by the
patterns of his or her life which figure in the memory of the
person after death. Atuot do not imagine a world awaiting
them after death in which they will find all their desires
satisfied, nor is there the image of a world where sinners
will suffer the consequences of their deeds. The individual
hopes, however, for the assurance of social immortality in the
memory of the dead among the living. In their words, a ghost
marriage is made for one without progeny "so his name will be
heard tomorrow." Ghosts, ancestors, and individuals thereby
participate in a single moral and spiritual world. The
essential distinctions between these states of being are
defined as a factor of passing time rather than as differences
in character, essence, or quality. This explains why
sentiments of the dead must be respected after life,
analogically identical to the manner in which individuals
assert their own independence in life. The person may live
beyond physical death, not as a soul in some other-worldly
abode, but as a memory among the living. And in every case
this memory will vary from individual to individual. To
conclude this brief overview of Atuot cosmology, and to recall
the epigraph that introduced this chapter, I would like to
suggest that one tenet of Atuot philosophy would be: As death
finds them in this world, so will they be in the next.

5.
INDIVIDUAL AND
SOCIAL EXPERIENCE

The discussion in the last chapter concluded by observing the
way in which the living and the dead form a single conceptual
unity of time and space. The individual is an embodiment of
the past living in the present who wishes, above many other
things, to be remembered in the future. Much of Atuot
religious dialogue turns ultimately inward toward individuals:
They seek peaceable relations among family and kin, but
reflect upon their own doings before asserting that personal
or collective misfortune has a source elsewhere. Their
acceptance of Divinity as the source of all creation and the
giver and taker of life is, even among many of those who have
experienced western secular education, implicit. I have no
basis, however, on which to suggest that they conceive of an
external constraining phenomenon we call "society." I rather
think they experience social life as being people in the
company of others (see Riesman 1977: 163). Through the media
of folktales and proverbs, younger children are presented with
images of behavior and sentiments which are "right and "moral"
(in context, laang or cuong). The same texts present
figurative images of people who become transformed into lions,
the antithesis of moral society. People-lions become wild (ca
waath) in folktales and actively seek to destroy individuals
and, by extension, the communities which they form. Within
this broad spectrum of psychological dispositions are people
who tend to be reserved, who speak few words. Others are
known in local circles as gwan aluope or "rumor mongers,"
known for their continual, often contradictory statements
about themselves and others. Still others, because they drink
too much, because they committed incest knowingly, or because
they appear to act without reason, are called abojek, or
"perverse" in its root meaning. I met many people in the
course of field work who reminded me of people I knew at home,
so that I would assert there are as many "personalities" or types of public/private selves in their communities as in our own. In any case, the individual person is
known by "their word," a simple phrase in English that invites
some further comment in regard to the intended Atuot
usage.
    Attention is focused in this chapter on the ways in which
individuals create and reflect upon the lives they lead

through public and private discourse.   Such things as ox-
songs, proverbs, personal names, and the amoral category of
the witch are cultural usages and representations expressly
oriented toward individual and collective expression, some in
public company and others in the guarded privacy of intimate
company.

The most challenging question facing social scientists
is, how is society possible?   Freely translated from English
into Atuot, this query might be stated, "How is it that people
come to bring their words together?"   A first presumption and
observation from the Atuot view is that individuals are
defined and known by their words, their statements and
observations that articulate the ways in which peoples
perceive social relations.   After the short ritual of formal
greeting one sometimes asks, "teke lat?"--literally, "do you
have a word?"--implying "what's up?" or "what have you heard?"
If the response is affirmative, one might then say be yi nong
rar, or "well, then, bring it out," or "what is it?"   In the
widest sense, the Atuot community is composed of individuals
who share and communicate common knowledge or, in their own
words, "people who share one word."   Recall the earlier
(Chapter 1) observation Atuot make that the Nuer are a people
"who have taken our language and made it crooked."   The
idiomatic usage of "the word" to connote a true community in
this case intimates that the Nuer are a people who cannot
fully be known, since they have a different word.   This is not
to say that the dialectic differences per se are taken to
define "otherness" or "foreigners" (though it may mean this in
context, as when a man suggested that "the Arabs are people
with a different word and you cannot follow it," or "you
cannot trust them").   It means to them that their "different
words" convey a different way of doing things, a different way
of being.   If they were to speak of their world in the
abstract notion of "society," I think they would first
emphasize that this would be a group in which "people bring
their words together."   Indeed, traditional spokesmen of Atuot
communities were called reth (from ruac, "to speak") who "kept
the words" of the people.

Understood in these terms "the word" implies common
knowledge in addition to collective expectations of
reciprocity and sociability.   As noted earlier, individuals
possessed by the heavenly power ring "keep the life of people"
and the truth and power of one possessed by ring is "in his
words" or "in his mouth."   One friend said, "If you have no
luck with anything you visit the person of ring.   He will
smear your mouth with ashes (thok buk, or "bless your word").
Then you will go and things will go your way."   In an
analogous manner, when a diviner is possessed by an earthly
power he or she does not claim to speak alone.   Rather, it is
the power that "brings the word" through the human medium, who
"catches the words" of the spiritual agent.   It is a basic
premise of exorcism rituals that "people do not hear the words
of the powers."   Those who "have the words," to put it another
way, are those who are publicly acknowledged to have greater
wisdom, perception, and vision than the common lot.   The
gossip or rumor monger, in contrast, promises only lies or
half-truths. As they say, "Many words hide the truth; few
words proclaim it."   Speaking, then, is as much an art form as
it is a requisite for their definition of society.   A.
Giddens' (1976: 127) remarks on the priority of language in

the definition of social experience are instructive in this
regard:

> Speech and language provide us with a series of
> useful clues as to how to conceptualize processes
> of social production and reproduction--not because
> society is like language, but on the contrary,
> because language as a practical activity is so
> central to social life that in some basic respects
> it can be treated as exemplifying social process in
> general.

In addition to the more numerous opportunities one has to
make evaluations of the person on the basis of conversation in
pedestrian contexts, the Atuot (along with other pastoral
Nilotes) engage in an art form they call tuar, or "making an
ox-song."

THE OX-SONG AND SOCIAL DISCOURSE

Entertaining, engaging, and creative public discourse is
highly valued in Atuot communities. To speak well is to
present one's self well. From the time they are young boys
and continuing through their formal initiation into young
adult status, Atuot males make great efforts to first mimic
and later master the style of public oration their role models
provide in the form of tuar. The ox-song combines a number of
elements which directly reflect the creativity of the
composer, the most important qualities being the use of
figurative language, the melodic line, and the texture of the
autobiographical narrative. Young children mimic the melodic
style and verbal form of the songs they hear during mornings,
afternoons, and evenings spent in cattle camps, though a
younger man will not sing in public until he has achieved
adult status. When they have become young adults, the amount
of time they devote to composing their own ox-songs is
commensurate with the aesthetic and economic value cattle hold
for them at this point in their lives. A young man even notes
this careful attention in one passage of this type:

> The song of Majok [his ox] is not made carelessly
> A man must sit and arrange the words properly

Young men take care to memorize the long passages of the songs
composed by their elders as a means of mastering the style,
but also as a means of coming to know more fully the person
who composes the song. The ox-song is equally a means of
masking identity since a good song conveys double meaning
through the use of figurative language. Indeed, metaphor is a
central element of good songs. A man named Makuei may compose
a song about his ox of the color configuration makuei; as a
result, the identity of the singer is continually transposed
with the identity of the beast, which serves as a medium of
his agnatic identity, the telescoped history of his family, as
well as the singer's self-perception. While he would be
regarded as a silly boastful youth if he were to draw
attention to himself this way in normal conversation, through
the use of metonymy and metaphor in an ox-song, the identical
end is achieved. The literal utterance of a song draws

attention to his ox, whereas he is in essence saying "look at me; see how different I am from the others; see the strength of the birth group to which I belong." Walking behind a herd of cattle in the open pasture he sings about his ox that leads the other animals toward the sweetest grasses. In the private company of his suitors he sings of his ox in the hope of impressing them with his social identity. On their part, young women assess the character of their potential lovers through the cleverness of their words. In cattle camps one often observes a man leading his ox around the perimeter of the clearing, in the pale light of early morning or in the evening after the cattle have been retethered, singing loudly about the beauty of his animal and how it will bring him all the happiness and luck in the world (see also Evans-Pritchard 1956: 194-95; Deng 1973).

Ox-songs have a common structure and melodic line. Each begins with what they call mien, a series of phrases the singer bellows rather than sings, which are followed by the actual text. Many of the songs I recorded run to more than 300 lines when transposed into print. Most of the songs I recorded were collected in cattle camps, where men would stand by their oxen as they sang. Occasionally the singer embellishes his performance by rattling the bell his animal wears around its neck. When one man takes the opportunity to sing, all others remain silent, listening closely to the narrative. Though the songs tend to be long, if the singer errs by forgetting or mispronouncing a passage, he will say in disgust ca ret, "I broke it," and will start the song once more from the beginning. As anyone who has attempted the task knows, recording, translating, and transposing extended texts of sung poetry is a time-consuming and sometimes tedious undertaking. For example, a single line from a song often requires considerable elucidation in the process of translation and, for the most part, the translation of a text was aided by the composer. Still, two singers will disagree about the "real meaning" of a passage, a fact which underscores the individual essence of each song. The composer is the "owner" of the song and those who are recognized as particularly adept in combining metaphor with melody are occasionally approached by others who seek assistance in their own compositions.

In the following pages I present a number of extracts from songs recorded in the process of field work. From my own perspective they have intrinsic ethnographic value as indigenous texts, but in this context the reader is asked to appreciate the manner in which the person is presented as being in the company of people. One song observes:

> My bull has fear like the fear of a cat
> When it is angered, its testicles run up
> My bull does not like the malicious words of
>   another man
> No one will look for you in the pasture [i.e., the
>   animal is so large it cannot be overlooked; by
>   analogy the singer's social presence is self-
>   evident]
> You protect yourself with your own horn
> The left horn of the bull never misses [Atuot will
>   sharpen the tips of horns so that when animals
>   fight, one is likely to injure another]

It gored the bull of Cep
It gored the bull of Cuot
It gored the big bull Mabor in the cattle camp at
     Naam [the singer here lists some of the men he
     has either fought or killed]
We are not people who are spoken of in whispers
My bull went wild like a lion
My bull went wild like a leopard
You, the sons of Nyanyong
Don't say that untethering the bull is an easy
     thing
The land of Nuer is the land of troubles
The troubles of Nuer destroyed our land long ago
You always want to go to the side of baar [a salt
     lick in western Nuer country]
But when the raiding of Nuer comes,
You will remain with only the ropes
This trouble with Nuer, you keep it on the left
When the move to the pasture of Nuer comes
I have no worry with the problem of cows
The ring of my father dances on the hump of the
     bull
The ring of my father knows how to keep cattle
The ring of my mother Inor followed us to the
     pasture
The ring of my father makes our name known to all
Oh Maduol [one of his oxen] nothing will touch you
Not even the eye of a witch
Maduol, mount the cows in the camp
Everyone is troubled by your left horn

Among other things, this passage conveys the deep pride the
singer holds for his lineage and ancestry. As a member of a
birth group that is possessed by or "filled with" the power
ring, he expresses the feeling that his family has been, and
will always be, blessed. The image of ring dancing on the
hump of his bull suggests celebration of his good fortune and
certainty that his name will be remembered by those who follow
him.

In another song,

Malith [pale grey ox-color] throws down the other
     bull
The big Malith of the village of Abuong
I deceive people with my fire
We went to bring Malith with the sons of Angainy
The huge Malith broke the rope
You keep dethier well [see below]
I took the big Malith to the land of Akot
The hornless bull remains in Akot
Malith sings throughout the land
I have not yet found the cow that looks ahead
In the season of rains, the great Malith slept
     under the roof

Unless the listener knew that the composer of this song was a
blacksmith it would not be known that the ox called Malith
refers in fact to the pale steely grey color of an anvil, upon
which he forms metal artifacts. The rope the "animal" broke

was not used for tethering but for carrying the anvil from
village to village. As a result, a sling made from parallel
lengths of bamboo (dethier) was manufactured to carry the
anvil to his homestead in the Akot section. The "singing" of
Malith, which would normally call attention to the manner in
which an ox or bull bellows, indicates in context the high-
pitched pinging that echoes when the anvil is struck. In the
next-to-last line the singer rues that he has no cattle--
anvils, unlike herds of cattle, do not reproduce! Atuot do
not build enclosed shelters for their cattle, unlike the
common Nuer and Dinka custom. Thus, when the rainy season
begins, he must move his metaphorical ox under the shelter of
his roof so it will not rust. Through the use of metonymy a
man who owns no cattle defines himself in relation to others
who do. In the absence of an ox or bull to praise, he still
has the opportunity to demand public attention for himself and
the work that maintains his life.

In the following song the composer suggests that his ox
"wants to carry the tassels." As noted in the text, Atuot
will pierce the tips of ox-horns with the heated point of a
fishing spear so that a small string attached to a tassel can
be affixed to the horn. The tassels are made from the tail of
buffalo and at the time of our first visit among them, Atuot
men were willing to barter them at the rate of six cows per
tassel. This immodest demand reflects the daring needed to
collect them. A group of young men will go off into the
forest to trail a herd of these animals. Once encountered,
they make the effort to separate one animal from the rest of
the herd, and as the men work toward this end, another man,
who carries a three-foot-long spear under his arm, runs ahead
in the direction of the moving herd. The lone man gains
distance on the animal, and at the appropriate moment lies
with his back on the ground and his spear in both hands. As
the buffalo runs in his direction he sits up so that the
oncoming animal impales itself on his spear. As such, the
line that appears in a number of songs, "I hung the tassel on
the horn of my ox" recalls this harrowing experience and,
understandably, draws attention to the singer's daring and
will:

> I left for the pasture of Makeui in the year of
>   floods
> The year when the grass refused to burn
> The year when the civil war ended
> When the morning breaks,
> Makuei will laugh like young boys
> Makuei will laugh like young boys who are satisfied,
> But ignorant about tomorrow
> Makuei will laugh like the man who is full of beer
> The ox is given life by my grandfather Athiokbec
> If you see the ox from afar
> You may think it appears as a flag
> Makuei will return from the pasture of Nuer with a
>   name that will be known by all
> The ox wants to carry the tassels
> I chose the ox like the handle of the blade of the
>   hoe
> What I found in Nyantoic [his suitor]
> Is what grain and beans find in the soil

They embrace each other and augment each other's
    life [in their gardens Atuot plant beans so
    they will grow up the tall stalks of grain]
Makuei was roaming through the cattle camp with the
    fishing spear in his horn
This is a spear that does not refuse to go through
It enters [the horn of the ox] like a circumcised
    penis
The fishing spear is like the penis that doesn't
    waste time once it has been shown the way
The earth is so wide, cows are kept like children
The back of my ox is as white as the grazing in the
    new grass [the image is that of morning dew
    glittering in the sun]
We are leaving for the camp of Maker in the
    morning--
The camp of Maker is like the smoke of the Nile
    Steamer [i.e., this is a large cattle camp, so
    that when all the dung fires are burning in the
    early evening, the billows of smoke resemble
    the clouds of exhaust from the river boat; by
    association, the singer is also indicating that
    his family and birthgroup own large herds, so
    that if his suitor agrees to a marriage, her
    family can be assured of receiving a sizable
    number of cattle as bridewealth]

Having attained the status of married adult, a man begins
to reflect on his life through song in a somewhat different
manner. He recalls through identification with a bull, more
commonly than with an ox, how he was involved in the settling
of one or another marriage or how his own valor was
responsible for a successful cattle raid. The change in theme
corresponds to an altered relationship with cattle in general.
Instead of actively herding them, he has more direct authority
over their allocation for other marriages; he is now an
individual who must be approached by younger men who seek
cattle for their own marriages. In short, the _tuar_ of older
men are retrospective. They sing about memories from the
corners of their minds instead of painting vistas of the
future reflecting youthful expectations. Since they have
lived through the very real difficulties of existence in this
taxing environment, it is time for the younger men to listen
to their words, to understand a mature view of social process.
While I initially doubted the veracity of assertions in ox-
songs, such as "Mayon shook like a fish at the end of my
spear" or "the horn of my ox is the one that never misses,"
experience gained living among them showed these statements to
be true. As I have stressed, the composer is saying, "this is
the way I see the world, and this is how I deal with it." An
older man in Kuek sang a song that included this passage:

Mangardit, the big ox laden with stripes
The ox of the daughter of Nyakuei [i.e., the animal
    that the man was given in the marriage of this
    woman]
Majok climbed upon the anthill among the cattle of
    Kuer Mac
You women with small families,
Don't trouble me with [your] words

On the day of drinking beer, women are all the same
On the day of drinking beer, women are all the same
I have released the ox to graze
Untethering the cattle is a hard thing--
It is confusing like a court case in the appeal
    court of Yirol
The ox of my brother,
People suffer just to look at it [i.e., he boasts
        that his ox is so handsome, people suffer
        thirst and hunger in their journey to see it]
When the day of drinking beer has come,
Women are all the same
Women are all the same
Mangar your head is covered with tassels
The tassels of my brother are in the house of
    Igaudit
The tassels of my brother, the tassels for dancing
The tassels of the ox of my brother Mabor Igai
The ox carries them like a man coming from Kuilamom
    and Anyanjok [these names denote camps where
    people in this region fish in the months
    before the dry season. The analogy suggested
    here is that the ox has as many tassels hanging
    from its horns as men have fish caught at these
    sites]
The ox of Kuek,
The ox that will make the diseases of cattle become
    cool
The tassels are in the house of my mother Igau
The tassels that I carry on my arm

As I have noted, the only animal that a man actually owns
amid the herd that he tends is his own personality ox. It has
also been noted that each animal tethered in a camp has its
own rope and this custom is reflected in song. The rope of
one's ox is not simply a utilitarian object, but is instead a
symbol of social relations. In song, a man sings about the
person who made the rope for his ox, and thereby conveys
information about the density of his own social network. This
theme emerges a number of times in a song composed by a widely
known man from the Apak section:

We decided to look for pasture for the bull
We decided to leave with Marang and Abolngar, the
    son of Majok Mer
We made the rope of my ox with the son of Turjok
Mayor Ayuicjok, the son of Ipoc Madet,
Your skill in making ropes is the skill of your
    father
Your uncles know the skill of making a fine rope
He made the rope and refused to take a gift of milk
When he worked the rope, he only smoked tobacco
If he paused to eat, his work may have been
    spoiled
He made the rope with the son of Adau
And the work finally ended in the evening
Lueth Mabolkuei, help the son of Durjok with the
    rope
It is a fine craft that they know
He made the rope well

Aleth Ngarker, a man whose words are good,
Aleth mentioned the question of the rope
He is a man who knows it well
He took to see after my rope
My father has a heart as hard as the hammer of
    blacksmiths
We made the rope, and made a hole in the horn
And brought a tassel
I made a hole and filled the horn with tassels
The big bull threw off the tassels
We took the ox, the people of Ayuol
And nobody joined us
We are troubled by the problem of Nuer
I call the son of Idour Bec to take the bull back
    to the end of the toic [i.e., to move the herds
    away from Nuer]
Makuai slept in the camp of Luac
Magainy, I took you to the grazing of foreigners
It ate the pasture of Jilek
We settled in the toic of Apak
The foreigners lit the camp with their spears
    [i.e., a raiding party arrived in the camp at
    night, and the light of the moon was reflected
    from their spears]
The vulture followed my path [i.e., where he
    walked, only dead remained behind]
And the coward ran deep into the toic
My people are covering the camp [protecting it]
When I heard the voice of the hyena
I followed it to kill the people who remained
    behind
The vultures followed me to the river
A man who doesn't know my name has run away
The age set of Awan has a sour heart
I killed so many people I nearly went mad
My father Jongbaai has the medicine of the vulture
I kill any man who tries to steal the ropes
I kill any man who steals the cow
I will run after him like a horse
I have frightened all the people in the camps
I will come like the thunder of the rain
I will fill my quiver with arrows
The hyenas will fill the cattle camp [i.e., they
    will consume the remains of the dead]
Awan is the owner of the land from long ago
I speared Makoi in the back of the head
I have spoiled the whole camp
Makoi buried the children in the fire

The song continues to name others he has successfully
fought. When transposing this text, the singer explained the
last line in this way: "In the old days before the government,
the purpose of a fight was to destroy a people completely.
When their defeat was beyond question, they would throw their
children into the fire so they could not be captured, so
everything would be gone."

Ox-songs often detail the ways in which relations between
groups of people are initially established through the
marriage and bridewealth of cattle. They are also a
legitimate and sanctioned medium within which insults can be

leveled against those who have not fulfilled the positive
expectations attending marriage. A direct verbal insult, in
other words, would most likely give rise to immediate physical
confrontation. The following extract illustrates this common
element of ox-songs:

My friend, we got to gather tassels
Those without tassels cannot boast of what is
    theirs
The women don't hear their words
The horn of Makuei nearly broke from all the
    tassels
We slept in the big toic of Mabor Ayual
The ox slept in a cold place
Major is eating the grass of a foreign land
Maker has black eyes like a witch from Ceic
Maker has black eyes like a witch from Ceic
Maker, see the descendants of Among Lual
Maker went to Abiang
I listened carefully and the sound of cooking
    lizard was there [most consider lizard
    inedible, indeed repugnant, as food]
Those of Among Lual always look for lizards
When I saw the woman of the family,
She was tired from cooking lizard all the night
The prostitution of the family is so great
Alek was fucked on the way
They fucked her continually for hours
They rested and fucked her again
It is like the prostitution of Arol [a section of
    Agar Dinka]
Arol fucked his mother
And then named the child!
Alek has given birth to children with black eyes
    [an idiomatic expression suggesting "a witch"]
Their sorcery is famous for killing cows
The fucking of Nyijong [another woman of the family
    he is insulting] is known everywhere
They took the penis to her under the tree
The big penis of Kot Rec made her run away

The extracts presented here are only small portions of
longer songs, and the songs themselves represent only a
fragment of texts I collected. Even this small sample
indicates, however, the way each individual attentively
reflects upon social experience through "his word," and in a
longer study F. M. Deng (1973: 84) observes that songs are an
essential means of affecting experience. Attention is here
again drawn to Giddens (1976: 107) where he suggests that
social meaning "is never fully taken for granted, and thus the
relevance of some particular element of an encounter may have
to be demonstrated, and sometimes fought for, by the
actor . . . it is not appropriated ready-made by actors, but
is produced and re-produced anew by them as part of the
continuity of their lives." I think it is fair to say, then,
that in the Atuot view of the "possibility of society" words
bind and separate individuals, just as birth groups, cattle
ropes, and relations are themselves bounded by bovine
transactions at the individual and social level. Clearly, the
ox-songs employ metaphors or idioms people live by, but they

further define the social meaning of experiences people live through, and thus indicate a local theory of how a social order is reproduced.

THE PERSONAL NAME AND SOCIAL EXPERIENCE

The primary matrix for the genesis of personal names occurs, of course, in conjunction with the institution of marriage, in its variety of forms. The personal name is a critical element in the definition of the person in Atuot as in all other societies. At the same time the name is a focal point of individual identity, it is a reflection of the social circumstances which surround birth so that in this light the personal name is also a social category.

It is customary in Atuot communities for the father to have the first say in the naming of the child. However, naming is not simply a matter of designation. As noted earlier, the word cak means in certain contexts "to create" and it is also the verb used to describe the naming of a child. The same usage is common among the Dinka. R. G. Lienhardt (1961: 41) notes that when a father names his son Majok, for example, "he is in fact making him into Majok and nobody else." The person is thus not simply given a name, but is created through a name. The first child of a union is customarily called after the color of an especially striking or beautiful cow given in bridewealth during the settlement of a marriage. In the case of a male, his name might be Makuei, or with a female, Akuei. Atuot call this the rin yang, the "name [of the color] of the cow." Thus in this context the name not only identifies the individual but also comes to act as a record of this marriage and bridewealth exchange and, by extension, to perpetuate the memory of those who were involved in this transaction. The way in which we were given new personal names amplifies this usage. In the village of Anuol, a man named Kulang gathered some of his age mates around us and said we would have to have new names since our own were "the names of foreigners." I was given the name Mayan, a common cow color approximating the color of my skin. Since we had no children, few accepted us as a married couple on first meeting. In Anuol, L'Ana's marital status had to be clearly understood before she could be renamed. Kulang first sought to establish how many cattle were exchanged at our marriage and what the colors of the animals were. I told Kulang we had been married without cows. His friend Anuer persisted, "How many cows were given?" I tried to explain that Americans exchange vows and wear rings on their hands after they are married. This was acceptable since Atuot admire bodily adornment. Anuer asked again, "How many cows?" Again I said, no cattle. Kulang suggested, "Oh . . . you must be like the Arabs. How much money did you exchange for her?" Some moments passed when Anuer stated, "Her name must be Alak." L'Ana's new identity was thus established, defined by the bluish (alak) coloring of the Sudanese paper currency.

Ethnographic evidence of this usage of a name acting as a marriage record appears commonly in song. A brother or paternal cousin of the groom may recall the marriage in an ox-song as "the marriage of the cow akuei." In a closely related sense, since the name given is derived from the color of a cow (rather than an ox or bull), it is symbolic of the expectation

of the continued growth of each family involved in the
marriage. The point I would wish to stress is rather simple.
The name given to the first child of the union reflects both
individual and social phenomena. By reference to the
transaction of bridewealth, the created personal name also
recalls an event of primary social significance, and in this
case there surfaces a correspondence between the perpetuation
of individual identity as well as collective immortality.

Children born later in the marriage are frequently named
in reference to an event that was co-terminous with birth.
Individuation of the social self is achieved in this manner
but I think what they have in mind through this usage is that
the circumstances of birth make an impress on the individual.
Rin jok refers to a category of names derived from the names
of different spiritual agents which are presumed to have
affected the well-being of the fetus prior to birth. For
example, if a woman has experienced difficulty in achieving
conception she may have consulted a gwan riang, a person
possessed by ring, so that he would offer his blessing and
life-sustaining power. Should she later give birth to a
healthy child, the baby will be called Ring, thereby drawing
attention to the circumstances of its birth. "It was Ring,"
they would say, "that brought out the child." In a similar
manner, if a woman experienced possession in the course of her
pregnancy, and was successfully attended to by a diviner, the
name of the child would be derived from that of the spiritual
agent that caused the problem. One younger man we met from
the Rorkec section was named Kenya. As he explained, during
the first civil war in their country his parents fled to
become refugees in Kenya where he was conceived and born.
After the passage of time his children and grandchildren will
learn something of that experience through the meaning of his
name. Lienhardt has similarly remarked on the circumstance of
a Dinka child named Khartoum, the capitol city of Sudan. He
wrote (1961: 150),

> Our view of the passage of time influences the
> value we attach to past events far more than is the
> case for the Dinka, whose points of reference are
> not years counted serially, but the events
> themselves. In the example of the man who called
> his child "Khartoum," it is Khartoum which is
> regarded as an agent, the subject which acts, and
> not as with us the remembering mind which recalls
> the place. The man is the object acted upon.

One is inclined to reason in light of this experience that
personal names are not so much selected by people as they are
imposed upon them: they might be called "metaphors of
experience."

A brief discussion of some common personal names may
serve to illustrate this point more clearly. Acithiec, the
name of a girl or boy, translates as "not requested, not asked
for," thus implying that the child was conceived unexpectedly.
I knew of a number of cases in which this name was given
wherein a young couple had conceived a child prior to a formal
engagement. Cagai, from the verb gai, "to be surprised," is
often the name of a child who survives infancy even though the
mother had miscarried a number of times before, and so they
are saying through the name "we are surprised with this life."

Dhuor is likewise an individual who was born after many others had died, or after it had been concluded that the mother was barren. One friend suggested to me that the name Dhuor "was a way of saying people have cried." In the same manner, the name Amer is derived from mer or "human tears"--tears of pain and tears of elation. Koryom, a generic word suggesting "catastrophe" or "drought," is given as a personal name to a child that was born in these circumstances. Acok (from the Dinka term "starvation") is an individual who was born in the midst of famine. An extreme form of resignation, one that borders on profound bemusement, is intended by the personal name Ayaang. This name was explained in these terms: "Divinity, surely you are joking, tempting us to imagine that this child will live." The common personal name Thuc refers to the act of sitting on one's haunches, with hands pressed against the forehead, a stance of resignation, indicating that the child was born in a time of great sorrow. A young boy we knew for a time was called Methalek. His father explained that some years earlier a British agricultural consultant had been in Atuot country to introduce a new strain of groundnuts. The consultant, whose surname was Lek, was recalled in this case by the father naming his child after him, since he was born at a time when these groundnuts were ready for harvest. I know of two other instances in which a novel circumstance was embedded into local social history. As she had endeared herself to smaller children, especially in the families of our own fictive identity, two women who gave birth during our visit named their daughters L'Ana, my wife's first name.

A child born with any type of physical abnormality or in a breech delivery is typically called Acao, or "of Divinity," from the verb cak, "to create." While all life is thought to emanate from Divinity, it is imagined that Creator made a special impress on these individuals when the fetus was still in the womb. In their view, twins are a special category of those who have been "touched by Divinity." As a social category twins are called diet (literally "birds"). The firstborn is called dit or "bird" and the second cien, or "the one that follows behind." Twins or birds are said to be associated with the species they call amor, a small bird that nests in mahogany trees. The birth of twins is a special event, one that is marked by women's dances and songs. Throughout their lives twins are treated as a single social category, a process I have discussed in more detail elsewhere (see Burton 1981a: 67-71). Soon after birth women gather in the homestead of the mother to perform the "dance of twins," bull acueo. As they dance the women sing,

> The spirit [of twins] has come between man and
>   woman
> And given them these twins
> The spirit has come between this man and woman
> And brought to them these twins
> Let us go to the mahogany tree and call out there,
> Eeeeeee, Eeeeeee
> Let us go to the palm tree of Nyawer and cry out
>   there,
> Eeeeeee, Eeeeeee
> The spirit has brought these twins
> When it came between man and woman

The sound represented here as "eeeeeee" is intended to mimic the song of a flock of the amor birds as they leave the trees and ascend into the sky.

Akec is another common name, in this case derived from the term kec, "bitter," and is given to a child born out of wedlock or one whose mother died in childbirth. A free translation of the image intended would be "the one left behind" or "abandoned." Cadong (from dong, "old" or "exhausted") may be the name given a child born after a prolonged and painful period of labor. Some other common names can be listed in a summary fashion:

    Akuo: "strong-willed"
    Kueric: "born in the middle of a path in the forest"
    Amuom: "the son who survives his dead brothers"
    Athildor: "the one with no birth group"
    Aruopiny: "remnant"; "tiny thing"
    Medeo: "tiny infant"
    Igalwang: "the only one to see" [others died at birth]

As is more widely the case, Atuot children are not given (one might also suggest, do not achieve?) personal names until the parents have a measure of certainty they will live, and during this interval the child is simply referred to as gat or "baby." In names of the type listed above, there is a reflection of the fact that life is hoped for, but is never a certain thing. Many of these names suggest surprise at life, a sentiment that recalls certain of their religious values. The traveler through their country learns not to comment upon the beauty or evident good health of a small child. A mother can be heard instructing her daughter, "Here, so and so, you take this thing [the baby] and care for it. I have other work to do now." To elicit direct attention to the child in public is to encourage envy of its good health, to attract the attention of those Atuot speak of as having an evil eye, or wang jeo. The goat- or sheepskin sling in which the mother carries the infant over her shoulder ensures that the child can be seen by others only when she wills.

A further category of personal names combines reference to images of suprahuman agents: the rin jao, or names that reflect the impress of these powers of human life, and rin atiep, children who are born in the name of ghosts. Atuot usage is quite like that Lienhardt (1961: 149) notes for the Dinka: "Dinka call children after Powers, and after the dead, who to the Dinka way of thought are less likely to return to trouble the living if their place and constant presence are thus explicitly acknowledged."

The foregoing discussion offers a partial inventory of Atuot personal names and indicates something of their experiential derivation. Atuot consider their personal names to be profoundly personal possessions. Unless one shares a strong and intimate relationship with another (and here, primarily between individuals of the same sex) it is utterly improper to refer to someone in public by their personal name. At the same time, it is something of an honor to be referred to by name in song. One might recall here the fact that when visiting her senior wife's homestead, a younger woman will address her as cek coude, "the wife of my husband." Were a husband to call his wife by name in public she will quickly become offended and refuse to prepare his meal that evening

and possibly for a few days more. In redress she will expect
a token gift from him, in the form of tobacco or a bracelet.
This is a way, they explain, of respecting (thek) one's
spouse. In the words of one woman, "You do not call someone
by their name because it is their name." In Chapter 3
attention was called to the practice of using relationship
terms between significant others in a public context.

The identity between the public person and the personal
name has a rather different and special quality with regard to
a man's rin theo or "ox-name." Ideally, as an adjunct to his
initiation into young adult status, a man's father will give
him his own ox and, as I have stressed, unlike the many other
beasts in a family herd, he has exclusive rights to ownership
over this animal. Age mates seldom refer to their peers by
anything but their ox-names. I admit a sense of inadequacy in
translating the personal and social significance of this
experience and usage. To own an ox is of unparalled value for
a young man. Young men often boast in their ox-songs,

> A man who has cows but cannot sing of an ox
> He is a man that can never be known--
> He will never be known anywhere

He is eager to bring his ox to be tethered in the camp of his
birth group so that he can smear dung ash across its back and
head, on its flanks and hump. He will then create a name
derived from some characteristic of his ox and from that time
on he will be known by this name in the company of his
compatriots. It is a name that is uniquely his own, and in
creating his name he is in effect creating a new social
status. In other words, the creativity he exhibits in the
"discovery" or creation (cak) of his ox-name will be a public
marker of his own sense of individuality.

There is some difficulty in describing how fitting the
use of ox-names is in the context of cattle camps. Possibly a
brief reference to a personal experience may be of some value.
My wife and I had been living in the camp called Wunarok over
a period of time, where I initially observed the habitual
reference to age mates by their ox-names. Seeking that sense
of collective participation any ethnographer might desire, I
acquired an ox and became known as Ayoicrial, after the rial
color configuration of my ox. One evening in August when the
rains had been especially heavy and lightning had been
particularly severe, the young men of our camp faced a
difficult task when herding the cattle through the forest on
return to the camp. As they explained, the thunderstorm had
startled the cattle, which then scattered in the forest. It
was past nine in the evening, long after the evening fires had
been lit, when the first animals began to make their way into
the camp. A short while later amidst what appeared to me as a
hopelessly confused collection of men and cattle, a friend
called to me, "Ayoicrial, thek e du ce ben," indicating that
my ox had returned and could be tethered at our gol. As I
understand it, the message was that amid about 1,500 cattle
and sixty adult males, my own ox could now be safely tethered,
insuring my own well-being. This point of digression can be
quickly summarized.

It is not uncommon for two people to share the same birth
name, and, indeed, it is inevitable that some will. But it
would be unthinkable for two individuals to have the same ox-

name, by the same logic that no two individuals have the same
"personality" or private/ public self. In the cattle camp a
man is known by identification with his cattle and his ox-name
further defines individual features of this relationship. In
the village or homestead setting he is more commonly known or
referred to by his birth name and in this setting he is a
father, responsible for the affairs of the homestead. His
divergent roles, in other words, correspond to different names
by which he is known. Lienhardt's (1961: 19) comments are
once again called to mind:

> The ox-name which a young man takes at initiation should
> not coincide with that he may bear as a birth-name. A
> man called Majok, for example, should not take as his
> song-ox a beast of the majok [color] configuration. He
> would not augment his social personality by doing so, for
> he would be known in manhood by nothing additional to the
> name by which he was known as a child.

Thus through the manipulation or altering of modes of address
as well as terms for self-reference, a different public self
is presented in different contexts and at different points in
one's life. In this sense I would argue that Atuot personal
names reflect social and individual experience and are at the
same time vehicles for the creation of experience and meaning.
Something of this quality was reflected in a further personal
context. Many ethnographers have likely had the experience of
being renamed by members of a local community so that they can
be "fit" into the social order. I was initially surprised to
find that Mayan Angainy (my Atuot name) appeared in a
genealogy I collected within my birth group. He was a man who
had died three generations earlier. Having been properly
named, I could then be known. The word, the name, the person:
Each of these categories merge in Atuot thought to create an
image and experience of the public and private self.

THE PROVERB: AN ASPECT OF COLLECTIVE THOUGHT

Thus far this chapter has been concerned with public
utterances that reflect individual perceptions and experience.
In a complementary fashion Atuot proverbs (kaang; sing. kang)
condense individual experiences reflecting more comprehensive
social truths. A number of these are offered here. By way of
introduction, proverbs are sprinkled through their oral
literature and commonplace conversation. Often Atuot
narratives and historical texts are embellished by a verse or
two of song which in effect abstract especially significant
events (or emphasize their consequence) for the listening
audience, in order that they might fully appreciate the finer
details of the text. Proverbs can be said to assume a similar
role in the more mundane context of daily conversation and, as
has been observed more widely, proverbs offer condensed
interpretations of received wisdom. The proverb is thus a
shorthand frame of reference on the moral and ethical
inclinations of a people. As a category of oral literature,
proverbs could be included in a class that comprises origin
myths, folktales, and song, each of which is related or sung
in particular situations. Songs accompany dances, courting,
initiation, birth, marriages, and a wide variety of

sacrifices. Folktales are most often recited by parents for children in the darkness of early evening when families are gathered around the hearth in the homestead, or underneath a shelter in a cattle camp. Proverbs figure primarily in conversation between mature adults in rather more diverse situations and, in light of this, the proverb is more often an element than a topic of social discourse.

I. **Lia era thang atel,** "there is death in spite of the pot for food." This proverb condenses an orientation in Atuot collective representations toward the acceptance of life as they know it, and of the existence of spiritual powers ultimately beyond their control and supplication. The phrase suggests that whatever effort may be directed toward subsistence, animate existence is in the final case a reflection of Divinity's will. The proverb also implicitly draws attention to an original world, as imaged in stories about creation, when Divinity withdrew from the human realm, deciding that whatever the extent of human labor to satisfy their needs, hunger would be a constant factor in human experience. For example, if there is a famine, it has been the work of Divinity, as the land was either flooded by water or gardens dried up because of a lack of rain. The proverb also hints that the greedy person, as well as the one who is able to just make ends meet, is not more assured than the other of a satisfying life.

II. **Aboth yene kai jao,** "hunger is the oldest and strongest of powers," expresses a sentiment much like the preceding proverb. When I heard this phrase the first time I interrupted the speaker to request a fuller explanation:

> A man named Malek had a very great wealth at one time and he boasted, "What is this called hunger? I have never seen it." Another man replied, "hunger is the oldest and strongest of the powers." After some time the wealthy man's cattle died. His children then had no milk to drink, so they died as well. Then Malek had seen the truth of the man's word.

The saying suggests that boastfulness begets want. This proverb is also a comment, and sometimes a conditional curse, uttered softly among those who have been refused an expected courtesy, as when a man with a large lump of tobacco does not share it with his fellows, or when a wife fails to offer guests food when she has an abundance to feed her children and husband.

III. **Ke ra buom te ne mei,** "these are the ancient hardships." When I asked the speaker for a better understanding of this proverb he said, "We cannot know how people began to say this. Maybe one day a man came and found people mourning and he said, 'Oh, you just forget about it. This death is an ancient thing, it has always been this way.'" I was satisfied with his response, yet he continued,

Sometimes there is no hope--so many things have
gone badly, and people will say _piny_ _be_ _duoth_ _ke_
iath, "just let the whole world remain with trees!"
Once a man lay dying and he did not have a good
word to say of anything. He saw nothing good in
what he was soon to leave behind, and he said, "let
all the land and our way of doing things be ended."

Clearly, in circumstances such as these, human optimism is at
a minimum. One who lives among them gains a feeling for this
possibility of resignation through personal names. The truest
translation of the Atuot usage in English approaches the
common shoulder shrug, and the suggestion, "eh . . . that's
life. What can you do?"

IV. _Nuer_ _thil_ _e_ _iok_, "a human being is not a dog!" is a
phrase that attends circumstances which test human capability
and persistence. Its common usage intimates that even a small
child, who is still ignorant in spite of what he or she may
have learned, is capable of worthwhile and productive effort.
While they speak of themselves as the "ants of Divinity" in
religious petitions, Atuot are confident of their ability to
provide for themselves as fishers, cultivators, and
pastoralists, a fact that is amplified in their strong values
of individual dignity and identity.

V. _Mieth_ _ka_ _yuic_ _thil_ _ke_ _mieth_ _iao_, "the first food is not
like the food behind" or "those who go first will have more
than those who follow." Some time after I recorded this
phrase a friend explained, "If I stay ahead of you, I will
arrive before you. You will never catch up with me. If we
are brothers and I am ahead [the eldest] the cattle of my
marriage are already there, but yours will only come later."
More generally in Atuot thought, things which are "ahead" are,
first, older and, second, superior. As noted earlier, the
first child of a union is said to "open the way" for the birth
of others. In the contemporary world, the first son of a
family is chosen to remain with the responsibilities of
keeping cattle while a younger son will be sent off to school.
Men are served the greater portion of a meal first, whereas
women are expected to eat what remains after a family has been
fed. When walking across the countryside, the husbands lead
while wives follow some distance behind. Those who arrive in
a dry season pasture first are assured of the chance to
exploit the finest grasses and settle near the best fishing
sites. Those who found a new wet season cattle camp will
always claim, along with their descendants, the highest ground
in the camp, which receives the best drainage during the
rains. Even while an ideology of equality is professed among
co-wives, the senior wife wields greater authority and enjoys
a greater measure of independence sooner in life. That which
is first, in other words, is considered to be more privileged
and superior. Ultimately, in view of their cosmology, this
sentiment characterizes Divinity.

VI. _Nuer_ _kue_ _ro_ _teke_ _iao_, "each person has his back" is a
proverb expressing the fact that the events of one's personal

history are an essential part, and likely cause, of one's
future. The attempt was made earlier on to understand how it
is that they see the world of ancestors, ghosts, and the
living as a single moral and temporal continuum. In a
different sense the usage implies that one will inevitably
confront the consequences of one's actions. The individual
who steals a cow, who commits adultery or who lies about his
true intentions to some other "will see his word tomorrow."

VII. _Era do ke me loic_, "every person keeps something in
their heart" is an Atuot proverb with very evident
similarities to the Dinka phrase, "what is inside a person is
like what is in the forest or in the river" (Lienhardt 1980:
74). The ethic that gives cultural value to pride and
independence is widely attested to in studies of Sudanese
Nilotes. On the one hand, this proverb states that people
have their own ends in mind, whatever their outward actions
might suggest or reveal to the contrary. In essence, one
never _really_ can predict the intent of some other since it is
an essential part of the private as opposed to the public
self, that the respect one demands from others obviates the
possibility of unfettered trust. With his head held at an
angle and with a smile in his eyes, a man explained,

> Every man is entitled to something of his very own.
> It happened once that a man was with his wife and
> decided to go on a journey. He started on his way,
> but decided to return to his home a short while
> later. In the meanwhile his wife had found a man
> to come and sleep with her in her husband's
> absence. When she heard her husband returning, the
> wife had time enough to hide the man under the
> sleeping hide. When the father returned and
> entered the hut a young child said, "Father, every
> person has something in their heart. I do, my
> mother does, you do, and so does the man under the
> sleeping hide."

A related proverb states _loic ke tau ne nien dial_, "the heart
is thinking all the days of a person's life."
     It should be self-evident that these few proverbs are
only representative of perhaps hundreds of others. A
consideration of these words in the present context draws
attention, once more, to the creative tension between the need
to share social and moral values and the constant effort, on
the part of the private self, to seek and define one's own
identity within these implicitly agreed-upon moral
constraints. Indeed, these few texts, along with extracts
from ox-songs and the discussion of personal names, represent
a broader morality that gives value to individual identity and
dignity on the one hand, and the supraindividual image of
Divinity, a being that makes human existence possible and
fulfilling. The creative tension between collective and
individual intent is constant. The individual in one sense
does not exist outside of the group. By way of illustration,
the social category "orphan" is one that creates feelings of
lament, if not horror. If one is taken ill in the company of
kin, there is some assurance that the afflicted will recover.
Conversely, to suffer similar misfortune far from one's kin

group is to find one's life quite on the borderline. An extreme example of this value is offered by Lienhardt (1981: 192). "On one occasion two young Dinka men met each other on a journey and were talking together in a friendly way when they found in conversation that they belonged to clans at feud with each other. One killed the other." At the other extreme is the situation where a wife takes offense at her husband's apparent lack of respect by referring to her by personal name in a public setting. It is unlikely that any human society professing such values could ever achieve a balance between such radical extremes. In any case, there are those individuals in Atuot communities who by their nature appear consumed by a passion to work forever against the values of community as well as the dignity of the individual. Collectively they form the amoral category Atuot term apeth, or witches, the topic of the concluding section of this chapter.

THE IMAGE AND REALITY OF THE WITCH

> Once, while discussing a different matter, I mentioned English owls, and was asked at once, "What, are there then witches also in England?"--to which somebody replied, "Of course, witches are everywhere" (Lienhardt 1951: 318).

The Atuot term ayuio can be translated in different contexts to mean jealousy, envy, covetousness, or greed. In the words of one man, "A person with ayuio may want to own something very much, even though it is not his nor could it be his. The thing itself will later go bad. It is like this. If you are cooking meat [and a person with ayuio sees it] the meat will burn in the fire or it will fall to a dog. It just happens like that." The illustration he chose may seem trivial, yet it points in any event to their view of a human tendency to seek gain at another's expense, or to act in vile self-interest. As a term that suggests some other as potentially responsible for a personal loss, the concept of ayuio is semantically contingent with the terms apeth and roadh, that is, "witch" or "sorcerer." An illustration of this semantic homology between the terms ayuio, apeth and roadh is provided through the examination of a very short passage from an Atuot ox-song:

> If a man has hated me
> He will see it later

This is sufficient and accurate as a literal translation though the intended commentary of the singer and composer invites additional comment. In the Atuot dialect, the term I translate as hatred, tiel, is cognate with the term for blood feud, ater. The beginnings of feuds are sometimes laid to the efforts of one person to possess something that is properly some other's. A desire to possess larger herds of cattle is certainly one of the most common illustrations offered by local peoples, but going back on one's word, literally "breaking a word," is another reason people offer for the genesis of long-seated hatreds between individuals and birth groups. In this sense the first line of the ox-song extract might also read, "If a man is covetous of me"; or "If he wants to claim or belittle what is properly mine." This gloss would easily shade into one meaning of ayuio, namely greed. Thus one could read in place of the Atuot text, "that greedy man." In their view, greed, covetousness, jealousy, and envy are all possible characteristics of the witch, so that the two lines cited above, if freely translated, would suggest,

> If this man is a witch
> I will see that he gets his own back

The song continues,

> The birds of prey will follow me to my pasture
> The hyenas will follow me

The gist of the message is that he will indeed get his own back: Scavenging animals will pick at and devour the rotting flesh of the man he will kill, the man who once tried to do him wrong. There are strong grounds on which to suggest that the singer will achieve his ends (see Howell 1954: 225; Howell and Lewis 1947: 158).

We might for the moment consider the proposition that "witches" and "witchcraft" are largely defined by words. An Atuot proverb that has a wider currency in the Nilotic Sudan suggests that the honest person speaks openly and in a direct manner: "Many words hide the truth, few words proclaim it." In contrast to this hopeful and trusting expectation is the image of the rumor-monger, gwan alope, who revels in the opportunity to spread lies about some other or to perpetuate accusations about the character of a person which have no basis in fact. The term aluope is here translated as rumor or gossip while related English usages would also be true to the Atuot meaning. The critical word is the adverb gwan, meaning genitor, hence the person who brings to life evil or otherwise malicious characterizations of some other: the person who tries to destroy, through his words, the public element of the self. This effort is conveyed in two lines from a different ox-song:

> Words are passed as whispers
> The words are not said straight

Here the singer invites public questioning of the moral integrity and unstated intentions of a suspected enemy. If one is not willing to be forthright and honest, in the Atuot moral imagination, one soon begins to question whether or not there is worthwhile reason to give that individual one's trust. Conversely, the Atuot phrase ca ling lat e du, "I hear [or understand] your word" implies some certainty in face-to-face relationships.

These observations have significance in a different context since it was my impression that Atuot rarely refer to some other as apeth directly. To do so would indicate that the slightest hint of trust had long ago evaporated between two individuals and that a violent confrontation between them was inevitable. The feeling is conveyed more commonly in song and it would be fair to say there is a social convention that encourages and condones this usage in the poetic and metaphorical medium of ox-songs in particular. As I have

noted, when individuals compose songs, the verse is often
memorized by others and in this way a larger group of
individuals learn of the experiences and reflections of their
elders in song. Thus, the individual perception of the vile
character of some other becomes a social fact. A short
passage from a song composed by Kuon Macek, a man with a well-
known reputation for protecting the dignity and property of
his family, provides a suitable illustration.

> This problem of Ngor continues to trouble me [as
>   indicated, the phrase "this trouble" or "this
>   hatred" is an idiomatic expression of a long-
>   lived animosity]
> Ngor is a man who has combined many things [i.e.,
>   his true intentions are unknown; he does not
>   speak plainly; he is devious, not to be
>   trusted]
> He is a man who defecates in the house
> And then waits so he can have intercourse with his
>   relatives
> Ngor does not know the shame of incest
> I ask the women of his family,
> What does the son of Baraic eat?
> How is he always able to satisfy his hunger? [i.e.,
>   why is he such a shameless glutton?]
> He is <u>apeth</u> that eats nuts and eels
> Ngor has many parts of his name
> He left behind sorcery [<u>roadh</u>]
> And took up intercourse with his uncle's daughter

It can be said with conviction that the singer is not implying
that the man in question is a witch, and thus behaves in this
manner. The meaning is, instead, he is a man so vile, he is a
witch. Similar images are conveyed in a different ox-song:

> The name of the family of Ajuong is known to all
> They have destroyed great families with their
>   witchcraft
> They bring only the problems of divorce
> When Ayuen opens his anus to defecate
> All the dogs run away
> The witch that walks with his tale . . .
> The family is remembered by the marriages they
>   would destroy
> Ayuen is the man who is a witch with his eye
> When he opens his anus to defecate
> The dogs howl

Here is the image of a man so vile, so base, so lacking in any
redeeming social value, that his insides are rotten. Even the
dogs who live off human refuse avoid him.
    Here I would like to repeat that in the course of field
work I collected only passing references to "witches" in
coversations I heard or participated in, even though such
references are not uncommon in the personal narrative of the
ox-song. I trust that any ethnographer in this region of the
southern Sudan would encounter a similar circumstance: Witches
and their activities do not consume the attentions of
pedestrian conversation. The following text was recorded in a
diary I kept:

We were sitting this afternoon in our hut drinking
millet beer and had just been talking about how
people used to attack an enemy's homestead, setting
fire to the thatched roof and then shooting people
with arrows as they ran from the hut seeking
safety. An older man said that if a person was
struck by an arrow he would urinate or defecate
immediately. I said something stupid: "Wouldn't
that be like a witch, defecating in a homestead?"
and the mood seemed to change quickly. I was told
to shut off the tape recorder so it wouldn't catch
people's words, and then another man said, "Apeth
is not spoken of just like that. When you say
something about apeth it is a serious word." Then
another man said if people even knew we were
talking about apeth we would become suspect of
being the same. When he was convinced that the
tape recorder wasn't running another man said,
"Apeth is passed along in a family. Such and such
a person is thought to be apeth so you do not want
to marry someone from that family. Apeth may be
the reason some people do not have cattle. Apeth
kills with his eyes and it is hard to ever catch
someone. Roadh works by night--you can see him
doing it. If a person enters a hut and someone
becomes sick after he leaves, maybe this is because
of apeth."

Although I did not know of a death that was thought to have
been directly caused by apeth, this does not mean that Atuot
do not entertain the possibility. One line from a song just
cited suggests that witchcraft destroys families, that it is
the cause of divorce. In this sense the image of the witch
strikes directly against a vital process of social
reproduction and thus images death. The point worth
emphasizing is that this is perceived in relation to the words
of an individual and his or her family. Their psychological
vocabulary leads to the suggestion that a witch is simply an
inherently untrustworthy person--one whose public self is
known through the combination of jealousy, greed, deceit, and
outright lies. Each of these dispositions is, in turn,
radically contrary to the values of individual identity and
community.

These cultural representations are found in neighboring
Nilotic communities in virtually identical form. According to
P. P. Howell (1954: 218), Nuer witches

are believed to cause harm and even death to those
who cross their path in anger, and sometimes
without any motive at all other than the inherent
evil of their personalities. . . . The peth might
be killed without grave danger of retaliation . . .
the act of revenge on the person of a witch by an
individual, or a few individuals who supported him,
was condoned by public opinion to such an extent
that the kinsmen of the deceased dared not to
retaliate, or perhaps themselves condoned the act,
considering themselves rid of a dangerous factor
within their own lineage.

The designation __apeth__ is but one of many possible assessments
Dinka make concerning the natural proclivities of the
individual.   To accuse someone of being __apeth__ is for them
among the worst of personal insults.   A common activity
attributed to witches by the Dinka is "eating" other people, a
metaphorical usage intended to suggest that the witch
"diminishes the good of those he attacks" (Lienhardt 1951:
305).   In Dinka tradition, a witch could have been killed
without fear of vengeance since such an individual "has
forfeited his value as a human being" (1951: 305).   Lienhardt
suggests that when an individual feels "envied, hated or
frustrated,   then   he   readily   thinks   of   himself   as
bewitched . . . a man who sees others as bearing malice
towards him is one who himself feels malice" (1951: 317).   The
same authority points out that by one measure the Dinka
concept __apeth__ can be interpreted as an imaginative fantasy--or
nightmare.   Yet by the measure of local knowledge the witch is
"indeed a reality which the Dinka know" (1951: 318).
     "Sharing a word" in the Atuot sense implies trust,
understanding, and even affection.   At the other end of a
spectrum of social relationships and the private self is the
reality of bitter animosity.   When one party to an implicit
social contract senses that he or she has been utterly
betrayed, in spite of hopeful confidence of some other
experience, then that person creates the other as a "witch,"
or what I think can also be understood as an inherently
untrustworthy individual.   Once the private self has lost
faith in another individual, one consequently begins to fear
that person, to distrust, in the most fundamental sense, the
real intentions of the other private self.   Lienhardt (1951:
102) offers the same interpretation of Dinka experience:

>   There is one more feature of witchcraft I should
>   mention too.   It is that generally, people suspect
>   those of bewitching them whom they suspect of
>   hating them, and whom, therefore, they hate.   As a
>   psychological   analysis   of   a   situation,   we
>   understand this perfectly.

If we do in fact understand this perfectly then the Atuot
image of the witch does not appear as a mystical fantasy but
rather as an objective characterization of one type of social
experience, created or interpreted by the individual.   The
witch is therefore not deviant but rather the monster, or the
nightmare, that potentially lurks in any social relationship.
     T. O. Biedelman (1986: 9) has recently reiterated an
important conclusion of comparative social studies, that in
all social environments, "we construct our scenarios of social
life from a complex mosaic of experience," configurations of
experience which combine collective images of the public self
with the self-conscious private person.   Though witches should
not be understood as deviant, they are in the Atuot view a
perverse extreme of unbounded individualism and thus manifest
public/private selves with no redeeming social value.   Mention
was made earlier in this chapter of the people-lions which
figure commonly in Atuot folktales.   A brief yarn explains
that "The lion does not reproduce many of its own kind because
it is harmful to human beings.   So Divinity cursed the lion so
that it would not be such a threat to human beings."   To my
understanding one of the morals embedded in this usage is that

Divinity is conceived of as a distant benevolent being that makes existence possible while there is no assurance that human character can be forever kept in check. So local life is also inspired by the Nilotic aphorism, "If you don't get it on the way, it will get you on the way back."

6.
NILOTIC PEOPLES IN A CHANGING WORLD

> Since all societies are constantly generating change
> internally or having it forced upon them externally,
> [social change] is more of a constant than
> extraordinary event. Looked at from this
> perspective any topic is one that is potentially
> seen from the standpoint of change. As a result,
> social change by its nature is a broad and ill-
> defined concept that cannot claim a distinct area of
> enquiry but rather allows for the choice of an
> infinite variety of areas for discussion (Arens
> 1976: 1-2).

The first chapter of this study reviewed some of the relevant
sources pertaining to external events which had a different
impact on the Atuot social world during the past two
centuries. For an even longer period, traders from the
northern Sudan perceived the southern environs to be an
unending source of slaves and exotic goods. During the latter
decades of the nineteenth century Nilotic peoples learned of
the Mahdi, a Muslim prophet who inspired the successful effort
to rid the northern Sudan of foreign political and military
domination. The Dinka in particular likened the Mahdi to one
of their own priestly figures, as a medium through which
Divinity speaks to human beings, even while Mahdist rule in
the Sudan was largely restricted to the northern part of the
country. The "recapture" of the Sudan by British-led forces
in 1898 set the stage for fifty-eight years of colonial rule.
This presence had no real impact on Nuer and Atuot communities
until the 1930s, save the losses of human and bovine life at
the hands of British punitive expeditions. Under the strict
directives of British administration northern and southern
regions of the Sudan were in effect governed as distinct and
separate colonies. Under the careful watch of bureaucrats in
Khartoum, a variety of Christian missionary societies were
given the task of "educating the natives" in western moral,
legal, and religious values (see Burton 1985a). No permanent
mission was ever established in Atuot country, and while few
Atuot entered the church to find salvation, many who attended
mission schools elsewhere in the south did learn of different
worlds through the medium of the English language. At the

time of our first visit to their country, members of the first
cadre of mission-educated boys then held positions of
leadership in the secular government of the southern Sudan.
Considered at a further remove, much of Nilotic history and
prehistory is a record of movement, of migration, and of
emergent dialects and ethnic categories. These internally
generated processes are, however, much different from the day-
to-day innovations introduced during the colonial period.

A vocal minority of northern Sudanese intellectuals led
the charge for Sudanese independence in 1956. Even though
many British officials imagined their tenure in the country
might last three or four more decades, they ceded their
authority to the Sudanese and left behind two countries, the
one defined by a common language, religious traditions, and
political organization and the other, in the south, comprised
of many distinct ethnic groups and languages whose sole
integrating factor was the presence of the British
administration. The constitution which detailed the
organization and structure of the new polity had been
conceived of largely by the intellectual and political elite
of the northern Sudan, almost entirely to the exclusion of
southern interests and input. In a majority of cases the
positions of administrative authority vacated by British
citizens were assumed by northerners. In retrospect it is not
at all surprising that civil war so closely followed the
independence movement.

In 1972 the war between the north and south was
officially brought to an end with the signing of a peace
treaty in the capital city of Ethiopia. In March of 1977 the
semiautonomous regional government of the southern Sudan
orchestrated a public celebration of the first five years of
peace that had followed the signing of the Addis Ababa accord.
The festivities in Juba were broadcast live by the radio
station there and included a speech by then President of Sudan
Jaffar Nimeri, shorter remarks by ranking officials in the
regional government, as well as songs and dances performed by
representatives of the many different ethnic groups in the
south. (A group of twelve young men and women from Atuot
communities placed first in the dance competition.) The
middle years of the past decade held forth great expectations
in the minds of southern leaders. At that time, the Sudan was
the second largest recipient of American foreign aid in Africa
and government ministries were buzzing with schemes and plans
for economic growth and "development." The process of
establishing peace in the southern region appeared to be a
success. When the former president visited the town of Yirol
in 1975, a large dance was organized in the small village
square and Akutei Muokjok, a local man of reknown who has
since died, led the gathering in song:

        Nimeri of Bahr-el-Ghazal
        Our high Premier, our high Premier
        Our high Premier of the South
        Premier of Sudan, I will dance
        You see our Premier come here
        The Premier of honor
        Come with your heads turned to him
        All of you greet him
        Greet the Premier with your heads

From the local perspective, Nimeri was the living symbol of the new government that was responsible for bringing about an end to the civil war. Indeed, "the government" and "Nimeri" were one and the same. A smaller entourage of southern officials visited the administrative towns on the Bahr-el-Ghazal Province following the Juba celebrations. In Yirol, they gathered at the new home of one of these officials, a man from the Luac section of Atuot. As we drank tea after a meal in his homestead, a number of officials expressed their real surprise that a number of localized skirmishes that had occurred in the province had not, in fact, renewed the fighting. In other words, five years after the establishment of peace the memories of war-related horrors were still very close to the surface.

Beginning in 1982 and continuing at the time of this writing, a second civil war has once again divided the fragile unity of the Sudan. It is useful to recall some of the experiences of Atuot and other Nilotic pastoralists from the period of the first civil war as a means of understanding the effects of present realities on local life. As I have noted, bitter memories of the war were very much a part of adult reflections at the time of our visit. In the village of Anuol in Kuek, an older man told us how a troop of northern Sudanese soldiers had arrived in the early hours of dawn.

> So many people--at least it sounded this way because
> of their guns--came out of the trucks and just went
> on shooting in all directions. What you see here
> now is just a road rebuilt since we first made it
> for the British. Before the war this was a good
> village, with many people and large gardens of
> millet. Then, on that morning, people died before
> they were even awake. I was one of the lucky ones.
> I escaped with my daughter to the forest. There was
> no time to look back. If you looked back, you would
> just be killed. No question on that. You just ran
> and hoped you would live. There were no Anya Nya
> [the common name of the guerrilla movement] in the
> village, but the Arabs destroyed the village anyway.
> Twenty-six people died that morning.

At the mention of the war it was difficult to find someone who had not suffered the death of a mother, father, sister, or brother. Others related how they had been arrested by northern troops in their homesteads. When they pleaded ignorance about the location of Anya Nya troops, the government soldiers smeared their eyes with the dust of crushed chili peppers and beat them in the head with rifle butts. At the time of field work, one sensed considerable trust and respect for those who had fought as guerrillas.

Perhaps the most common recourse for survival was to abandon village settlements and live in the forest, where herds could be protected, and then move to the <u>toic</u> with the coming of the dry season, living here on milk and riverine resources. Only a very few people we spoke with returned to their homesteads and found them intact. More commonly it was the case that huts had been burned along with standing millet cultivations. A typical rationale for open and wide-scale destruction (quite like the situation in the early decades of colonial rule) was the government suspicion that local peoples

were offering food to guerrillas thought to be in the area.
Those who did not flee to the forest, or seek refuge in Zaire,
Uganda, or Kenya, built small huts on the periphery of
administrative towns which grew considerably at the time.
Those who were encountered by government patrols on the open
road were immediately held suspect.

By the nature of their occupation, individuals involved
in the cattle trade of the southern Sudan (see Burton 1978a)
were often met by such patrols. Even in the best of times and
conditions, the cattle trade is an arduous undertaking. A
number of younger men often drive a herd of thirty cattle up
to a distance of 200 miles. During the first war, cattle
traders were caught in a peculiar relationship with the Anya
Nya and Arab merchants in the small towns. One man summarized
the experience of many others he knew.

> A man had to possess two licenses. The first was
> given by the Anya Nya and the other by the Arabs.
> When you traveled with the herds through the forest
> and on roads you had to hide these in a cloth by
> your penis. If you met Anya Nya you took out their
> certificate. When you met Arabs on the road you
> showed them the other one. When Anya Nya tried to
> steal cattle you had to give them money and a bull.
> Then they would let you go on your way. You could
> pass by. With the Arabs, they asked you if you had
> seen the Anya Nya in the forest. If you said never,
> they took all your cattle and put you in prison. In
> the morning you would go to the court and say you
> did not see any of the Anya Nya in the forest. Then
> you had to show the court your certificate. The
> Arabs said, "If you walk through the forest, you
> must see the Anya Nya." They would never believe
> what you said, so you always had to pay a fine.

In Juba we spoke with a number of Dinka from the Bor area who
said it was common during the war for people to live on the
Nile, drifting on the floating islands of vegetation called
sudd. Historically the sudd vegetation had been a natural
barrier, clogging the Nile and its tributaries, thus
protecting southern Sudanese peoples from hostile assaults
from northern traders and slavers. As one man said,

> In 1965 my family lived on a floating mound of
> papyrus reeds. We had to do this for two reasons.
> First, the Arabs would just shoot you and there was
> no place to be safe. The only food we had was fish.
> Second, the land became so flooded cattle could not
> live and people could not make gardens. Even if we
> tried to make a garden, then it would would just be
> destroyed.

Experiences such as these became historicized in song. In one
of his ox-songs Acinbaai Takpiny, an adult man of Luac,
recalls,

> The cattle camp was deserted in my absence
> The people have become confused
> I led all the people in the fight of the black
>   people

Against the soldiers of the North
Now the people have been helped by a woman who bore
    Nimeri
We slept in the forest like buffalo
Our land is now calm--
But it was robbed by the Arabs
You see them--
They have intercourse with their sisters
Our land was robbed by the Arabs

A related experience is remembered in a song translated by F.
M. Deng (1972: 150):

How does the spoiling of the land come about
Our land is closed in a prison cell
The Arabs have spoiled our land
Spoiled our land with bearded guns
Is the color of skin such a thing
That the government should draw its guns?
A country we took back from foreigners
A country for which we fought together

With assistance provided by a number of international
agencies people began to move back to their home territories
and modest efforts were made by the government to encourage
faith in the new regime. One morning over tea in our hut, the
man in charge of resettlement in Atuot country said

Only a small number of people from the Atuot area
became refugees. Most stayed in the area and moved
away into the toic or away from the roads into the
forest. People did not receive any compensation for
their homes that had been destroyed or for their
gardens or herds. Many people came into the town to
collect free clothing, cooking utensils and seed,
but there was no one to know who really needed these
things most. Too many of the government people who
were supposed to give these things kept too much for
themselves.

During the 1977 celebration of five years of peace, Deng spoke
with an Atuot elder in Juba about his perception of past
events. His remarks are atypical in that he had been a
ranking official within the Anya Nya. Conversely, they
positively reflect a quality of the relationship between
northern and southern Sudanese at the time. According to
Stephen Thongkol Anyijong (Deng 1980: 130),

The war is going on. We [the north and south]
cannot say we are relatives. The war is still on.
There is no relationship. . . . Many things are
already showing themselves. For instance, our
children are being prevented from learning English
in school. Respect toward people is missing . . .
we are still being insulted. Some people still call
us slaves. Some of us are still actually slaves.
We cannot marry their daughters. . . . They take our
girls and turn them into prostitutes, and when they
have made them prostitutes, they send them back.
They are still controlling our economy: they are the

people who own the shops; and all the money is still
in their hands. The only thing which has improved
is security. . . . Southerners are only children.
If they are told that this has gone well, they
celebrate and sing and say "Oh, it's wonderful, it's
wonderful" and they don't know what is going
on. . . . So, the way I see things, problems have
not ended. The worst is still to come; the worst is
in our hearts . . . this war has not ended; the
problem has not ended. It is Nimeri who is
containing it. If Nimeri were not here, people
would die.

Anyijong concluded his observations with these words (1980:
132):

What has been given to us [in the Addis Ababa
agreement] is the little portion that is given to a
dog, the portion that is thrown on the ground. This
Regional Automony is one in which food is thrown to
the ground and dogs jump on it and start eating. A
clever dog bites a bit and looks around. He takes a
piece of meat and looks around. But if a stupid dog
goes in and eats without thinking about being
attacked by something like a hyena, eating
everything without worrying what's going on around
him, he may die. . . . We should look around so that
we get good doctors, so that we improve our roads,
so that we improve our education. We must improve
our cultivation so that if hunger comes, we don't
have to depend on the north.

In many ways these comments, like the views of others who
had similar experiences during the war, have proven to be
prophetic. In the mid-1970s the Sudan had become the meeting
ground of Arab petro-dollars and Western technology and one
often read that with some 200 million acres of arable land
that was largely undeveloped, the country could soon become
the "breadbasket" of Africa and the Middle East. During the
same period, the Sudan was the second largest recipient of
American foreign aid in Africa. The United States State
Department saw this as a practical means of thwarting Soviet
influence, or at least countering the socialist governments of
Ethiopia and Libya. The Shell Oil Corporation began drilling
for promising oil reserves in the area south of Bentuei in
Nuer country. A consortium of European companies began work
on the so-called Jonglai canal, a vast, artificial channel
imagined since the first years of colonial rule that would
divert flood waters from the Nile swamps northward, to further
agricultural development schemes in the northern Sudan and
Egypt. President Numeri visited Washington and returned with
promises to revamp and revitalize his aging Soviet technology
with new American products, such as aircraft and munitions
systems. However, in the last years of that decade, as Deng
(1984: 171) notes, "debts began to mature, oil bills began to
soar, the International Monetary Fund began to impose economic
measures [and] the gap between aspirations and realities
became unbridgeable."

To the educated southern elite an inordinate proportion
of funds and manpower for development were restricted to the

northern region. When oil finds were in fact made, the
Khartoum government announced that the resource would be
refined and distributed from the north. As further studies
were undertaken and assessed, it appeared that the professed
benefits for southern peoples were an illusion and that in
this case as well, the north rather than the south would reap
the benefits. Studies indicated that the diversion of Nile
waters would radically affect everything from rainfall
patterns to riverine resources to the migration of game. In
essence, the economic and social systems of Nuer and Dinka who
lived in the path of the projected canal would be destroyed.
Meanwhile, in Khartoum, a $9-billion debt on interest payments
for loans had forced the government to revalue the Sudanese
pound, and basic resources such as gas, flour, sugar, and tea
quadrupled in price in the space of a few months. Many of the
same products became scarcer and scarcer in the southern
regions. As a final effort to consolidate his weakening
government and political alliances, Nimeri decreed in 1983
that the regional autonomy of the southern region, as outlined
in the Addis Ababa accord, was now defunct. In the place of
regional autonomy and traditional courts of law, the entire
Sudan would follow the Sharia form of Islamic law wherein a
suspected thief has a hand amputated in retribution, an
accused adulterer is stoned to death in public, and so on. As
Deng (1984: 171; see also Malwal 1985) writes, "The reaction
was a spontaneous return to the conditions of the seventeen-
year civil war and the establishment of the Sudan People's
Liberation Movement, with its military wing, Sudan People's
Liberation Army." Soon after, in April 1985, a popular
uprising in Khartoum transformed Nimeri from president to
political exile. More recently, virtually all forms of
transport and communication between the northern and southern
Sudan has ceased, and beyond the towns of Wau, Malakal, and
Juba, the countryside has been occupied by the new guerrilla
army. The town of Yirol now stands as a scattered pile of
rubble following a successful guerrilla attack on a small
government outpost there. When northern soldiers occupied the
small hospital seeking refuge, the guerrillas destroyed these
buildings as well. The government evacuated the remaining
residents of the town, primarily itinerant Sudanese merchants,
in December 1985.

The popularly acknowledged leader of the southern army
and the People's Liberation Movement, John Garang (who was
awarded his doctorate in economics in the United States),
professes two major objectives, one of which has already come
to be. His first goal was to overthrow Nimeri "and his
repressive dictatorship by force of arms. . . . The second
objective follows from the first: to install in Khartoum a
government of the majority of Sudanese who have been oppressed
by the minority for so long" (cited in Malwal 1985: 41).

Against the background of this series of facts one can
only wonder about, rather than predict, the way in which the
traditions of Atuot and neighboring peoples will be affected.
The contemporary situation is quite different from that during
the first civil war, since government troops are not widely
dispersed in the countryside. Further, popular support of the
guerrilla movement is more widespread, more entrenched, than
with the Anya Nya. Localized warfare in certain regions of
the south, particularly to the east and west of Juba, has
interrupted local life to the extent that some 100,000 people

are now living in squalid refugee camps in Ethiopia, Kenya, the Central African Republic, Uganda, and Zaire (Sudan People's Liberation Movement, 1985). Recent reports on conditions in Atuot country beyond Yirol indicate, in contrast, that many people have simply taken the time-honored recourse of moving with their herds deeper into the forest, relying primarily on riverine and bovine resources to sustain their livelihood.

The immediate consequences of renewed warfare are varied. Among the more obvious is the fact that a generation of young people will not have the opportunity to gain a formal education. The already meager medical supplies once provided by the government are no longer available in the abandoned rural clinics, and as the cultivation of millet decreases while people abandon homesteads, prospects of prolonged hunger may be expected. Each of these events alone has serious implications for the future, but as they now work in combination there will be dire, if localized, conditions. But one must remember at the same time that some measure of suffering has always been expected and confronted in Atuot as in other pastoral Nilotic communities. As subsistence horticulturalists and pastoralists, they have always provided for their own means in the absence of external support. Indeed, for as long as they have been exposed to exotic and novel elements of culture, Atuot have adopted only those elements which they find to be valuable in supplementing tradition. Surely others who have lived in Nilotic communities in the Sudan are aware that local peoples regard strangers as truly human only to the degree that they acknowledge or adopt local values. This is one of the reasons older people recall the days of British administration with sad longing. Even though the local official rarely if ever tried to mimic local usages, Britons were appreciated because, to a large measure, they left people to live as they wished. Conversely, northern Sudanese are not trusted since they have always sought to impose their own language, religion, and law. As W. Arens notes in the epigraph to this chapter, social change is a constant rather than extraordinary process, and surely this is one of the most dominant themes in Nilotic ethnology and prehistory. What has remained constant in their experience is a mode of cultural identity, especially as this applies to language usage. One would like to imagine that with the resources of their cultural heritage, and in the possession of their herds, the Atuot, like the Dinka and Nuer, will survive the present war as they have other violent confrontations in their history.

Appendix I.
BRIDEWEALTH CATTLE

Adult men are quick to offer general statements about the
proper distribution of cattle between families that publicly
and legally establish a marriage, and even younger children
speak of relatives in terms that elucidate the manner in which
cattle establish kinship. The ideal figures offered, however,
should be understood as a useful abstraction or guide since
there is considerable variation in any particular case. The
primary variables in each case are (1) the number of animals
exchanged and (2) the pattern of their distribution. The
following discussion draws upon data collected in a survey of
Atuot marriages, volunteered information from open-ended
discussions and firsthand observations. All three sources
provide useful data though, by itself, no single source is
particularly reliable. This results from a number of factors.
On the one hand, few individuals are willing to offer
information about the number of animals which comprise a
family herd, nor do they wish to volunteer information about
the location of particular animals. A second problem in
collecting valid data is that the Atuot, like many other
peoples, sometimes seek to achieve certain cultural ideals but
fall short of the mark. Nonetheless, they may boast of the
number of cattle exchanged as bridewealth while the actual
number of cattle was significantly less. The data in my
survey in which I have the greatest confidence was provided by
men with whom I felt I shared honest and candid intentions.
Even though the number of cattle exchanged as bridewealth may
have been inflated in a number of cases, the cultural ideal
expressed, ranging from thirty to forty animals, has intrinsic
interest for different reasons (see Kelly 1985: 189-225). E.
E. Evans-Pritchard (1951: 74) addresses a closely related
matter in writing "if one asks a Nuer how, on marriage, the
bridewealth is divided, he gives at once its ideal
distribution and it will be found that the actual distribution
in any particular marriage is made to approximate as far as
possible to this ideal."

In the attempt to standardize "traditional" usage, the
local government has defined bridewealth as "cattle payable
[sic] as compensation" to the family of the bride by the
family of the groom. In the words of the local court, "The
relatives of both parties to a marriage shall be free to fix

the number of bridewealth cattle as well as the manner and
time of their delivery." Where a man and his agnatic kin have
failed to make an offer that is acceptable to the wife's
family, the local court now has the power to order that he and
his relatives provide thirty cows and six bulls as
bridewealth. If nothing else, the court decree standardizes
the traditional ideal. Before the formal exchange of
bridewealth cattle, the future mother-in-law of the groom
asserts her claim to what Atuot call apet piny, a promise of
five to ten cows. These cattle may not be handed over until
the formal exchange, but establish the marriage to be as a
social fact. At the same time, the father of the groom agrees
to give an ox to the father of the bride, echoing a similar
intent. The mother of the bride is then given an additional
ox, "to ensure a peaceful settlement of the marriage. The cow
is slaughtered by the elders of the girl's family, who ask
that the marriage will be seen and blessed by Divinity and
that it will bring many children."

The ensuing process is characterized in a text offered by
an adult man. "On the evening before the day chosen for the
settlement of cows, the family and relatives of the girl come
to the man's homestead and are fed milk, millet porridge, and
millet beer. That evening a bull called buol [lit., a gift]
is sacrificed and is eaten by both families. In the morning
they begin to put down [i.e., count] the cows, beginning with
the bulls. Those who have a right to a small part of the
bridewealth are counted, and their claims are made." As among
the Nuer the interests of ancestors and ghosts must first be
recognized (see Evans-Pritchard 1951: 81). Another text
continues, "The counting of cows comes to those who have the
right to the greatest number of cattle, the girl's father, his
brothers, and the brother of the mother of the bride. After
the father, the eldest brother has a claim, then the younger
brother, then the brother of the girl's mother. Each has a
right to claim ten cows. The remainder of the cows will be
claimed by the elder and younger brothers of the girl. But
before they speak, the brother of the mother must be heard."
Based on a number of texts collected in the course of field
work, an ideal distribution of bridewealth cattle would be as
follows:

        Father of the bride: 10 cows
        Elder brother of the bride: 10 cows
        Next brother of the bride: 5 cows
        Paternal uncle of the bride: 10 cows
        Maternal uncle of the bride: 10 cows

In local circumstances, at the time of the bridewealth
exchange, one often hears the phrase "so and so will be given
a cow of no color (thil ciet). This is in effect a promise to
exchange some animal at some point in the future. The phrase
indicates that the donee agrees to a claim, but has no cattle
at hand at the time and thus implies, "I promise to come up
with this animal as soon as I am able." On both sides of the
exchange, individuals are calculating what they can give or
claim, and what use they will make of the animals. For
example, a man will make a promise to give a cow of a certain
color in the expectation that he will soon receive such an
animal through the marriage of a sister. On his part, the
maternal uncle may be adamant in his claim for a specific

number of cattle as he is in the midst of settling a marriage
of his own, or to gain animals he may be expected to exchange
in the marriage of one of his paternal kin. As noted in the
text, a family that enjoys wealth in particularly large herds
can expect demands of larger-than-normal bridewealth, but will
also expect to supplement herds through the marriage of a
daughter. In the examination of more usual exchanges, one
realizes that the ties that bind families together are often
based upon promises and stated intentions. When, after some
time has passed and a woman has given birth to a number of
healthy children, demands for cattle yet to be exchanged are
less frequent. In other words, bridewealth exchanges can be
understood in one sense as representing reciprocal relations
which all hope will emerge, a fact which further underscores
the local meaning of the institution.

Appendix II.
ATUOT RELATIONSHIP
TERMINOLOGY

PATERNAL SIDE

Father: Gwar
Father's Sister: Wac
Father's Brother: Gwalen
Father's Father: Gwadong
Father's Father's Father: Gwadong
Father's Father's Brother: Gwadong
Father's Brother's Sister: Wac
Husband of Father's Sister: Cou Wac
Husband of Ego's Sister: Cou Imar
Sister's Son: Gatimar
Sister's Daughter: Gatimar
Sister: Imar
Brother's Son: Gat Demar
Brother: Demar
Father's Mother: Madong
Father's Mother's Brother: Ner
Father's Mother's Sister: Iman Madong
Father's Mother's Brother's Child: Gat Nere
Husband of Sister's Son: Cou Gat Imar
Husband of Sister's Daughter: Cou Gat Imar

MATERNAL SIDE

Mother: Mar
Mother's Sister: Malen
Mother's Brother: Ner
Mother's Mother: Madong
Mother's Mother's Mother: Madong
Mother's Mother's Brother: Ner
Mother's Brother's Sister: Gatnere
Mother's Sister's Husband: Cou Malen
Mother's Brother's Wife: Ceknere
Mother's Sister's Daughter: Iman Malen
Mother's Sister's Son: Gat Malen
Mother's Father: Gwadong
Mother's Father's Brother: Gwadong
Mother's Father's Sister: Iman Gwadong

REFERENCES

al-Rahim, M. 1969. _Imperialism and Nationalism in the Sudan_.
    Oxford: Clarendon Press.
Arens, W. 1976 (ed.). _A Century of Change in Eastern Africa_.
    The Hague: Mouton.
Barth, F. 1961. _Nomads of South Persia_. New York: Little,
    Brown.
Baxter, P. T. 1972. "Absence Makes the Heart Grow Fonder:
    Some Suggestions Why Witchcraft Accusations Are Rare
    Among East African Pastoralists." In M. Gluckman (ed.),
    The Allocation of Responsibility. Manchester: Manchester
    University Press.
Beidelman, T. O. 1986. _Moral Imagination in Kaguru Modes of_
    Thought. Bloomington: Indiana University Press.
Beltrame, G. 1961. "Some Notes on the Distribution of
    Nilotic Peoples in the Middle 19th Century." _Sudan Notes_
    and Records 42: 118-22.
Beshir, M. O. 1969. _Educational Development in the Sudan,_
    _1898-1954_. London: Oxford University Press.
Brown, R. G. 1969. _Fashoda Reconsidered: The Impact of_
    Domestic Politics on French Policy in Africa 1893-1898.
    Baltimore: The Johns Hopkins Press.
Bryan, M. A. and A. N. Tucker. 1948. _Distribution of the_
    Nilotic and Nilo-Hamitic Languages of Africa. London:
    Oxford University Press.
Burton, J. W. 1974. "Some Nuer Notions of Purity and Danger."
    Anthropos 69: 517-36.
___. 1977. "The Peoples Called Atuot." _Sudan Now_ 12: 42-44.
___. 1978a. "Ghost Marriage and the Cattle Trade Among the
    Atuot of the Southern Sudan." _Africa_ 48: 398-405.
___. 1978b. "Ghosts, Ancestors and Individuals Among the
    Atuot of the Southern Sudan." _Man_ (N.S.) 13: 600-617.
___. 1979. "The Wave Is My Mother's Husband: A Piscatorial
    Theme in Pastoral Nilotic Ethnology." _Journal of Asian_
    and African Studies 14: 204-18.
___. 1980a. "Atuot Age Categories and Marriage." _Africa_ 50:
    146-60.
___. 1980b. "Atuot Totemism." _Journal of Religion in Africa_
    11: 93-105.
___. 1980c. "The Village and the Cattle Camp: Aspects of
    Atuot Religion." In I. Karp and C. Bird (eds.),

Explorations in African Systems of Thought. Bloomington: Indiana University Press.

Burton, J. W. 1980d. "Women and Men in Marriage: Some Atuot Texts." *Anthropos* 75: 710-20.

____. 1981a. "Atuot Ethnicity: An Aspect of Nilotic Ethnology." *Africa* 51: 496-510.

____. 1981b. *God's Ants: A Study of Atuot Religion*. St. Augustin: Anthropos.

____. 1981c. "The Moon Is a Sheep: A Feminine Principle in Atuot Cosmology." *Man* (N.S.) 16: 441-51.

____. 1981d. "Pastoral Nilotes and British Colonialism." *Ethnohistory* 28: 125-33.

____. 1981e. "The Proverb: An Aspect of Atuot Collective Thought." *Folklore* 92: 84-91.

____. 1981f. "Sacrifice: A Polythetic Class of Atuot Religious Thought." *Journal of Religion in Africa* 12: 83-94.

____. 1981g. "Some Observations on the Social History of the Atuot Dialect of Nilotic." M. L. Bender and T. Schadberg (eds.), *Nilo-Saharan*. Leiden: University Press.

____. 1981h. "Sudanese Independence and the Status of Nilotic Women." *Africa Today* 28: 54-61.

____. 1982a. "The Divination of Atuot Philosophy." *Journal of Religion in Africa* 13: 1-10.

____. 1982b. "Figurative Language and the Definition of Experience: The Role of Ox-Songs in Atuot Social Theory." *Anthropological Linguistics* 24: 263-79.

____. 1982c. "Gifts Again: Complimentary Prestation Among the Pastoral Nilotes of the Southern Sudan." *Ethnology* 21: 55-61.

____. 1982d. "Lateral Symbolism and Atuot Cosmology." *Africa* 52: 69-85.

____. 1982e. "The Names People Play: Atuot Metaphors of Self." *Anthropos* 77: 831-51.

____. 1982f. "Nilotic Women: A Diachronic Perspective." *Journal of Modern African Studies* 20: 467-93.

____. 1983. "Same Time, Same Space: Observations on the Morality of Kinship in Pastoral Nilotic Societies." *Ethnology* 22: 109-19.

____. 1985a. "Christians, Colonists and Conversions: A View from the Nilotic Sudan." *Journal of Modern African Studies* 23: 349-69.

____. 1985b. "Why Witches? Some Comments on the Explanation of 'Illusions' in Anthropology." *Ethnology* 24: 281-96.

Buxton, J. 1955. "The Mandari." in P. P. Howell (ed.), *The Equatorial Nile Project*. Khartoum: Government Printer.

____. 1963. "Girls Courting Huts in Western Mandari." *Man* 56: 49-51.

____. 1973. *Religion and Healing in Mandari*. Oxford: Clarendon Press.

____. 1975. "Initiation and Bead Sets in Western Mandari." In J. Beattie and R. G. Lienhardt (eds.), *Studies in Social Anthropology*. Oxford: Clarendon Press.

Collins, R. O., 1963. *The Southern Sudan, 1883-1898*. New Haven: Yale University Press.

____. 1967. "The Aliab Dinka Uprising and Its Suppression." *Sudan Notes and Records* 48: 77-90.

____. 1971. *Land Beyond the Rivers*. New Haven: Yale University Press.

____. 1985. *Shadows in the Grass*. New Haven: Yale University Press.

Comyn, D. C. 1911. _Service and Sport in the Sudan_. London: Duckworth.

Crazzolara, J. P. 1933. _Outlines of a Nuer Grammar_. Vienna: Anthropos Institut.

___. 1950. _The Lwoo_. Verona: Missioni Africane.

David, N. P. et al. 1981. "Excavations in the Southern Sudan." _Azania_ 16: 7-54.

Dempsey, J. 1956. _Mission on the Nile_. New York: Philosophical Library.

Deng, F. M. 1966. "Property and Value-Interplay Among the Nilotes of the Southern Sudan." _Iowa Law Review_ 51 (3): 541-60.

___. 1971. _Tradition and Modernization: A Challenge for Law Among the Dinka of the Sudan_. New Haven: Yale University Press.

___. 1972. _The Dinka of the Sudan_. New York: Holt, Rinehart and Winston.

___. 1973. _The Dinka and Their Songs_. Oxford: Clarendon Press.

___. 1974. _Dinka Folktales: African Stories from the Sudan_. New York: Africana Publishing Co.

___. 1978. _Africans of Two Worlds: The Dinka in Afro-Arab Sudan_. New Haven: Yale University Press.

___. 1980. _Dinka Cosmology_. London: Ithaca Press.

___. 1984. "Epilogue" in _The Dinka of the Sudan_. Prospect Heights: Waveland.

Evans-Pritchard, E. E. 1935. "The Nuer: Tribe and Clan." _Sudan Notes and Records_ 18: 37-38.

___. 1936. "Daily Life of the Nuer in Dry Season Camps." In L. H. D. Buxton (ed.), _Custom Is King: Essays Presented to R. R. Marett_. London: Hutchinson.

___. 1937. _Witchcraft, Oracles and Magic Among the Azande_. Oxford: Clarendon Press.

___. 1939. "Nuer Time Reckoning." _Africa_ 12: 189-216.

___. 1940. _The Nuer_. Oxford: Clarendon Press.

___. 1945. _Some Aspects of Marriage and the Family Among the Nuer_. Lusaka: Rhodes-Livingston Institute.

___. 1950. "Nilotic Studies." _Journal of the Royal Anthropological Institute_ 80: 1-6.

___. 1951. _Kinship and Marriage Among the Nuer_. Oxford: Clarendon Press.

___. 1956. _Nuer Religion_. Oxford: Clarendon Press.

___. 1960. "The Sudan: An Ethnographic Survey." In S. Diamond (ed.), _Culture in History_. New York: Columbia University Press.

___. 1971. "Sources, with Particular Reference to the Southern Sudan." _Cahiers d'Etudes Africanes_ 11: 129-79.

Fergusson, V. H. 1921. "The Nuong Nuer." _Sudan Notes and Records_ 4: 146-56.

Gessi, R. 1892. _Seven Years in the Soudan_. London: Sampson, Low and Marston.

Giddens, A. 1976. _New Rules of the Sociological Method_. New York: Basic Books.

Gluckman, M. 1956. "The Peace in the Feud." In M. Gluckman, _Custom and Conflict in Africa_. Oxford: Basil Blackwell.

Gray, R. 1961. _A History of the Southern Sudan_. London: Oxford University Press.

Grunnet, N. 1962. "An Ethnographic-Ecological Survey of the Relationship Between the Dinka and Their Cattle." _Folk_ 4: 5-20.

Harrison, M. H. 1955. _Report on a Grazing Survey of the Sudan_. Khartoum: Government Printer.

Henderson, H. D. 1953. _The Making of the Modern Sudan_. London: Oxford University Press.

Hill, R. 1965. "Government and Christian Missions in the Anglo-Egyptian Sudan." _Middle East Studies_ 1: 113-34.

Howell, P. P. 1953. "Some Observations on Earthly Spirits Among the Nuer." _Man_ 53: 85-88.

____. 1954. _A Manual of Nuer Law_. London: Oxford University Press.

____. 1954. (ed.) _The Equatorial Nile Project and Its Effect in the Anglo-Egyptian Sudan_, Vol. 2.   Khartoum: Government Printer.

____. 1955. (ed.) _The Equatorial Nile Project and Its Effect in the Anglo-Egyptian Sudan_. Khartoum: Sudan Government.

Howell, P. P. n.d. "Colonial Rule and Nuer Response." Paper Read in a Seminar on Colonial Rule and Local Response, School of Oriental and African Studies.

Howell, P. P. and B. A. Lewis. 1947. "Nuer Ghoals: A Form of Witchcraft." _Sudan Notes and Records_ 28: 157-69.

Jackson, H. C. 1923. _The Nuer of the Upper Nile Province_. Khartoum: El Hadra Press.

Johnson, D. 1979. "Colonial Policy and Prophets: The Nuer Settlement, 1929-30." _Journal of the Anthropological Society of Oxford_ 10: 1-20.

____. 1980. _History and Prophecy Among the Nuer of the Southern Sudan_. Thesis, University of California, Los Angeles.

____. 1986. "Judicial Regulation and Administrative Control: Customary Law and the Nuer, 1898-1954." _Journal of African History_ 27: 59-78.

Joshni, N. R. et al. 1957. _Types and Breeds of African Cattle_. Rome: United Nations.

Kelly, R. 1985. _The Nuer Conquest: The Structure and Development of an Expansionist System_. Ann Arbor: The University of Michigan Press.

Kiggen, J. 1948. _Nuer-English Dictionary_. London: St. Joseph's Society for Foreign Missions.

Lévi-Strauss, C. 1974. _Tristes Tropiques_ (trans. J. and D. Weightman). New York: Atheneum.

Lienhardt, R. G. 1951. "Some Notions of Witchcraft Among the Dinka." _Africa_ 21:   303-18.

____. 1958. "The Western Dinka." In J. Middleton and D. Tait (eds.), _Tribes Without Rulers_. London: Routledge and Kegan Paul.

____. 1961. _Divinity and Experience: The Religion of the Dinka_. Oxford: Clarendon Press.

____. 1963. "Some Dinka Representations of the Relationship Between the Sexes." In I. Schapera (ed.), _Studies in Kinship and Marriage_. London: Royal Anthropological Institute.

____. 1970. "The Situation of Death: An Aspect of Anuak Philosophy." In M. Douglas (ed.), _Witchcraft Confessions and Accusations_. London: Tavistock Publications.

____. 1974. "Primitive Religion." _Encyclopaedia Britannica_, pp. 1040-47.

____. 1975. "Getting Your Own Back: Some Themes in Nilotic Myth." In J. Beattie and R. G. Lienhardt (eds.), _Studies in Social Anthropology._ Oxford: Clarendon Press.

____. 1980. "Self: Public, Private. Some African Representations." *Journal of the Anthropological Society of Oxford* 11: 69-82.

Lienhardt, R. G. 1981. "The Sudan--Aspects of the South. Government Among Some of the Nilotic Peoples, 1947-1952." *Journal of the Anthropological Society of Oxford* 12: 185-198.

___. 1985. "From Study to Field, and Back." *Times Literary Supplement* (London) June 7: 647-48.

Lowie, R. 1935. *The Crow Indians.* New York: Holt, Rinehart and Winston.

Malwal, B. 1985. *The Sudan: A Second Challenge to Nationhood.* New York: Thornton Books.

Mauss, M. 1972. *A General Theory of Magic.* London: Routledge and Kegan Paul.

Millais, J. G. 1924. *Far Away up the Nile.* London: Longman, Green and Co.

Nebel, A. 1954. *Dinka Dictionary.* Wau: Verona Fathers.

Needham, R. 1975. "Polythetic Classification: Convergence and Consequences." *Man* (N.S.) 10: 349-69.

Petherick, J. 1869. *Travels in Central Africa.* London: Tinsley Brothers.

Poncet, J. 1863. "Notice Geographique et Ethnologique sur la Region de Fleuve Blanc." *Annales des Voyages Geographique* 4: 5-62.

Riesman, P. 1977. *Freedom in Fulani Social Life.* Chicago: University of Chicago Press.

Sacks, K. 1979. "Causality and Chance on the Upper Nile." Pub. in *American Ethnologist,* Vol. 6, pp. 437-48.

Sahlins, M. 1961. "The Segmentary Lineage: An Organization of Predatory Expansion." *American Anthropologist* 63: 322-42.

Sanderson, G. N. 1976. "Some Problems of Colonial Rule and Local Response in the Southern Sudan, c. 1900-1920." Paper read in a Seminar on Colonial Rule and Local Response, School of Oriental and African Studies.

Santandrea, S. 1967. *Luei e Ombre dell Amministrazione Britannica nel Bahr-el-Ghazal.* Bologna: Editrice Nigrizia.

___. 1968. *The Luo of Bahr-el-Ghazal.* Bologna: Missionari Comboniani.

Schweinfurth, G. 1873. *The Heart of Africa* (trans. E. Frewer). London: Sampson, Low and Marston.

Seligman, C. G. 1932. *Pagan Tribes of the Nilotic Sudan.* London: Routledge and Kegan Paul.

Southall, A. W. 1976. "Nuer and Dinka Are People: Ecology, Ethnicity and Logical Possibility." *Man* (N.S.) 11: 463-91.

Sudan Peoples Liberation Movement. 1985. *Sudan Today: A Collection of Talks Given at the Africa Centre, London.* Sudan Peoples Liberation Movement.

Tedlock, D. 1982. "Anthropological Hermeneutics and the Problem of Alphabetic Literacy." In J. Ruby (ed.), *A Crack in the Mirror: Reflexive Perspectives in Anthropology.* Philadelphia: University of Pennsylvania Press.

Trimmingham, J. 1948. *The Christian Approach to Islam in the Sudan.* London: Oxford University Press.

Tucker, A. N. 1935. "A Survey of Language Groups in the Southern Sudan." *Bulletin of the School of Oriental and African Studies* 7: 861-96.

Verdon, M.   1982.   "Where Have All Their Lineages Gone?
    Cattle and Descent Among the Nuer."   American
    Anthropologist 84: 566-79.
Wall, L.   1976.   "Anuak Politics, Ecology and the Origins of
    the Shilluk Kingship."   Ethnology 15: 151-62.
Wilson, B.   1973.   Magic and the Millennium.   London:
    Heinemann.
Zahan, D.   1979.   The Religion, Spirituality and Thought of
    Traditional Africa   (trans. K. E. Martin and L. M.
    Martin).   Chicago: University of Chicago Press.

INDEX

About the Author

JOHN W. BURTON is Associate Professor of Anthropology at Connecticut College. He is the author of *God's Ants: A Study of Atuot Religion* and has published numerous articles in *Man, Africa, Journal of Religion in Africa, Ethnology, Ethnohistory, Journal of Modern African Studies, Anthropos, Journal of Asian and African Studies*, and *Folklore*.